# YOGA
## FOR PREGNANCY
### & to get back into shape

# YOGA
## FOR **PREGNANCY**
### & to get back into shape

**Françoise Barbira Freedman**

Doriel Hall

HERMES HOUSE

This edition is published by Hermes House

Hermes House is an imprint of Anness Publishing Ltd
Hermes House, 88–89 Blackfriars Road, London SE1 8HA
tel. 020 7401 2077; fax 020 7633 9499; info@anness.com

A CIP catalogue record for this book is available from the British Library.

Publisher: **Joanna Lorenz**
Managing Editor: **Helen Sudell**
Project Editors: **Debra Mayhew, Ann Kay**
Designers: **Ruth Hope, Lisa Tai**
Photographers: **Christine Hanscomb, Alistair Hughes**
Stylist: **Sue Duckworth**
Illustrator: **Samantha Elmhurst**
Production Controller: **Wendy Lawson**

Previously published in three separate volumes, *Prenatal Yoga, Aqua Yoga* and *Postnatal Yoga*

10 9 8 7 6 5 4 3 2 1

**Publisher's note:**
The reader should not regard the recommendations, ideas and techniques expressed and described in this book as substitutes for the advice of a qualified medical practitioner or other qualified professional. Any use to which the recommendations, ideas and techniques are put is at the reader's sole discretion and risk.

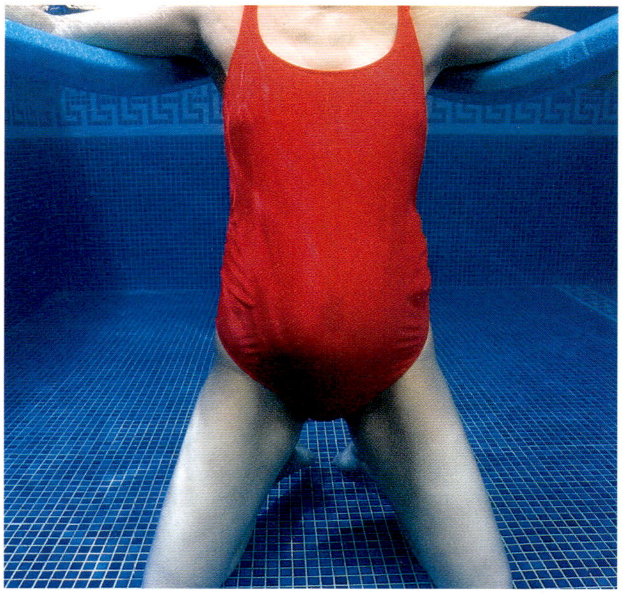

# Contents

# introduction



Yoga is an ancient system of self-help that can bring health and a feeling of "lightness" into every level of your being – physical, emotional, mental and spiritual. You may have been practising yoga for years, and if so, you will already be aware of how helpful it can be in any demanding situation. If you are absolutely new to yoga, approaching the birth of a baby is a wonderful time to start, just when you need all that it has to offer to adjust to the joys and challenges of pregnancy, birth and motherhood. It can be the beginning of a lifelong practice.

Birthlight is a practice of yoga that enables women to "birth lightly", making use of the breath to increase the efficacy of uterine contractions in labour. It allows you to release fear and tension while your baby is born. The prenatal yoga sequences in this book focus on opening the body to let energy flow freely, to nurture your growing baby. Gentle stretches, working with your deepening breath, foster the fluidity and flexibility of your changing body, while developing strong supportive muscles and a healthy cardiovascular system.

Yoga breathing exercises develop inner strength, stamina and serenity, by acting on the nervous system. As you gradually develop the habit of deep, slow breathing, you are encouraging your nervous system to make you feel good about yourself and your life. This is the yoga way to breathe. Negative feelings disappear when you learn to change the way you breathe. If they return, as they probably will from time to time, you can simply breathe them away again.

▷ Lifting one bent leg allows you to extend your spine more, raising yourself on your toes before bringing the bent leg to the floor in a "tall walk".

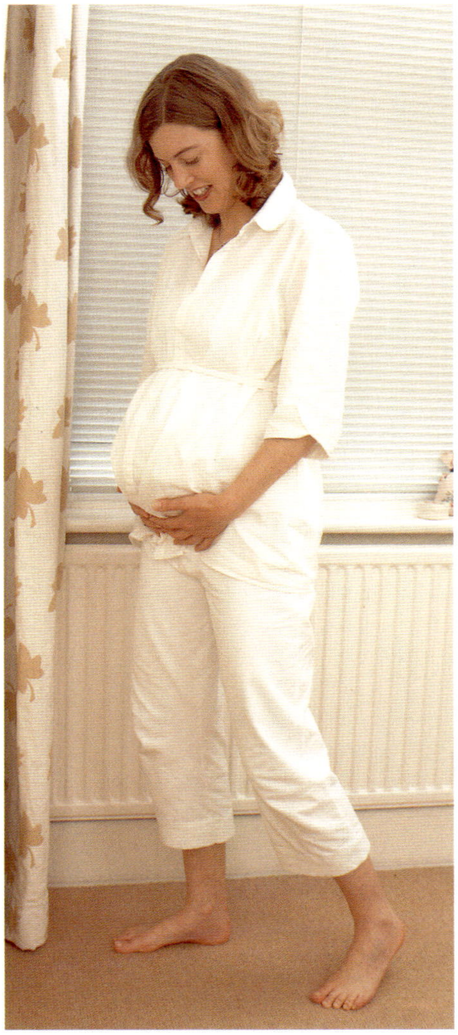

◁ Good breathing practices help greatly throughout pregnancy and labour.

## supportive water

The exercises designed for the prenatal period have been specially adapted from classical yoga poses. The use of movement and rhythm, together with additional supports such as chairs and cushions, is designed to alleviate strain and fatique. The aqua yoga sequences use water to support the body fully during exercise, allowing joints and muscles to move freely, unhindered by gravity. Aqua yoga is an adaptation of yoga practice that offers particular benefits in pregnancy. Adapted swimming strokes concentrate on slow, relaxed movement, to stretch the body, deepen the breathing and calm the mind.

There is increasing awareness of the advantages of water during labour and birth, and this book includes suggestions for using

▷ **Being supported in water enables you to relax really deeply. It is advisable to always have someone watching you while relaxing in a pool in case you lose track of time.**

aqua yoga techniques in a birthing pool, as well as presenting other ways in which yoga can help you through the experience of birth, as you lightly breathe your baby out into the world.

## strength and vitality

Whether this is your first, second or third baby – or if you are expecting twins – the postnatal exercises and advice given in this book will help you. They have been specially designed to address your needs as a new mother, and take you safely from the earliest days after giving birth towards full fitness and confidence in your maternal role.

△ **Relaxation gives you the deep rest essential to renew your energy.**

The gentle movements of yoga will help to restore tone in the deepest muscles, to streamline the figure and to build up your strength and vitality after giving birth. During pregnancy, your body was required to "open out" to accommodate your growing baby. Your abdominal muscles and pelvic floor muscles became very elastic, so that the baby could be born. All the emphasis in prenatal yoga practice is upon facilitating this opening and elasticity. After birth, the situation is reversed. It is time to "close up" your body while maintaining and developing the physical suppleness and the openness of heart and mind that birth brought. This is a gradual process, but by about nine months after the birth you can expect to feel better than you felt before.

Each exercise is numbered so that you can refer easily to an earlier sequence. Use the sequences to suit your own needs and those of your baby or babies. Each family is different, of course, but every resourceful and determined new mother can find a few moments, several times each day, to practise the movements, the breathing exercises and the relaxations that are shown in this book: you will find that it is time well spent.

Involve the family. Have fun together. Be lighthearted. Yoga brings "lightness" to mind and body, and spreads it all around. Yoga relaxation will help you to rest and unwind, so that you can enjoy your baby and your family life. Yoga helps you to feel happy, secure and light-hearted. Your own ability to relax teaches your baby how to relax as well, so that you can enjoy life together. Physical, emotional, mental and spiritual well-being after giving birth requires that you learn to nurture yourself in deep relaxation. Only then can you truly nurture anyone else.

◁ **Doing yoga together integrates the whole family and creates additional closeness.**

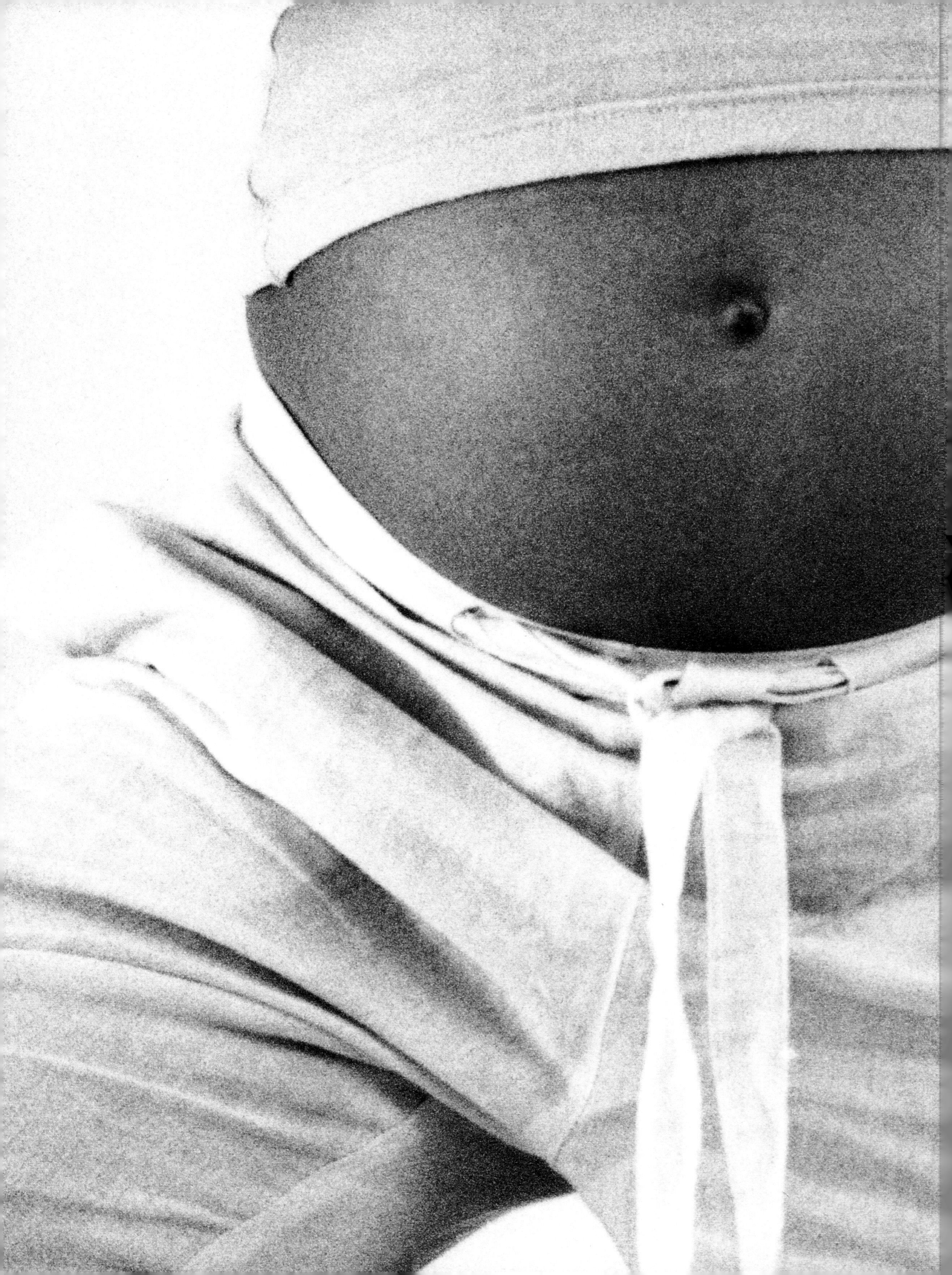

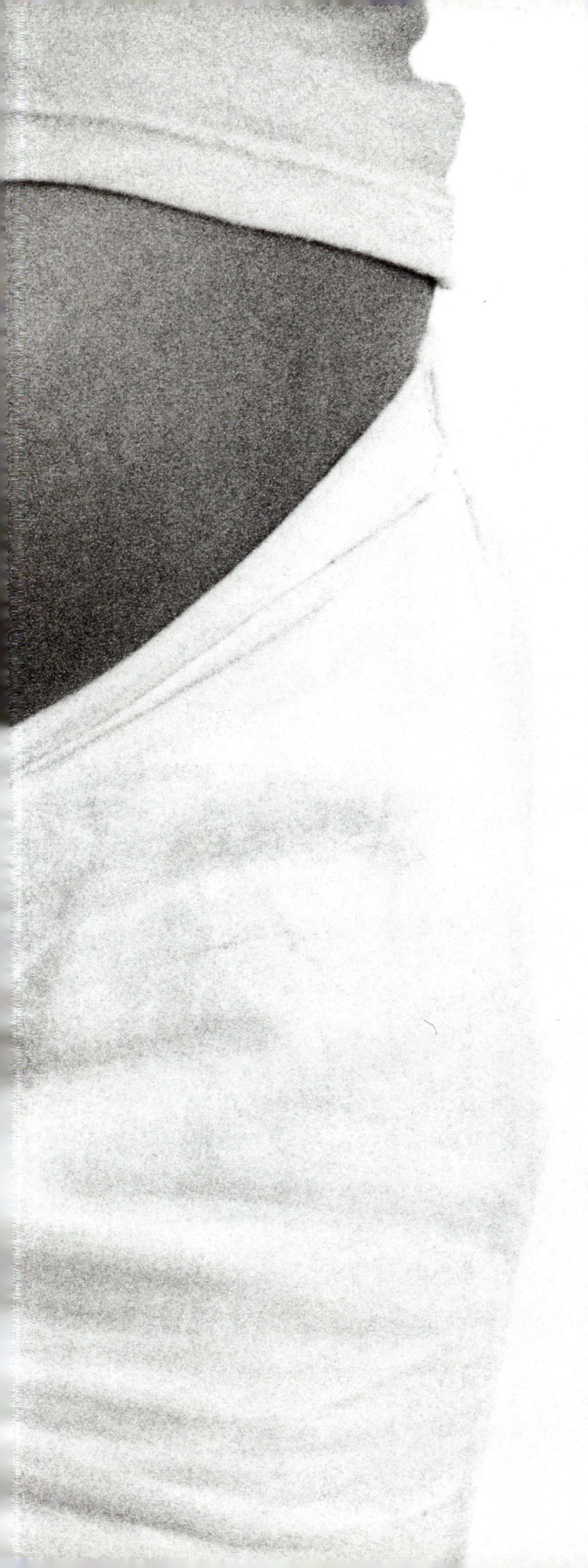

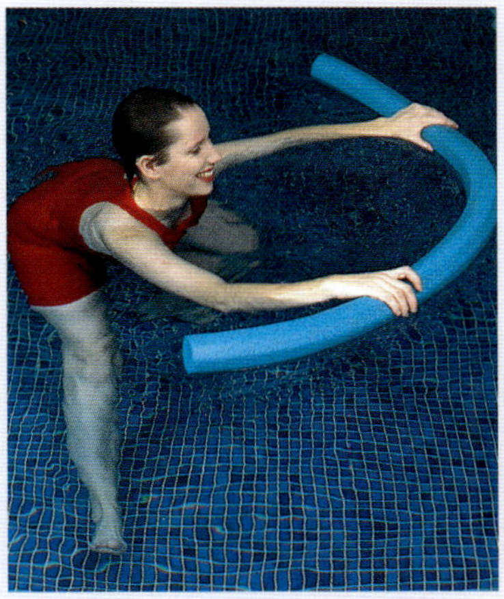

# introducing yoga and aqua yoga

Yoga is a holistic life practice that will greatly help you to enjoy your pregnancy, right from conception through to the birth. It will increase your vitality, reduce your stress levels and make you feel close to your growing baby long before he or she is born. In aqua yoga, stretching, breathing and flowing become one in water, allowing you to approach birth in a vital, energized, yet profoundly relaxed way.

# Why yoga is the best form of exercise for you





Today, women have much more choice about when, and if, they conceive children. Yet conception is still a mysterious and unpredictable event that has much to do with our personal well-being and mental outlook.

Conception and pregnancy bring great changes. First there are the hormonal ones. Then there are the mental and emotional changes involved in altering your life so you can focus on the joy of motherhood and your baby's needs. Yoga can help you sail through all these changes with a light step, a happy heart and a clear mind.

## how yoga will help you

Regular yoga practice can help enormously at all stages of pregnancy, birth and parenthood, bringing you to a physical, emotional and mental peak. Strong, supple, focused, relaxed and happy, a woman will be well placed both to conceive and to carry her baby joyfully right through to the birth – provided this is what she wants and there are no major medical obstacles.

The yogic routines in this book are specially adapted to suit your needs, both before and after the birth of your baby. They are easy to follow, and have been designed with your safety, and that of your baby, as the first priority. If you feel uncomfortable with any exercise, don't persevere. Trust your instincts: deep self-awareness is the essence of yoga. There is plenty of choice throughout the book and the exercises are designed to make you feel great – at work, at home, anywhere.

## a new way of being

Yoga can transform your life, making you feel happy and fulfilled not just at this special time, but in future years.

- Feel well in yourself, with energy and enthusiasm for life, despite the hormonal changes and the inevitable anxieties of pregnancy and mortherhood. Yoga will ease the emotional tensions that can cause physical blocks – aiding conception, and helping you to cope serenely with pregnancy, birth and parenthood.
- Be present in the moment – yoga is based on the practice of awareness, of living in the here and now. As you stretch and breathe and relax you will be living more fully than you ever could without this yogic awareness. Creating a baby is a wonderful experience. So make the most of every moment and enjoy it.
- Relate more deeply to those you love. Because yoga focuses on relaxation and breathing it opens our hearts to those around us, so that we draw them into our sphere of harmony and contentment. Your partner will appreciate being part of preparing for conception, enjoying pregnancy and giving birth. Friends, too, can enjoy practising yoga with you all through this time. Above all, your unborn baby will bask in your love as the foundations are established for a strong bond of love between you.
- Become more self-aware. You will find that you are constantly observing how you sit, stand, walk, breathe and relate to those around you, and that you are making subtle adjustments where needed. Change is cumulative – you will be amazed at the subtle changes you find in yourself.

**△ Pregnant and happy. Regular and carefully adapted yoga practice gives you a light step and a light heart.**

**▽ Do not overstretch yourself when practising yoga. Here are three possible variations of the Dog Pose (see also 16). All are equally beneficial, as long as you do the one that is right for you.**

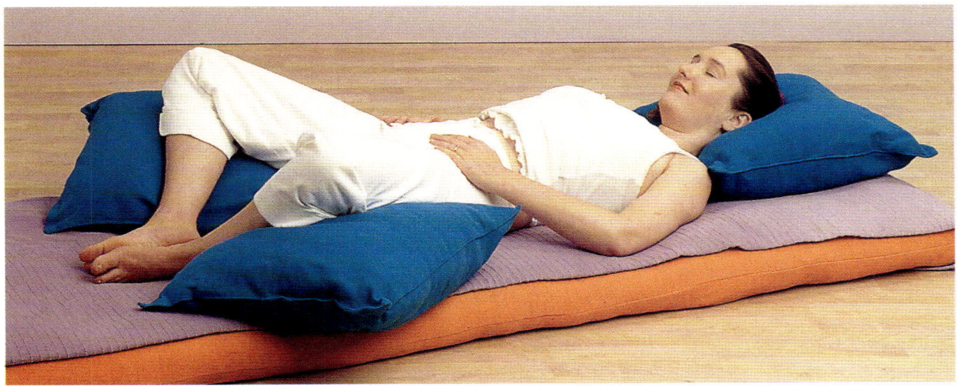

◁ ▽ To aid conception, yoga poses such as these two positions make space for the baby by opening up the hips.

- Become more fully who you are, as you become more relaxed and supple in body, mind, emotions and spirit.
- You can continue to do this kind of yoga at any age, at any time, anywhere, every day of your life. You will gain most from it with regular practice, but even a small amount is beneficial.

## tailoring yoga to suit your needs

Yoga is infinitely adaptable – provided it remains holistic and no element is left out, and the principles of classical yoga that have been followed for millennia are respected. If the exercises shown in this book are followed mechanically, without attention to breathing or the natural rhythm between activity and relaxation, they simply become "keep fit". This can, of course, still be beneficial, but yoga gives you so much more. It creates a wonderful sense of deep-down well-being as well as increasing your physical fitness.

## aqua yoga

Water is the source of life on this planet. It is an environment that is familiar to us from before birth, as babies grow in amniotic fluid. Water is an ideal medium for yoga, allowing stretching and breathing beyond anything that is possible in land-based postures. In pregnancy, particularly, water gives freedom of movement. It is a powerful toner and a vitalizing environment.

The aqua yoga exercises presented in this book may look easy, but they are very effective in toning and increasing the flexibility of your pelvic muscles as preparation for birth. All the sequences can be practised from the start of your pregnancy and continued throughout. Postnatal aqua yoga sequences, like the land-based exercises, concentrate on closing the body. Aqua yoga sessions in the pool can include your baby, and are an ideal way to introduce him or her to the water.

Aqua yoga swimming opens the pelvis and stretches the whole body. The focus is not on speed, but on maximum relaxed stretching, full use of your breath and a symmetrical use of joints and muscles. You are actually encouraged to swim slowly, yet with an efficient technique that aims at generating a very smooth rhythm and movement. The third element of aqua yoga, floating relaxation, opens access to an anxiety-free state of harmony with the surrounding world.

◁ During the last few weeks of pregnancy, yoga helps you to get in training for the birth. Here, a friend and a chair are used for support while practising birthing positions.

# How yoga works for you





Yoga is a holistic discipline so it benefits you at every level, not only the physical one. Yoga philosophy maintains that a human being operates at several well-defined levels.

## the five levels

There are five principal levels in yoga, and these are as follows.

**Physical structure** This includes bones, joints, muscles, skin and internal organs. Yoga develops physical strength, stamina and suppleness but these qualities are also developed at mental and emotional levels. Movement and posture are key elements.

**Life processes** This is the working of all the bodily systems, such as the respiratory and cardiovascular systems, the various branches of the nervous system, the hormonal system, the digestive system and, of course, the reproductive system that will first create your baby and then support it in the womb. Breathing is the key element.

△ Yogic stretching, relaxing and unwinding with your partner helps you open up to each other.

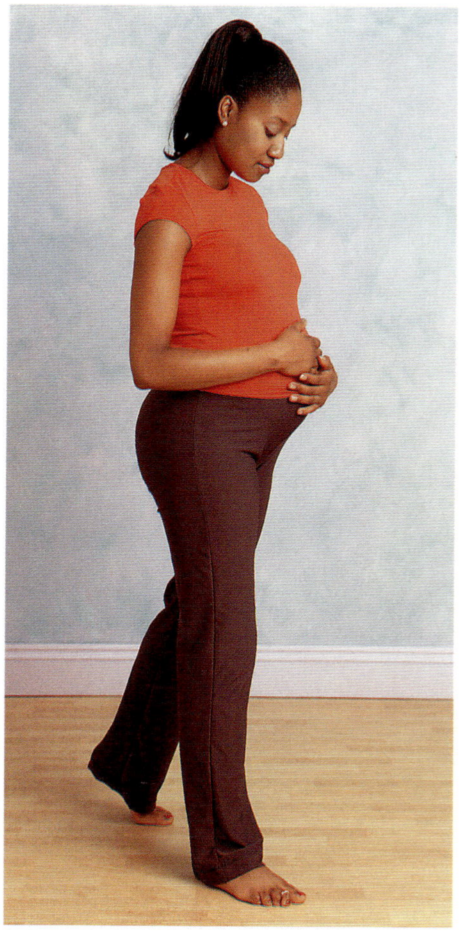

△ Take time to relax and commune with your baby. This Walking Meditation (24) will help you to focus on the most important things in your life.

**Internal organization** This governs the workings of the brain and nervous system, so that all other body systems get the energy they need to do their jobs, just when they need it. In this way, internal harmony (also known as homeostasis) is sustained and we enjoy a state of contented well-being. Relaxation is the key element.

**Clarity of mind** This involves the ability to sort out our priorities, to concentrate on just one subject at a time until we are ready to turn our attention to another, rather than being too easily distracted by conflicting demands. In this way, we use our energy in a focused fashion, alternating periods of activity with those of relaxation. Being aware of posture, breathing and relaxation, and bringing them together in yoga practice, is a form of meditation, and meditation is a key element here.

**Emotions and deepest desires** Yoga differentiates between automatic reactions and considered responses. We choose to respond warmly and positively to life rather than spin from one knee-jerk reaction to another. In this way, we take control of our lives and cultivate qualities of the heart. We develop mental stamina, plus emotional as well as physical suppleness and strength. Taking time and trouble to make a resolution that is meaningful for us, and confirming it while in deep relaxation, helps us to live more fully as the person that we choose to be – truly living our choices.

## the Chakras

In simple terms, the Chakras are the points where the five levels of being, already described, meet and work together to produce the person that we are. The Chakras correspond to nerve plexuses along the spine in the physical body, and yoga aims to bring them into balance with each other in order to keep us healthy, happy and growing in wisdom and serenity.

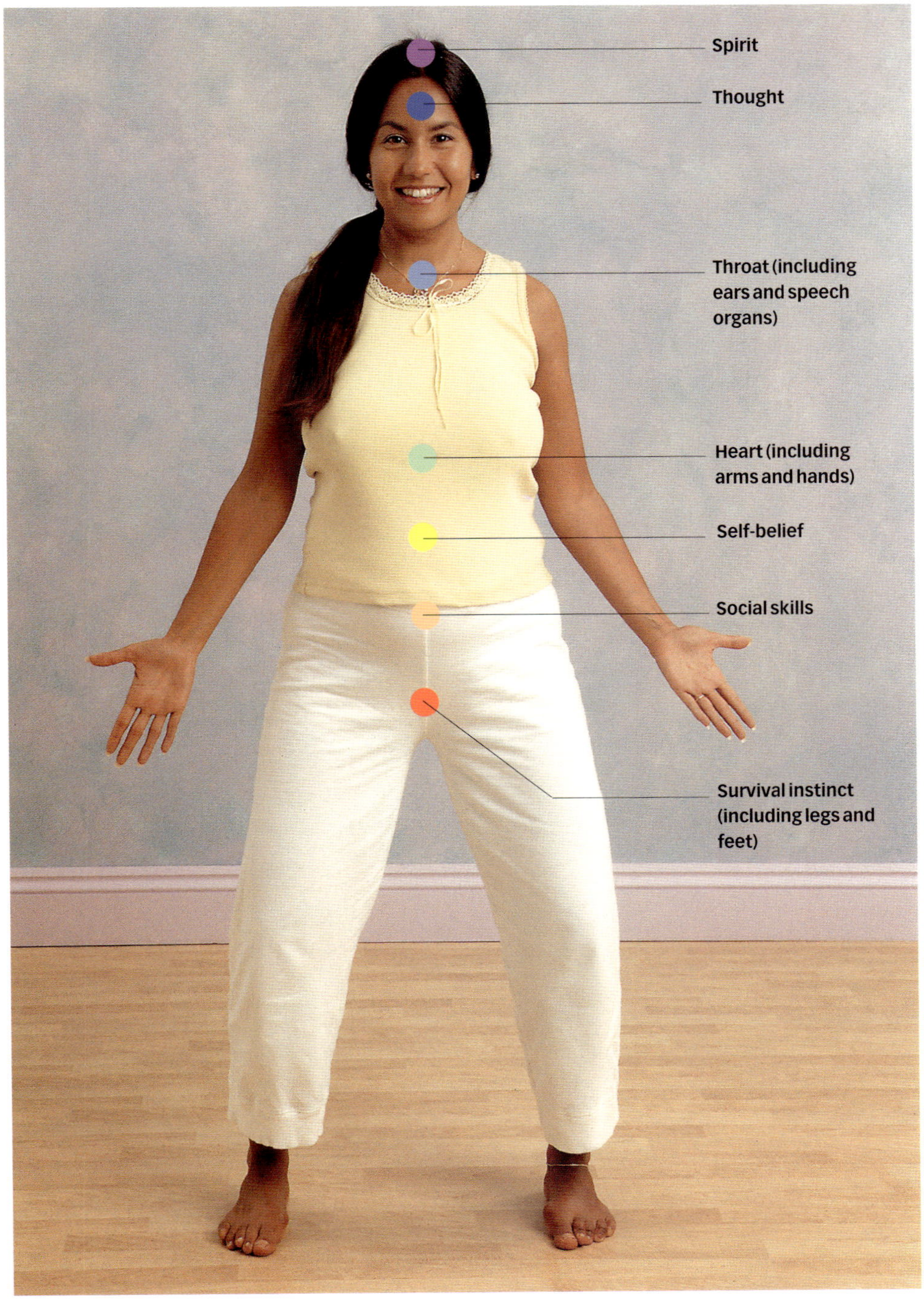


◁ The position of the Chakras in the human body. These fall into three main areas: the Life area (waist to toes), the Love area (chest and throat), and the Light area (head).

**Love energies** The two Chakras in the chest area are concerned with relationship, or Love energies. The heart is often called the "organ of feeling", and we express those feelings through the voice box in the throat. How we breathe profoundly influences our nervous system, which in turn determines to a large extent how we are feeling in ourselves and towards other people. Breathing with awareness could be said to be the heart of yoga, as all the other practices are linked with the movements of our breath. Relaxed breathing and deep relaxation practices allow us to open our hearts in welcome to all those beings we interact with, as well as to ourselves.

**Light energies** The two Chakras in the head are concerned with our mental, or Light, energies. It is these that sustain the clarity of our thought processes, our powers of observation and awareness, our focus on the job in hand, our choices and our decision-making. Practices that work with focus, awareness and meditation are all exercising our Light Chakras.

All yoga practices help to harmonize the energies of the Chakras and to maximize their combined energies.

**Life energies** The three Chakras in the abdominal cavity are concerned with vitality or Life energies. These include the energies that operate in the reproductive system to prepare for, conceive and create a baby, and the energies in the digestive system that nourish the body (and foetus) and clear away the waste products. These systems all lie in the abdominal cavity. Quite a lot of our prenatal yoga practice is aimed at enhancing vitality, to facilitate conception and later to make more space in the abdominal area as the baby grows larger. We also focus on the spinal and pelvic muscles that hold the reproductive organs in place and on bringing vitality to the whole reproductive system.

◁ Spinal stretching for alignment is always an important part of yoga practice as it encourages the flow of energy through the Chakras. This aspect needs special attention during pregnancy as the body shape and weight are constantly changing.

# opening your body and your self

Whether you are trying to conceive or are already pregnant, it is vital to remain open at all levels. A woman is probably at her most welcoming at this time, offering her love, her body, her womb, her breasts, her nurturing ability, her home and her whole self as a safe haven. This openness is the pinnacle of femininity – and no experience could be more feminine than welcoming and nurturing the baby growing in your womb. Yoga for conception and pregnancy focuses on staying open and creating more space – more space in the lower abdomen for the baby, more space for the digestive organs to process the food needed by mother and baby, more space for the lungs to provide oxygen for mother and baby.

## letting energy flow freely

Openness is a yielding, welcoming quality, but it is not a shapeless "giving in", nor a collapse, for it is literally backed up by the strength and support of the spine. A key focus in yoga for both conception and pregnancy is to increase and maintain the alignment of the spinal and pelvic bones in order to provide free flow of vital energies and to protect the growing baby. This is vital for several reasons:

- To enable all the systems of the body to perform their functions without pressure or congestion. This is especially important when you are planning to conceive.
- To hold the baby in place, to create space for movement as he or she develops, and to make room for vital nourishment to pass through the placenta to the baby without any hindrance.
- To allow free passage through the spine of energies that activate the Chakras, as well as the mechanisms that are vital for the smooth running of the nervous system.

All our bones are held in place by muscles and ligaments. Muscles need to be exercised in order to remain strong and flexible and to have the stamina to go on doing their job for as long as necessary. Muscles that are not exercised at first become stiff and then atrophy, which can lead to greater fat deposits. The muscles that support our body's weight are the biggest and strongest ones. In classical yoga, we exercise them a great deal by doing standing poses where the weight of the trunk is taken by gravity through the legs and feet, which are firmly planted on the floor. In pregnancy, however, movement and rhythm are introduced to avoid the strain of holding

△ **In many poses, cushions placed under the knees protect your ligaments from undue strain.**

> "Open the window in the centre of your chest and let spirit move in and out."
>
> *Rumi*

## THE THREE MAIN STAGES OF PREGNANCY

**Here you can see how the spine changes shape and the organs get increasingly squashed. Yoga helps to keep the organs working well and strengthens the all-important, supportive spine.**

At 8 weeks

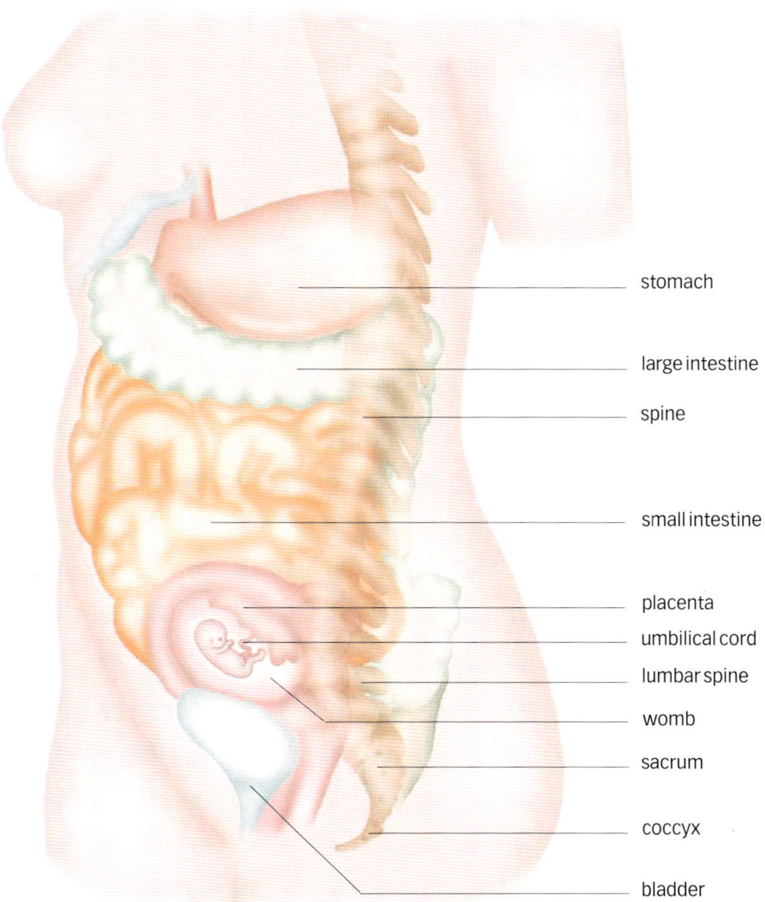


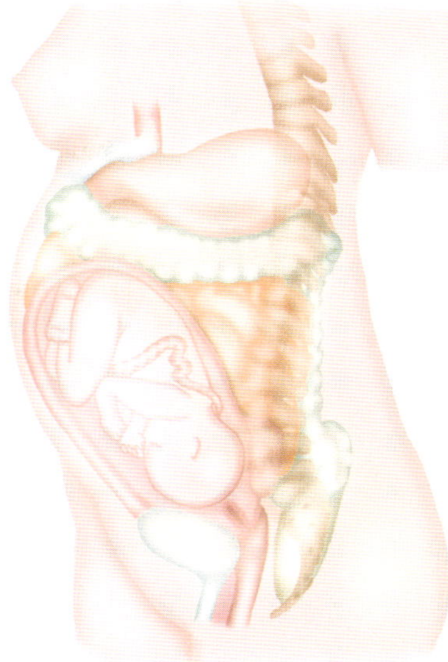

At 24 weeks

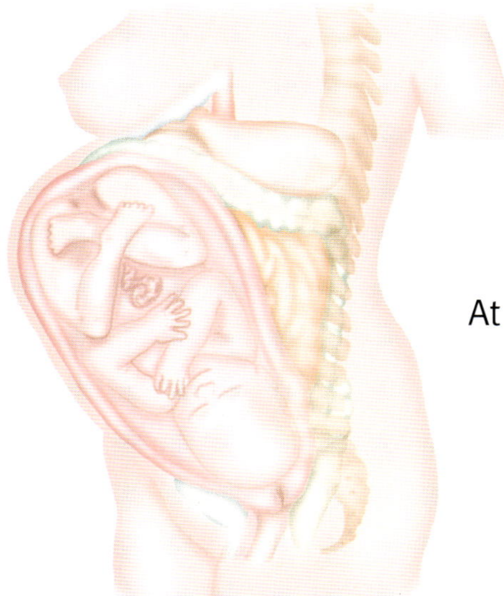

At 40 weeks

the classical positions. Various supports may also be used, to avoid tiring or straining while standing. Many poses are performed either sitting down (less tiring than standing) or lying down (where gravity works with you and the ground supports you).

## posture and breathing

Yoga creates a virtuous circle whereby the more you become aware of good posture and alignment of the spine, the more you will pull yourself up whenever you notice you are drooping. The more you stand tall, the better you will breathe and the more vitality you will have. The more vitality you have, the less you will droop and the more you will naturally stand well and move with a spring in your step. Yoga is a holistic discipline, so improvement in any area affects all other areas for the better.

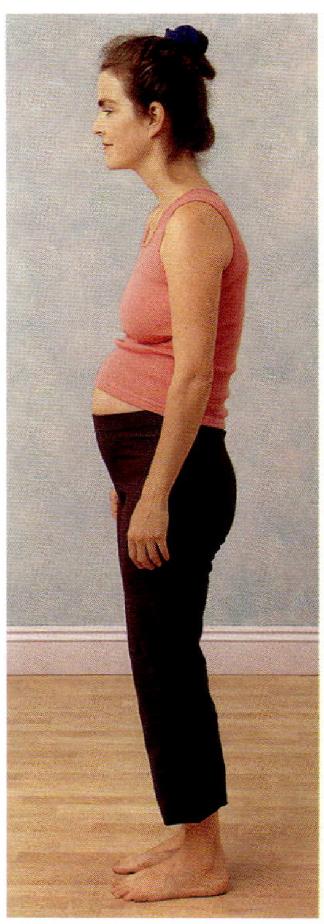

**◁ Poor posture can spark all kinds of problems. Compression of the spine leads to pain in the neck and upper back as well as the lower back, while poor breathing from congestion of the lung space inevitably contributes to tiredness and low vitality. Slack abdominal and pelvic muscles lead to congestion in the abdomen and possibly lower back pain and swollen ankles.**

**▷ Good posture means that your head and neck are erect and balanced between the shoulders, and your spine and pelvis are properly aligned. Your abdominal and pelvic muscles are strong enough to support the baby and your chest is open so that the breathing muscles perform fully and fill the body with a positive vitality. Finally, your legs are strong, springy and balanced.**

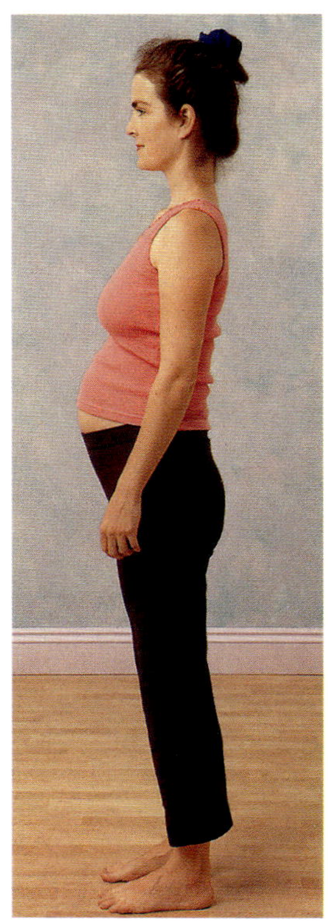

# How to get the most out of your yoga



It is better to practise yoga for a few minutes each day than not at all. Some days it may be possible only to stretch your spine while standing in the kitchen waiting for a kettle to boil, or to practise your breathing at your desk after a prolonged spell on the telephone or computer. Do, however, find a quiet space and the time to practise whenever you can, daily if possible. When you use a particular place for yoga, a wonderful atmosphere builds up. Your yoga corner welcomes you and surrounds you with peace and safety, so you immediately relax, and this makes your yoga session a deeply fulfilling experience. Anywhere quiet and comfortable is suitable. Adorn it with flowers, pictures and other things that make you feel happy, and you will soon transform it into your personal haven.

## getting started

You will probably find most of the equipment for your yoga practice around your home. A list of handy items follows.

- A yoga mat, or a similar-sized piece of non-slip carpet, to practise on.
- Several cushions, large and small – to put, for example, behind your back or under your head or knees.
- A beanbag to lean against.
- A variety of seats at different heights to sit on or place a foot on.
- A firm, upright chair for breathing exercises and meditation.
- A tape recorder and tapes to make your own recordings for deep relaxation.
- A light rug or blanket to cover yourself during relaxations.
- Several surfaces to push or pull against, such as a wall or a kitchen counter.

◁ You don't need special, expensive equipment to practise yoga. Choose props that will support you so that you can be as comfortable and relaxed as possible.

## deep relaxation

Relaxation is a key practice in yoga and should not be omitted, whether you rest completely after each sequence of movements or practise deep relaxation at another time in the day. Ideally you should do both, so that you learn how to switch off at will. By restoring the natural rhythm of activity and rest in your life, you restore the body's natural balance. To do this, you need to alternate exertion, which achieves

△ Achieving a deeply relaxed state is a key element in good yoga practice. Help this along with cushioned supports and soothing tapes.

short-term benefits, with the rest needed to achieve long-term benefits. These benefits include good digestion, repair of bodily tissues, release of stress, communication with your own inner world (meditation), and balancing and realigning the energies of body, mind, emotions and spirit.

The structure of your relaxation will depend on whether it is to last 10, 15 or 20 minutes. Many people make an audiotape to guide them in and out of their relaxation. This means that you can relax without worrying about missing out any parts of the session or overrunning. It is a really good idea to make several tapes, varying in length, to cover any eventuality. Whether you are making your own tape or not, be guided by the relaxation suggestions that follow.

## a tailor-made relaxation session

During this session, you will plant a positive seed-thought deep into your mind, so think carefully beforehand what it is to be. No one can create this for you because it arises from deep within you but affirmations might include, "I feel ready to conceive", "I am enjoying my pregnancy", "I feel confident and happy about becoming a mother", and "life is wonderful". The affirmation should

▷ **A meditation corner filled with peaceful and beautiful vibrations is an ideal setting for yoga, and anyone can set up a simple corner at home.**

address any doubts or fears you may have and help to dissolve them. Such positive affirmations are extremely powerful, especially when repeated daily while in a state of deep relaxation. Gradually, it will replace any negative seed-thoughts that you may have been harbouring for years, perhaps since early childhood. Just let go and forget about this early conditioning, for you are an adult now, ready and able to choose for yourself how you wish to be.

Experiment to find your most comfortable position (remember that this will change as your pregnancy advances), with cushions for support where appropriate. Now either switch on your tape or start to run mentally through these instructions, in this order:

- Take your focused attention to every part of your body, especially hips, shoulders, neck and face, to check that it is comfortable and relaxed. Wherever you find tension, breathe out deeply into that area to release the blockage.
- When your body is settled, turn your attention to your breath. Watch the process of breathing, how the air comes in through your nose cool and dry and moves right down into your lungs. How it then changes its quality and feels warm and moist as it is breathed out. Focus on your breathing for a few moments.
- Breathe into your heart space, building up feelings of welcoming love for the baby that you hope will come, or has already come, into your womb.
- If you are already pregnant, move your attention to the baby growing within you and delight in its presence in your life. Tell your baby of your joy, and feel how he or she is responding to your love and nurturing attention.
- While you are feeling deeply relaxed, open and receptive, repeat your seed-thought to yourself three times, slowly and clearly, so that it takes root and grows in your mind and in your heart.

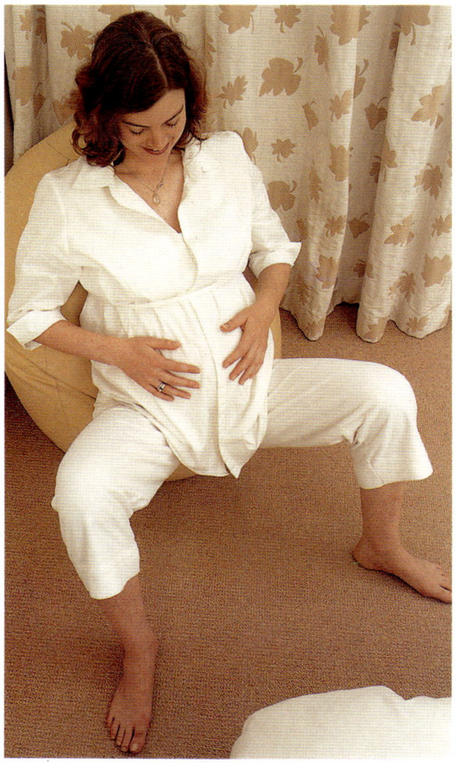

◁ **You may wish to vary where you do your yoga sessions – perhaps doing breathing or relaxation practices in one spot, and exercises in another.**

Now, instruct yourself to come out of the relaxation slowly, reversing the sequence with which you went in, but moving through it much faster.

- Tell your baby or hoped-for baby of your complete love.
- Return your attention to your breath and watch its flow. Then start to expand your breathing to wake up your body slowly. Your eyes will open automatically when your breathing has woken you up.
- To start bringing movement to your body, move ankles, wrists and neck gently. Now have several good, long stretches, yawning or sighing with long breaths out.
- Roll on to your side before coming up on to all fours. Rock your pelvis a little before getting up slowly.

# breath awareness

As well as energizing the body, our breathing has a profound influence on the nervous system. Fast or shallow breathing makes us feel anxious and stressed, whereas slow, deep breathing immediately relaxes us. If you are to practise active relaxation, you need to be aware of your breathing patterns, so that you can use your breath to consciously reduce stress and promote well-being. Note that the awareness of exhalation comes first in yoga, avoiding any forceful inhalation.

## 1 Deepening the breath

**Sit upright on a sturdy chair, with your feet apart and planted firmly on the floor. Feel your breathing muscles working by placing your hands on your ribs, then lower chest, then abdomen. The lower you can take the breathing movement the more energized and relaxed you will feel, and the more efficiently your abdominal organs (digestive and reproductive) can function. In yoga you should always breathe in and out through the nose unless instructed otherwise.**

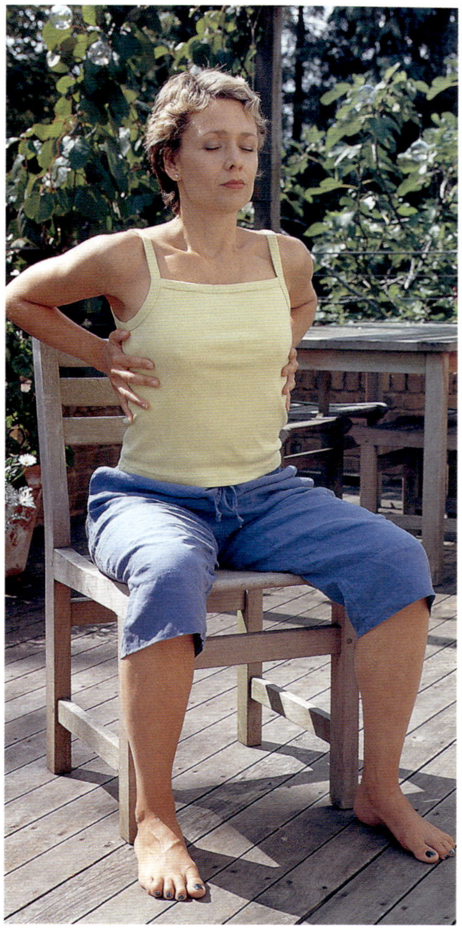

△ **1** Bring your elbows back to open your chest, and place your hands on the sides of your ribs with fingers pointing forward. Breathe in deeply, expanding your ribcage against your hands. Breathe out, keeping the lift and openness in the chest. Be careful not to collapse, even though your ribcage contracts a little. Repeat several times.

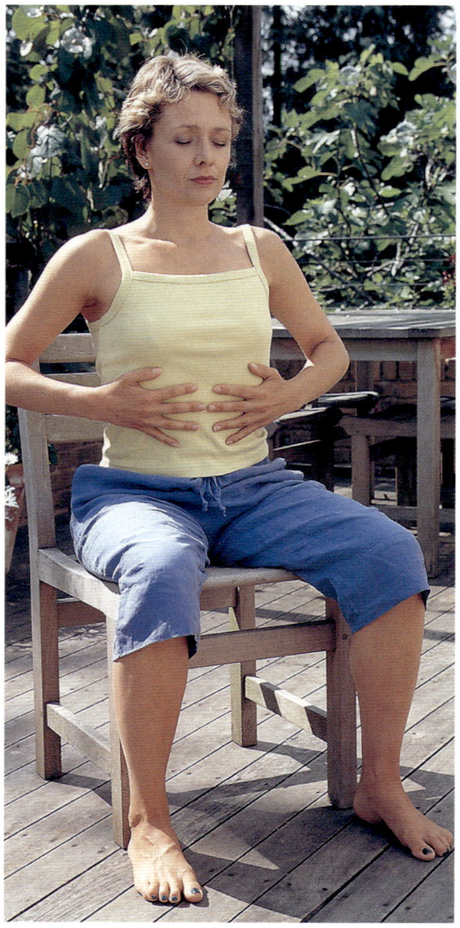

△ **2** Still with elbows wide and chest open, bring your hands forward with fingers pointing toward each other and little fingers against your lowest ribs. As you breathe in feel your lower ribs expanding outward and your diaphragm contracting downward against your abdominal organs. As you breathe out feel the ribs relaxing inward and the diaphragm relaxing upward. Repeat several times. If you blow the air out forcibly through your mouth you will also feel the corset muscles around your waist contracting sharply.

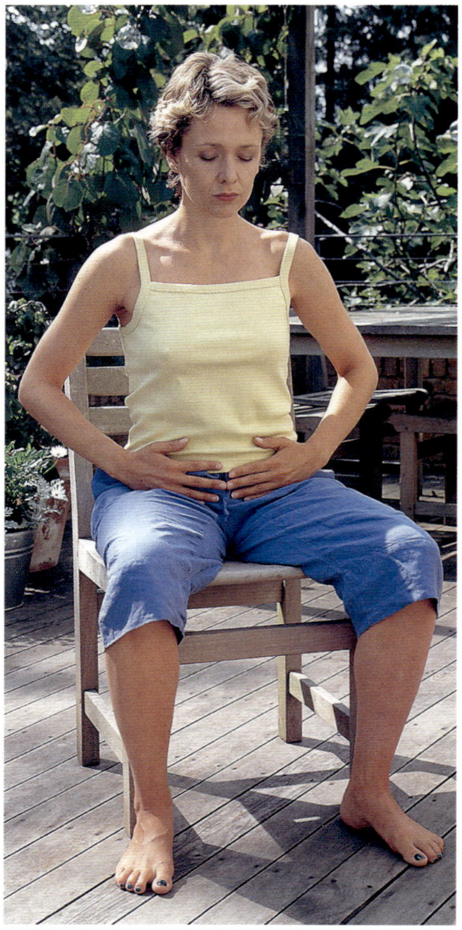

△ **3** Now move your hands below the navel to feel the effect of deep breathing on the abdominal organs. As you breathe in, contracting the diaphragm, the downward pressure massages and flushes away stale blood from these organs. As you breathe out this pressure is released and fresh new blood rushes in, bringing a new supply of oxygen and nutrients. Feel the movements of your breathing reaching right down through the abdomen and pelvis to the muscular pelvic floor. Repeat a few times, keeping neck and shoulders relaxed, and then rest.

## 2 Stretch, bend and relax

**This exercise sets the pattern for all your yoga practice – alternating active movements with a pause to relax. If you can arrange your daily life to the same natural rhythm you will find that you can undo stress before it has a chance to build up. Either sitting or standing you can rid the lungs of stale air, open the chest and massage the abdominal organs.**

△**1** Make sure that you are seated comfortably and use a firm bolster or similar as a foot support. As you breathe in raise both straight arms above your head.

△ **2** As you breathe out fold forward like a rag doll, dropping your head between your knees and hands loosely to the floor.

△ **3** Breathing naturally, relax your neck and shoulders to ease out any tension. Repeat this exercise several times.

## 3 Lengthening the out breath

**The breath out relaxes the nervous system, whereas the breath in is energizing. First, sigh or yawn to release tension. Always remember to make the breath out last a little longer than the breath in. An enjoyable way to lengthen the breath out is by using the voice. A lower pitch usually resonates better than a higher one and is more relaxing.**

▷ With spine erect and chest open, breathe in deeply and let the air out slowly as you chant "A...E...I...O...U...".

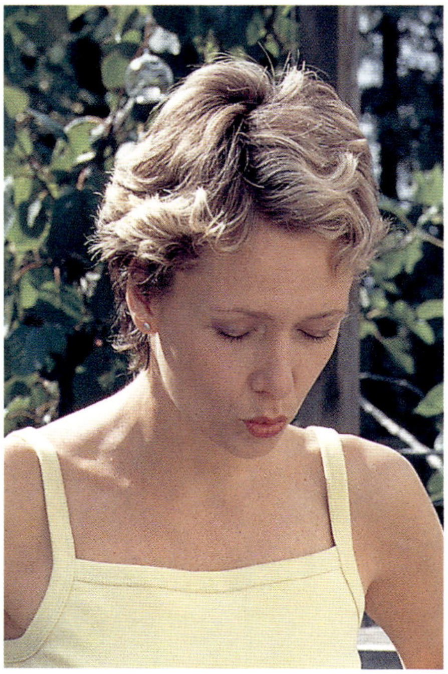

## 4 Alternate nostril breathing

**This breathing exercise is a classical yoga practice. It is remarkable for soothing the nervous system and balancing our extrovert and introvert tendencies – calming us when we are anxious or overexcited and lifting our spirits when we are tired or depressed. Ideally, it should be practised for a few minutes each day.**

▷ Sit with spine erect and chest open. Place the right hand in front of the face, with the index and middle finger resting lightly on the centre of the forehead, the thumb in position to close the right nostril, and the ring finger in position to close the left nostril. Now concentrate and follow these steps:

- Close the right nostril with the thumb and breathe in through the left nostril.
- Close the left nostril and open the right.
- Breathe out through the right nostril.
- Breathe in through the right nostril.
- Close the right nostril and open the left. Breathe out through the left nostril.

This is one round. Repeat, gradually building up the number of rounds over a few weeks.

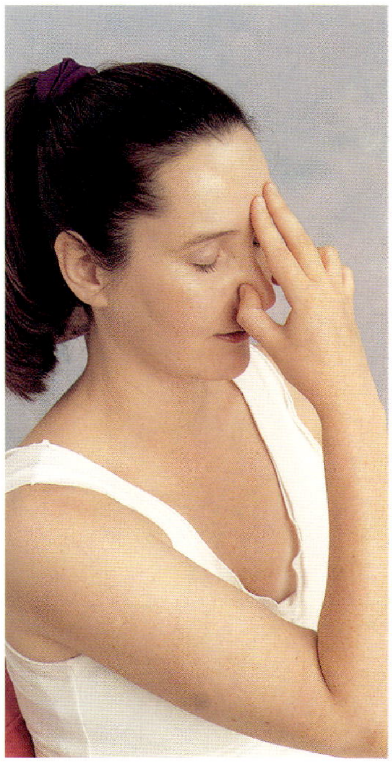

# The benefits of aqua yoga

Aqua yoga is a natural and all-encompassing way to promote and sustain fitness and health. It offers a gentle and easily available way to enjoy movement and breathing by using the supportive element of water. Many aqua yoga exercises are classical yoga postures adapted to water. Adaptations of swimming strokes have also been found to be especially beneficial to mothers-to-be and new mothers, and they too are presented in this book.

Good health is far more than simply an absence of disease: vitality and contentment are required to enjoy pregnancy and the postnatal period fully. The power of water for revitalization and therapy has been known and used since ancient times by both humans and animals. The Greeks and Romans gave a high priority not only to baths but also to exercise in water. Massage in water can also be used therapeutically for healing injuries, as well as on specific areas of the body that need loosening, toning, strengthening and shaping.

▷ **The supportive medium of water allows strain-free, ample movements of the hips while on your front ...**

## swimming for health

It has been shown that swimming can strengthen the immune system, and can help to heal a wide variety of conditions. People with chronic illnesses, such as asthma, benefit from its effects on their breathing, even finding that they shake off infections and other problems in no time at all. There are very few people who will not benefit from swimming and for whom it may be unsuitable. It is rated as the top exercise for stamina, suppleness and strength, as it exercises the whole body simultaneously, rather than working on parts of it separately.

Everyone can swim, regardless of their age or state of fitness. Supported by the water, joints and muscles can move freely, unhampered by gravity and protected from the jarring and knocking that can happen in land-based exercise. It is ideal for all conditions, such as pregnancy, where weight-bearing exercise is best avoided.

The general benefits of swimming are well known. It increases lung capacity and improves breathing performance, increasing the tidal volume of the lungs as well as their blood supply. It also improves the proportion of muscle to fat, while strengthening the connective tissues (cartilages, ligaments and tendons), intermuscle and organ-supporting tissue. Lower-back problems and painful arthritic or inflamed joints can be alleviated.

◁ **... and on your back, floating with a support if needed.**

Cardiovascular function and muscle tone are enhanced, and both the pulse rate and recovery period are reduced: this is really helpful during labour. The number of capillaries increases, as does the haemoglobin. Your recovery after surgery or from a weakened condition will be improved, which may be important if you have a traumatic birth or Caesarean section.

In summary, swimming not only improves the circulatory and respiratory systems but develops mobility in the muscles and joints and increases muscular strength and tone. Of all exercise forms, it performs these functions in a most effective and enjoyable way within a short time span.

## major skeletal muscles and ligaments for posture in pregnancy and after birth

**Both in pregnancy and after birth it is extremely important to strengthen and elongate the muscles of the back, buttocks, thighs and abdomen. In aqua yoga, as in classical yoga, this is achieved through a combination of breathing and stretching, but greater elongation of muscle is possible in water.**

**Your deep spinal muscles, together with your leg muscles, adjust your posture through pregnancy and after birth by holding your pelvis in the right position at all times, supporting your baby comfortably.**

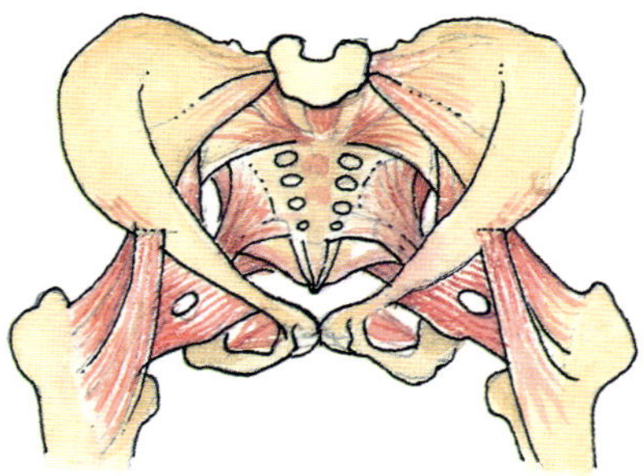

The ligaments of the pelvis

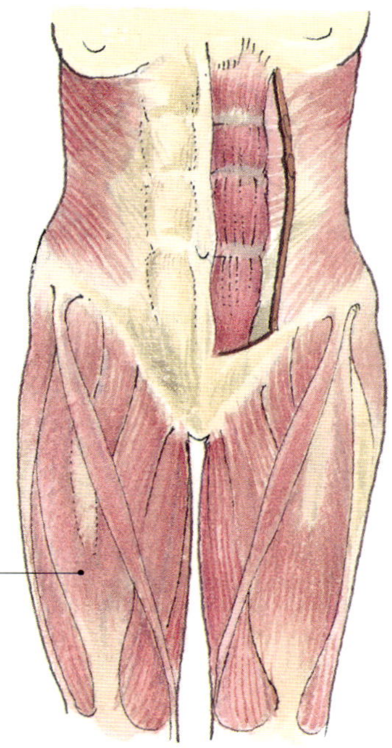


Anterior view

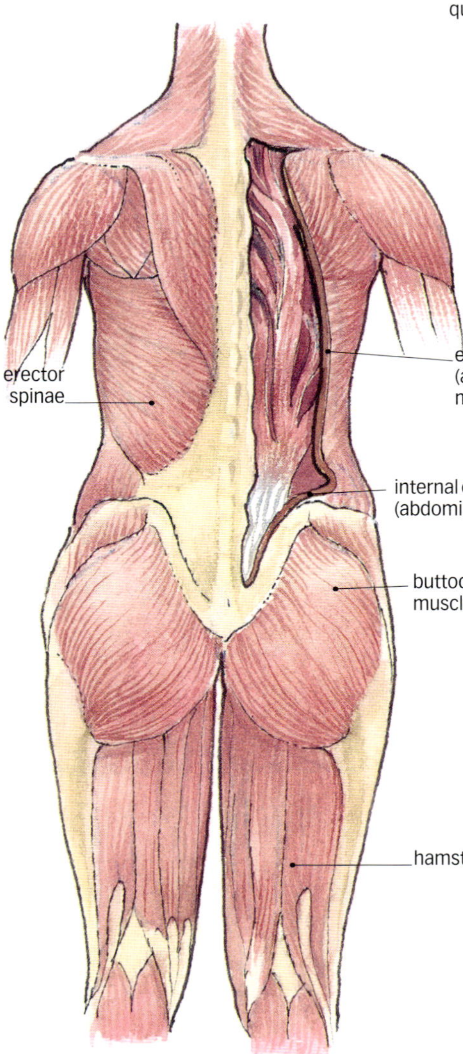


Posterior view

## breathing is what matters

Aqua yoga combines slow stretching with the use of breathing and relaxation, as the water provides resistance for the muscles to work against. Bodies feel virtually weightless in water, so that stretches that might not be possible on the ground can be achieved without strain. Although it is not yet practised widely, aqua yoga is a perfect combination of the benefits that yoga and swimming each can bring. Both share the practice of deep breathing. Swimming, involving exercise of the whole body with the deep breathing necessitated by its rhythmic movement, promotes the health of all tissues. Swimming that deepens breathing, stretches the body and calms the mind becomes the type of yoga described in the classic Indian texts.

Aqua yoga is aimed at developing your fluidity. By cultivating a "go with the flow" attitude to life, you can simultaneously be active while surrendering to outside influences. Water is eminently supportive to yoga's pursuit of the essential inner balance, without which spiritual and physical harmony cannot exist. The time of creating a new life and bringing a child into the world, requires this unified harmony in a special way, and aqua yoga can uniquely respond to this.

▽ Supported by water, the baby feels free and easy.

# The essence of aqua yoga

The benefits of swimming, as a very efficient means of keeping the body in good condition and rapidly returning to fitness, apply well to women during pregnancy and after birth. It may be the only form of exercise that remains comfortable until the moment of birth.

In pregnancy, women do better if they exercise. The human body developed over many thousands of years in a harsh world, and it continues to need physical activity to stay in good order. Many of the common complaints of pregnancy are due to an inactive lifestyle. Aqua yoga makes it possible to get the exercise you need without undue strain or risks and in a relatively short time, achieving results with two half-hour sessions per week.

Both yoga and swimming are ideal forms of an overall fitness programme during pregnancy and postnatally, but aqua yoga is more than the sum of its parts. It will enhance your health and well-being while you are pregnant, and help to prepare both your body and your mind for birth.

Pregnancy requires special training of the body to respond effectively to the added strains and stresses placed on it by weight increase and hormonal changes. If they are handled correctly, these changes can be experienced positively and greatly enjoyed during pregnancy and right through to the time when your baby is born.

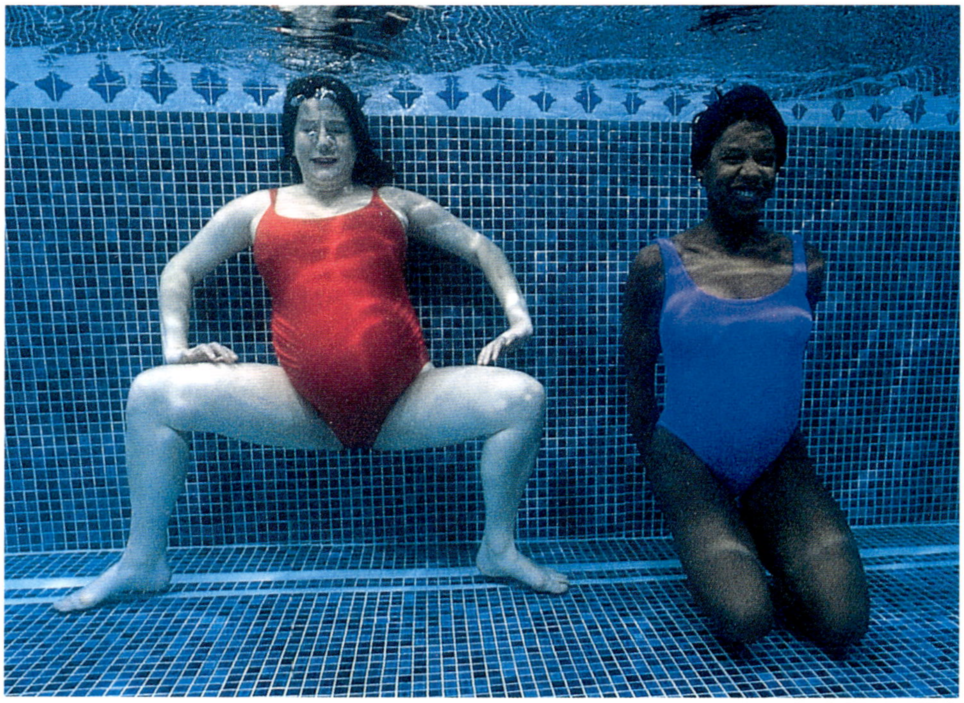

△ **Yoga helps you to open your body for birth, and then close it afterwards.**

## exercising during pregnancy

A study in the United States showed that pregnant women who exercised in water had lower heart rates and blood pressure than women who did ordinary exercises. The babies also benefited by having lower foetal heart rates after water exercises than when the same exercises were done on land.

Because of buoyancy, water makes the body virtually weightless, so all pregnant women immediately feel more comfortable and free to move. The aches and pains in the lower back, neck and knees that are common in pregnancy, due to imbalance in the hips and poor posture, can be eased or cast off, and while you are in a horizontal swimming position your blood pressure is lowered and the risk of exhaustion from exercise is greatly diminished.

◁ **In aqua yoga, the four layers of abdominal muscles are exercised effortlessly around the growing uterus.**

## Elongation

**Aqua yoga promotes isokinetic contractions of the muscles as they are moved at constant speed in the water. This is better for women than exercise that tends to shorten muscles by developing tension through isotonic and isometric contractions.**

▷ Legs can be actively stretched in water right up until giving birth.

Aqua yoga combines the efficiency that both yoga and swimming confer on muscles in extracting oxygen from the blood and discharging waste products into the lymph. The uterus works most efficiently if it has a plentiful supply of richly oxygenated blood to wash away the toxins and carbon dioxide which build up with muscle action. Invigorating exercise improves your vitality and the tone of your body. It makes you feel attractive and fit and promotes sound sleep.

## A strong heart

**Aqua yoga is even better than yoga at increasing cardiovascular fitness without a decreased blood flow to the uterus. In water, body temperature is not raised during exercise, which is also beneficial to pregnant women.**

## preparing for birth

Whether or not waterbirth is an option that you have chosen or that is open to you in the particular circumstances of your pregnancy, aqua yoga can be beneficial for you not only before the birth of your baby but also during your labour, when water can be your main source of pain relief.

Aqua yoga integrates the physical, emotional and spiritual. Pregnancy is always a time of intense changes and personal transformation, and aqua yoga can put your mind at peace. It facilitates relating to your baby in the womb and promotes powerful relaxation. It is good for the baby too, toning foetal muscles and inducing greater alertness long before birth.

The water facilitates the release of pent-up emotions that can create tension at the time of birth. Aqua yoga, even more than yoga, has direct effects on the nervous system, both calming and stimulating, which is needed for an ideal balance. It increases the occurrence of an optimal foetal positioning and presentation at birth, using pelvic rocks, rolls, swings and loops which are easier to achieve and therefore more effective in water.

It is also valuable postnatally to tone the muscles in depth around the newly contracted uterus, reshaping the figure and restoring health and firmness. So once you have given birth, return to the swimming pool – and why not involve your baby too?

◁ From late pregnancy until the period following birth, yoga in water helps you keep your spine aligned in a sound posture.

△ Your new baby is a welcome companion in postnatal aqua yoga.

# Where and how to practise aqua yoga

You can do aqua yoga in the sea, in a river or a lake, but you are most likely to choose a swimming pool. The depth needs to be between waist and shoulder level: chest level is ideal. For aqua yoga swimming, a length of at least a few metres is needed, but for the aqua yoga sequences you will not need much more than the size of a yoga mat.

There may be several pools near where you live or you may have to make do with the only one within reach. In this case, it is better to adapt to a less than ideal pool than not to do aqua yoga at all.

△ **The practice of aqua yoga makes it easy to help your baby develop her natural swimming ability. She will enjoy accompanying you in the water through another pregnancy.**

## choosing a pool

Indoor heated pools are not affected by the weather and offer a guaranteed basic temperature and standard of sanitation. However there are many variables that can affect your enjoyment of aqua yoga:

**Water quality** Most pools are still disinfected by chlorine, rather than ozone treated. Chlorine may affect asthma sufferers and ozone is far preferable for babies. Some pools are treated using a combination of ozone and sodium hypochloride; the latter acts as a residual disinfectant with fewer side effects than chlorine. The overall standard of hygiene is important. Not only the water but the edges of the pool and the changing rooms should be clean and inviting.

**Temperature** The ideal temperature is 30°C/86°F. Training pools where children learn to swim are perfect for aqua yoga as they are usually slightly warmer than average, yet not as warm as some hydrotherapy pools, in which women in late pregnancy may feel too hot. If you wish to take your baby swimming, the pool needs to be as warm as possible.

**Depth** Training pools may be between 0.8m/2ft 7in and 1.45m/4ft 9in in depth throughout. Other pools may slope gently from a shallow end to a deep end.

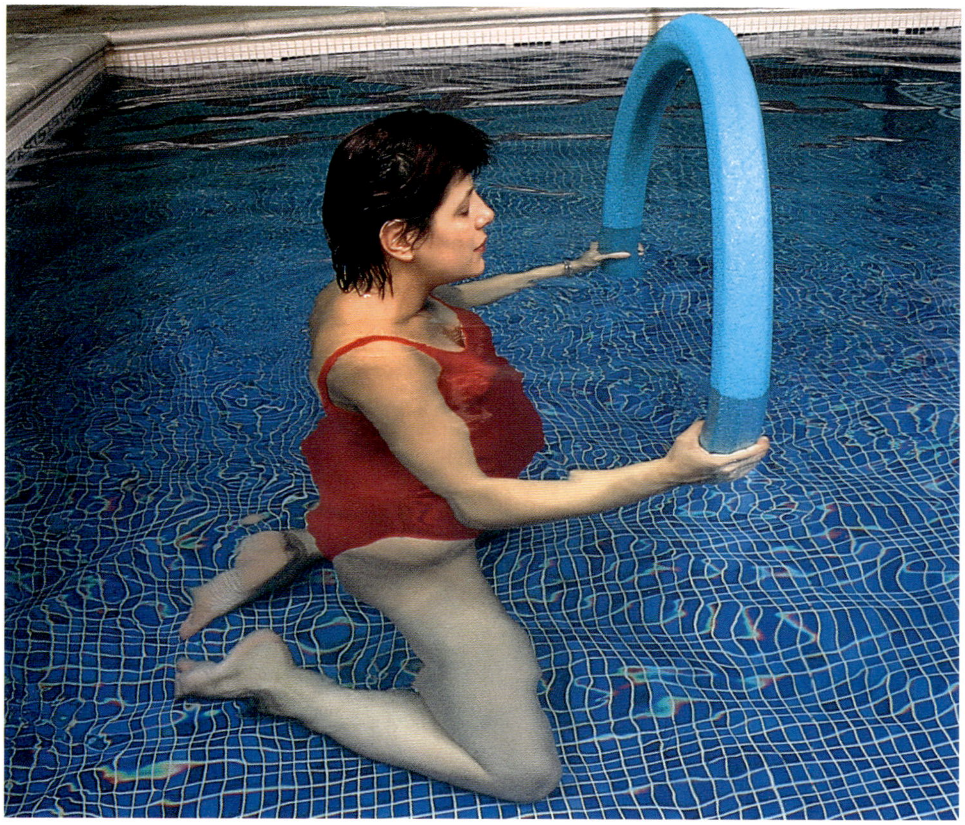

◁ **A shallow pool is more comfortable to sit and kneel in, particularly for non-swimmers, but swimmers need to have access to deeper water.**

**Fixtures, access and safety** Many training pools have bars that offer a steady support for hands and feet in the aqua yoga stretches. Other pools have a raised edge which can be used in the same way. Access into the pool may be by a ladder fixed to the side or by steps into the water. Steps are preferable to ladders in late pregnancy and if you are carrying your baby in and out of the pool. If there is no lifeguard in attendance, it is prudent to have someone with you at all times.

▷ **Avoid dehydration. Drink while you are exercising in the pool if you need to, particularly if it is warm.**

**Size (for swimmers)** Most modern pools are 25m/27yd in length, and training pools range from 8m/9yd to 12.5m/13½yd. Generally, a training pool is most suitable for aqua yoga. Doing lengths is fine if you are a confident swimmer, but forget about your ego and stay in the slow lane at least for your aqua yoga practice.

**Convenience** Take into account the distance you will have to travel, but seek out a well-managed pool. Many pools offer season tickets for regular swimmers and have special quiet slots in their timetables when you can stretch freely without being hemmed in by crowds. Some pools have times reserved for group bookings and it may prove cost-effective to arrange a weekly session with friends from your antenatal class or clinic.

## equipment for practice

Aqua yoga is a relatively cheap form of exercise, as very little equipment is needed. Buy a comfortable swimsuit that allows for growth not only around your abdomen but also on the bust. Goggles will protect your eyes under water and provide clearer vision. Make sure they fit comfortably, particularly if you wear contact lenses.

Brightly coloured foam "woggles" (also known as "fun noodles" in the United States) are becoming an increasingly common sight at swimming pools and are ideal for supporting you during your aqua yoga sessions. If your local pool does not provide them, it is worth buying your own as they are fairly cheap. Refer to the end of this book for details of suppliers.

◁ **Even if you are a good swimmer, it is worth investing in a pair of foam woggles (fun noodles) and a pair of floats that will give you full support to practise aqua breathing and relaxation. Some pools make these items available to swimmers on request.**

## how to practise

A session of 30–45 minutes is ideal. This will give you 10 minutes for exercises, 10 minutes for swimming and about 10 minutes for aqua breathing and floating relaxation. Always pay attention to the signals your body is giving you and stop when you feel you have had enough, which may be after only a few minutes in both early and late pregnancy.

Regularity is most important. It is better to visit the pool twice a week for half an hour than for one hour once a week. In late pregnancy, three short practices a week are most effective.

Besides observing general safety rules, take sensible precautions related to your pregnancy: be careful with temperature changes, rinse chlorine off your skin after swimming, allow more time to settle if you are driving home from the pool in late pregnancy. It is not advisable to swim if you have an infection, a rash, if you are bleeding or feel nauseous. Ask your midwife or doctor if you are unsure about whether you should keep away from the pool and for how long.

Most important of all, make sure you are swimming for fun; this way you will get the most benefit from your practice. If you don't enjoy it, don't do it, but don't be deterred if you don't feel like swimming for a week, or a month, as hormonal changes can temporarily put you off. Try again later.

# Choosing the best aqua yoga sequence





All the sequences presented in the sections on aqua yoga, like the land-based exercises, give equal importance to exercise, relaxation and the emotional preparation for birth and parenthood. You may feel that you wish to concentrate specifically on just one or two of these aims, and this is possible: use the sequences in the way that seems most comfortable and beneficial.

Aqua yoga in pregnancy can be effective whether you are a keen swimmer or not, and you will find variations to suit you whatever your ability, even if you do not usually enjoy the water. Do not be limited by preconceived ideas about your competence as a swimmer – just try it. Many women start aqua yoga tentatively during their pregnancy, find that they begin to enjoy it, and go on to improve their swimming skills after giving birth. Some of the exercises are vigorous and dynamic, others gentle and relaxing, but all the antenatal sequences can be practised throughout pregnancy, indeed right up to the beginning of labour.

▽ **The adapted swimming strokes encourage you to swim slowly, generating a very smooth rhythm and movement.**

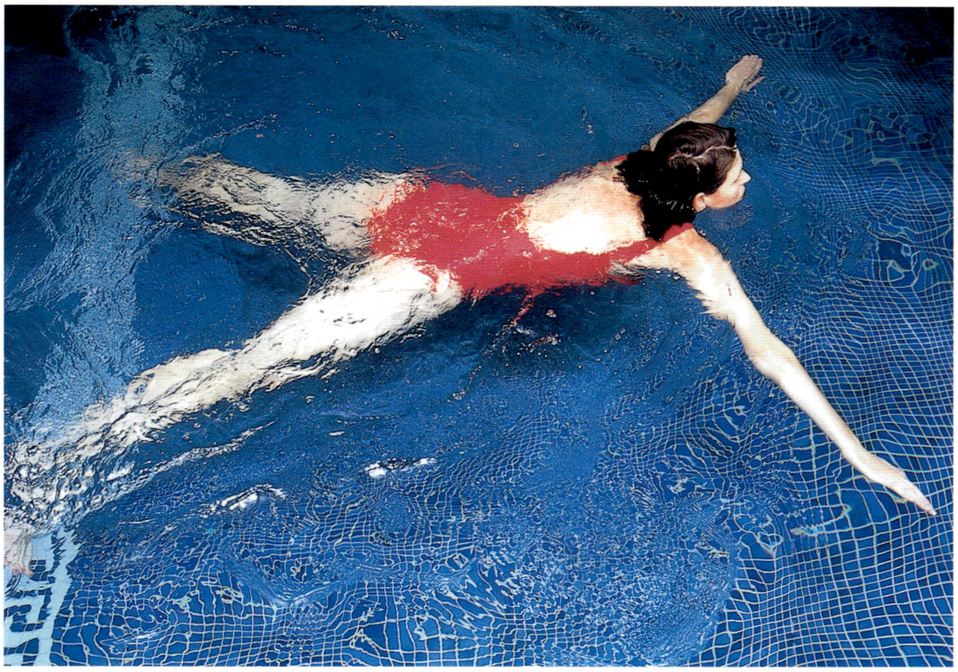

For maximum benefit, all the aqua yoga exercises follow the basic breathing pattern of yoga, in which you inhale as you begin a stretch, extend fully on the beginning of your exhalation and release the stretch as you end your exhalation. Take your time to get used to this pattern, which may be unfamiliar to you. However, with practice you will come to feel that it helps you find a very natural and effective rhythm. If you find it difficult, read the section on aqua breathing for a fuller explanation of how to use yoga breathing in water so that you familiarize yourself with it first of all. Exercises 31–33 are designed to help you practice the technique.

Check your breathing at the beginning of each session, clearing both nostrils with a few rounds of Alternate Nostril Breathing (4). This will also help to deepen your breathing before you get into the water. If necessary, learn to clear your nasal passages in water before getting into the pool. Fill a washbasin with water – salt water is best, so add some sea salt – then lower your face into the water and exhale sharply through your nose. You are now ready to begin your aqua yoga exercise, so enjoy!

## antenatal aqua yoga

The aims are:

- to enjoy a gravity-free environment
- to open the pelvis
- to stretch and strengthen the spinal and abdominal muscles
- to gain control of the pelvic floor muscles so that you can relax them while giving birth
- to expand your breathing capacity
- to relax more deeply and release worries and fears
- to "tune in" with your growing baby.

### About the antenatal exercises

The exercises fall into two main groups. For the first, you are mainly standing in water, holding on to the bar or the edge of the pool, or to a foam woggle. These sequences are equally suited to swimmers and non-swimmers and, if you do not float, you can use supports for relaxing comfortably and safely in the water. The second group of exercises takes you away from the edge and involves more swimming skills, including adaptations of strokes combined with yoga stretches. For women who are both competent swimmers and familiar with yoga, some classic yoga postures are adapted for water. Each woman should choose her practice according to her ability and how she feels on the day: there are no "set" programmes to follow.

The sequences involve going underwater, but you can also complete them without putting your face in the water if you dislike doing this. Going under water gives you greater freedom and helps to expand your breathing in a powerful way. Do not be limited by your perceptions of past experiences; many women find that these can be overcome. A good pair of goggles, and in some cases earplugs, may make being underwater more comfortable.

Some very good swimmers may prefer to swim lengths in their accustomed way rather than practise aqua yoga swimming.

◁ **The antenatal aqua yoga exercises activate the deeper muscles in the lower back and the pelvic area too.**

If practised well, swimming can only be beneficial. Yet the aqua yoga swimming sequence aims particularly at opening the pelvis and preparing the body for giving birth. It is useful to try the adaptations and the slow motion suggested, particularly in the third trimester of pregnancy, to get the full benefits of aqua yoga. Swimmers who do this find it helpful not only to prepare for the birth but also to refine their technique and expand their breathing.

If you intend to have a waterbirth, or to use water as pain relief during labour, the dedicated section of this book will be helpful. The earlier you start, the more effective aqua yoga will be to facilitate your labour and birth. If you are not a swimmer and dislike swimming pools, you can gain a great deal from practising the pelvic floor exercises, breathing and relaxation at home in your bathtub. Bathtime is popular with babies before they are born too.

## postnatal aqua yoga

The aims are:

- to realign the spine and strengthen the spinal muscles
- to tone and strengthen the abdominal muscles
- to regain full tone of the pelvic floor muscles
- to energize without strain in a short movement, relaxing at the same time
- to tone and remodel your figure safely
- to get ready to swim with your baby.

### About the postnatal exercises

Aqua yoga helps you close and tone your body again after giving birth, through sequences that mirror the antenatal ones. It is possible to start with these if you are reading this book after having your baby, though it may be helpful to look at the "opening" exercises in order to understand the reason for the "closing" ones.

## planning your practice

Start with the basic exercises (spinal alignment, pelvic floor and abdominal muscles, use of the breath) and progressively add on the other exercises when you feel ready, perhaps exploring two or three more each week. Be careful not to overdo it and do not stay in the water for more than 45 minutes, particularly in late pregnancy. Ideally, your selection should include some standing exercises, some aqua yoga swimming and a relaxation in each session. If you are not water-confident, make breathing your priority in the basic exercises so that you can feel your confidence increase at the same time as your buoyancy. Floating relaxation is also the foundation of supported swimming; this may gently but surely lead you on to unaided swimming.

After aqua yoga, you will be stimulated and your nasal passages will be clear. This is a good time to practise pranayama, the special breathing techniques of yoga, particularly if you have asthma or more general difficulty with breathing. A few minutes of Alternate Nostril Breathing (4) will again add greater benefit to your aqua yoga practice. You should always allow a few minutes of rest at the end of each session. As you may well be hungry after aqua yoga, it is nice to sit and enjoy a healthy snack at the pool rather than rushing out in a hurry.

▽ **Relaxation is an essential part of your aqua yoga routine both before and after having a baby, particularly if this is your first child.**

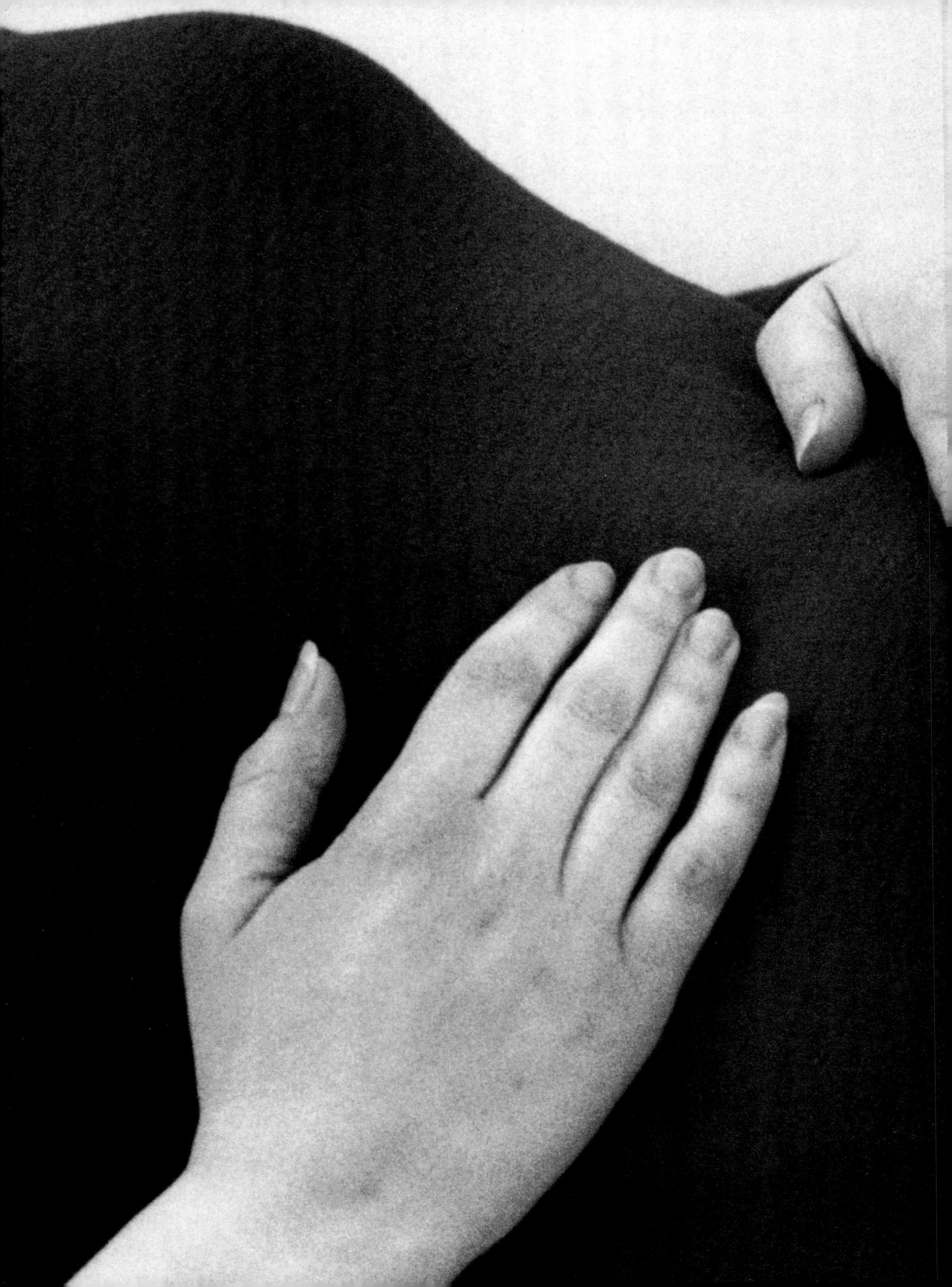

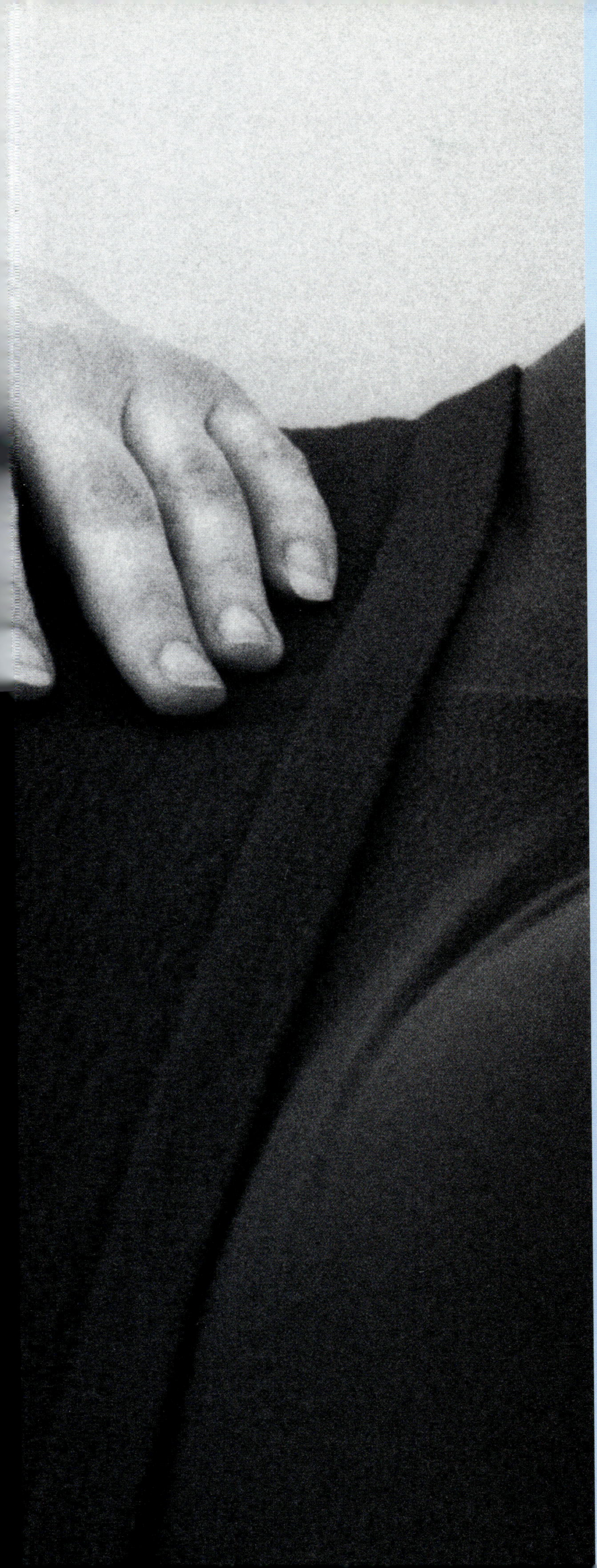

# yoga for conception

Conception is a miracle of energy, timing and receptivity. These qualities are enhanced through regular yoga practice, which improves the smooth functioning of the reproductive system. Then, when a ripe ovum (egg) is claimed by an eager sperm and slips into the prepared, waiting womb, the two will fuse into one and a unique new person can grow within the nurturing embrace of the mother's body.

# How yoga can help you conceive

Stress can impede conception because it ties up so much of our vital energy – and this is detrimental. If stress is claiming energy for keeping our muscles uptight, our minds on overload and our emotions all churned up, the other systems of the body have to manage on the energy that is left over. If conception is eluding you, stress is the most likely culprit. Indeed, long-term stress can even cause medical problems that require medical solutions. Regular yoga practice is a simple preventative measure and can also be a cure. It increases your energy supply and channels it to all the body's systems to keep them in balance so that you become fit and relaxed, living each moment to the full.

## what your body language tells you

The way you sit, stand and move can reveal a lot about your state of mind, health and emotional well-being at any time. If most of your energy is tied up either in your mind (your work, for example), in your emotions (say, problems that may be weighing on your mind) or in your hectic lifestyle, your body becomes depleted. There just may not be enough energy left over to work your reproductive system properly. It can be as simple as that. This stress can be reflected in your body language – legs tightly crossed, upper spine hunched over, or arms crossed over your chest.

"This state, in which the senses are steady and at rest, is known as yoga, the state of union."

*Katha Upanishad VI 9*

The yogic answer to stress is to rebalance your nervous and endocrine systems so that all functions are enhanced. Use yoga to stretch, strengthen, open and relax. This releases locked-up energy, and so eases conception, pregnancy and birth.

△ The "uptight" body language here says it all. This posture displays feelings of fear and vulnerability. The arms and legs form a shield across the trunk, blocking the flow of energy. The chest and abdomen are closed, so that breathing is restricted and energy to the pelvic area is blocked.

△ The body language here shows a relaxed mind, peaceful emotions and an erect, vibrant spine. The shoulders, neck, hips and pelvis are relaxed so that energy can flow freely throughout the body.

## breath is the key

The respiratory and cardiovascular systems bring oxygen (the prime source of energy) into the body from the outside air and circulate it to every cell. Good breathing habits, therefore, increase the total supply of energy available for the body's systems to use. The diaphragm is the large muscle that separates the abdomen from the chest cavity. It is the chief breathing muscle. If its movement is restricted through poor posture it cannot pump enough air into the lungs and so not enough oxygen is available to the body. Shallow breathing, which does not draw in enough oxygen, is one of the main causes of feeling below par. Deep breathing (using the diaphragm fully) is instantly energizing.

As you breathe in, the diaphragm contracts strongly downwards, massaging and energizing the abdominal organs and increasing lung capacity so that air rushes in, through the nose, from outside. The diaphragm springs back up again as you breathe out, releasing the abdominal pressure and decreasing the lung capacity so that air is forced out through the nose. This contraction and release reflects the whole momentum of yoga – activity followed by rest, followed by activity, in a continuous, balanced cycle. Practised with awareness, deep breathing reconnects us with this rhythm of life and helps us to learn how to relax deeply between all bouts of activity. It also helps to create a calm strength.

## 5 Tuning in to your breath

**A deep breath in recharges both body and mind. A deep breath out releases muscular tension, chemical waste products and tired, strained feelings. Mentally, take your breath in to the very base of your spine. Taking time to practise breathing slowly, deeply and fully induces calm, positive feelings.**

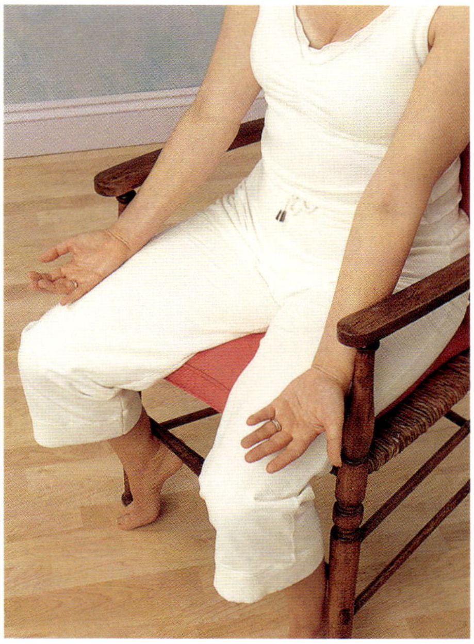

◁ Sit at the back of a firm chair with spine erect, knees apart and feet on the floor. Rest your hands with palms up in an open, receptive gesture. This position opens the trunk, so the diaphragm can move freely. Take several deep breaths with awareness of what is happening to your body as you breathe. Repeat the exercise frequently.

**CAUTION**

Deep breathing is strenuous, especially if it is new to you. Stop at once if you feel tired, breathless or light-headed. Rest for a while before starting again. Very gradually build up the number of deep breaths you take at any one time.



## 6 Flexibility in the pelvis

**The reproductive system lies within the lower part of the abdomen and is protected by the bony pelvic girdle. This area needs to be open and relaxed so that energy can circulate freely through the reproductive system and conception is unhindered. Regular movement of the pelvis brings energy, flexibility and strength to this area.**

◁ **1** Sit on the edge of a sturdy chair with feet apart and set firmly on the floor. Place your hands on your thighs above your knees, with fingers turned in and elbows turned out. Lean forward, bend your elbows and take your upper body weight on your thighs. This frees the pelvis – think of it as a bowl and tip it forward at the front "rim" (the pubic bone) and up at the back "rim" (where the sacrum joins the spine).

▷ **2** Open the front of the body by spreading your arms with palms up, lifting your chest and tucking your pelvis under so that the front pelvic "rim" rises and the back "rim" is lowered. This movement stretches the spine and releases tension. It also tightens the lower abdominal muscles that hold the pelvis in place. Repeat these two movements several times and practise frequently in order to increase mobility in the pelvic area.

# Yoga poses to release tension



For many people, tension settles in the pelvic region, causing stiffness in the hips, pain in the lower back, and general congestion and an uptight feeling in the lower abdominal area. Yoga stretches relieve all these conditions and allow energy to circulate freely. They also work on the whole body, so remember to keep the spine extended and the chest open in all these exercises.

**CAUTION**
Make haste slowly. Locked-in tension impedes movement. As you release the tension through yoga movements, you will find it easier to move much further. All yoga stretching should be performed with active relaxation and not force.

## 7 Pelvic movements with focused awareness

**These relaxing movements encourage increased awareness, blood flow and flexibility in the pelvic area. Feel that you are opening up to new healing energy and letting go of any tension there.**

◁ **1** Lie on your back, with a large book and three cushions beside you. Place one cushion under your head and tuck your chin in to lengthen the back of your neck. Bend your knees and plant your feet hip-width apart on the floor. Place the book on your lower abdomen, so that it is evenly balanced upon the hip bones and the pubic bone, then stretch your arms alongside your body with the palms down to support you.

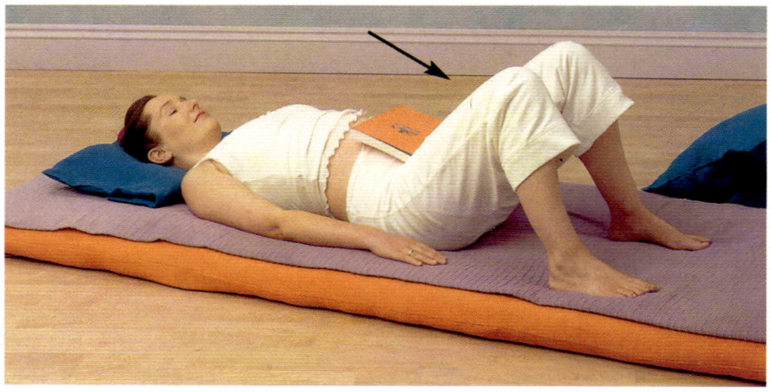

△ **2** As you breathe in press on your hands and arch your lower back as much as you can, so that the navel and hip bones rise and the front "rim" of your pelvis (and the book) is tipped towards your feet.

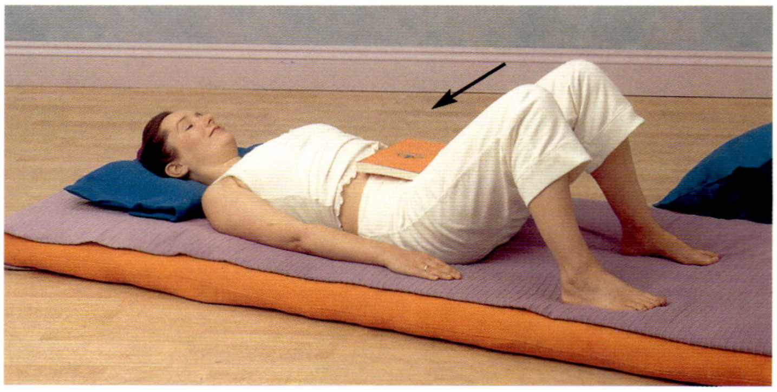

△ **3** As you breathe out pull the navel against the spine and press on your hands to lift the coccyx just off the floor, so that the pelvic front "rim" (and the book) is now tipped backward, towards your head. Keep your waist against the floor and move the lower spine only. Repeat steps 1–3 several times.

△ **4** Now place your hands, in a relaxed pose, on top of the book and breathe deeply. Feel the movements of the book over the pelvic area as you breathe in and out slowly for several minutes.

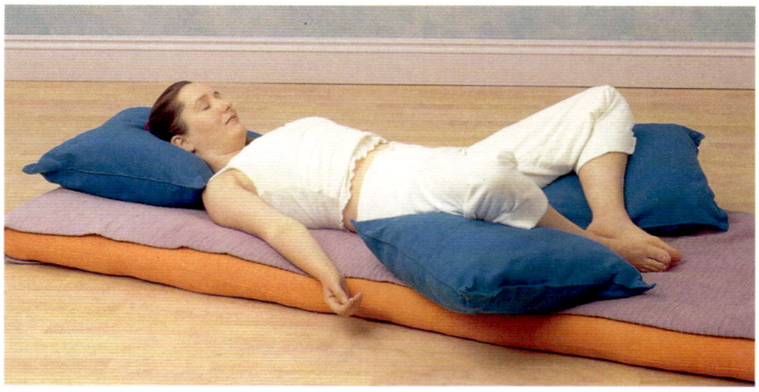

△ **5** Remove the book and bring the soles of your feet together so that your knees fall outward. Support them with the remaining two cushions. Place your hands, palms up, beside you in a gesture of openness and complete surrender. Relax for several minutes.

## 8 Seated looseners

**Let your partner encourage and help you. It is fun and relaxing for both of you. The closeness of trying to conceive can permeate all aspects of your life together.**

△ **1** Sit on the floor with legs extended and feet apart. Bend your right knee and bring your foot to rest against your left inner thigh, with your heel close to the pubic bone. Flex your left ankle and straighten your left knee. Raise your right arm overhead and stretch up through your right side, breathing in.

△ **2** Breathe out as you lean to the left over your left leg, with your left arm sliding gently along your leg and your right arm stretching up. Breathe in as you sit up, lowering your right arm. Breathe out as you bend to the right, walking your hands along the floor each side of your bent right leg.

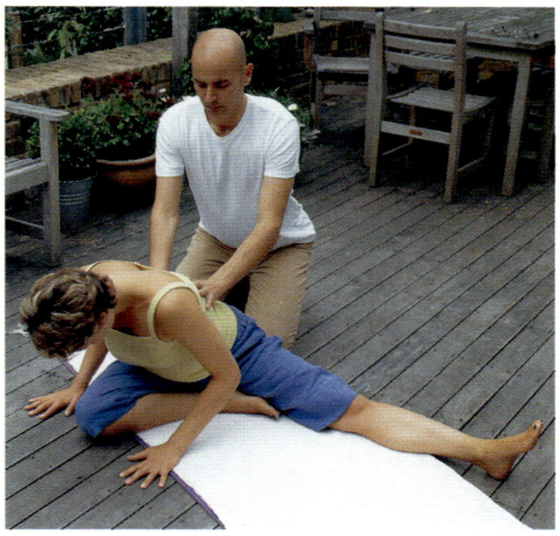

△ **3** Keep the left ankle flexed and stretch right through your left side as you bend over your right leg. Breathe in as you sit up straight. Repeat these movements a few times on the same side. Then breathe naturally as you change legs and repeat the movements with the left knee bent.

## 9 Happy womb poses

**It is important to focus your attention in the lower abdomen and to create space there in order to bring more energy to the reproductive system. Sit on the floor or a chair and open your hips, with your knees wide apart, as often as possible. You can sit comfortably on the floor to read, talk on the phone, watch TV and do most of those things you normally do sitting in a chair – except that in a chair the pelvic area is apt to be constricted, especially if you cross your legs.**

◁ **1** Lie on your back, bend your knees and hold one knee in each hand. Keeping your chin tucked down and your waist against the floor (using the abdominal muscles), rotate your knees outwards with your hands, relaxing and opening the hip joints. Circle the knees out and in again for a few moments, several times a day.

△ **2** Sit upright with your legs loosely crossed and a scarf around your middle, crossed over at the abdomen. As you breathe out pull the scarf ends loosely to create pressure. Breathe in deeply against this pressure to open the scarf and bring the breathing movements down into the lower abdomen and pelvic floor. Continue for several minutes.

△ **3** Sit with your knees bent and your feet apart and flat on the floor. Now bring your palms together with bent elbows. Keeping your chest open, gently press your elbows against your inner thighs for a few moments to open the hip joints. Breathe slowly and deeply.

△ **4** Remaining seated, lean forward and place your hands on the floor with palms upwards. Gently press your knees apart with your upper arms. Breathe deeply, lengthening the out breath for as long as you can.

# Sharing energy with your partner





Do you lack quality time with your partner? It may be that you are both so busy that you hardly ever have time simply to enjoy each other's company. Yogic stretching, relaxing and unwinding together may be all that is needed to make your womb, and his sperm, more "conception friendly".

Nature often works on a subliminal level, and an openness and emotional intimacy with each other can increase the likelihood of conception. Remember too, that prolonged stress can adversely affect the reproductive systems of both sexes, and that yoga gradually dissolves the effects of past stress and also helps to prevent new stress from building up.

Couples are very often disappointed if conception does not occur exactly when they are ready for it, especially as preparing for a baby involves great shifts in outlook and investments of energy. Yoga helps to deepen harmony and acceptance between hopeful parents at this difficult stage.

▷ **Teach your partner the joys of yoga relaxation. Stress affects his reproductive capabilities too.**

## 10 Moving energy into your reproductive system

**Every single message passing along your nervous system between the brain and the body has to go through the neck. It is hardly surprising that the neck and shoulders often get tense and energy-congested. Massage releases this congestion and allows energy to move freely around the body once again.**

△ Encourage your partner to massage your neck and shoulders to restore energy flow while you place your hands on your abdomen and focus on "charging" your ovaries with deep breathing. Then change places so that you can massage his neck and shoulders.

## 11 Synchronizing your energies

**When both partners are relaxed, synchronized and emotionally ready for conception – "two hearts beating as one" – a favourable energy field will help conception to take place.**

◁ **1** Sit back to back so that the flow of energy in your spines can synchronize, bringing you closer together on an energy level. You will find that your breathing also synchronizes as you relax into each other and become much more intimate.

◁ **2** To become even closer, sit facing each other with spines straight. Place your legs over your partner's legs, snuggle up, place your palms against his and gaze into each other's eyes. Your energies will synchronize and pass from one to the other through your eyes and your joined palms.

# A sample practice for promoting conception

1

▷ Tuning in to your breath (5)

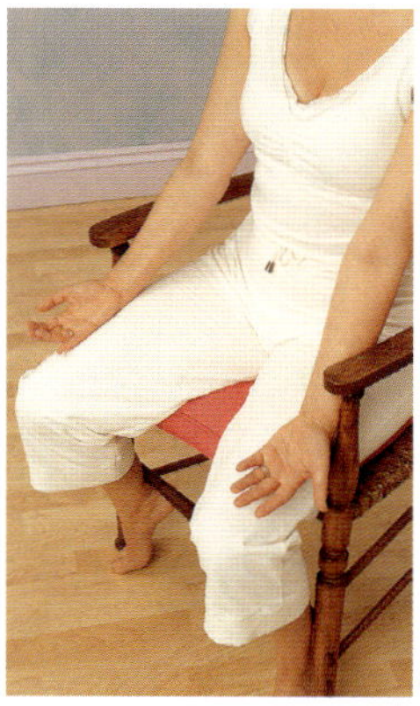

2

△ Happy womb pose (9)

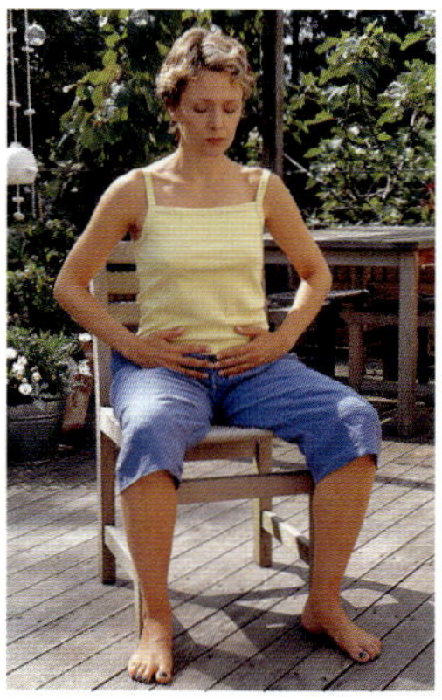

3

◁ Deepening the breath (1)

4

◁ Stretch, bend and relax (2)

5

▷ Flexibility in the pelvis (6)

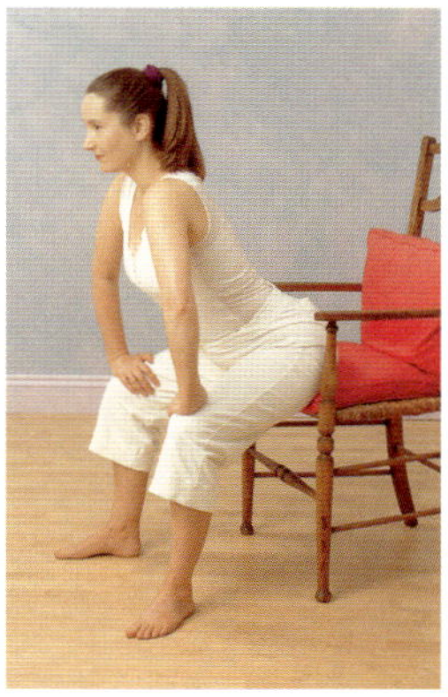

6

▷ Lengthening the outbreath (3)

## Questions and answers

**• Roughly how long should we try to conceive before consulting medical experts?**

If you have been taking oral contraceptives for years and then stop in order to conceive, your reproductive system may take up to a year to re-establish its natural rhythm. If you and your partner have stressful jobs you may need to take steps to change your lifestyles so that you can both reduce your stress levels. Yoga practice speeds up the rate at which you de-stress. Medical intervention may ultimately be needed but remember that medical procedures are in themselves stressful - so do what you can to help yourselves first. Remember also that there is no definite answer – everyone is different.

**• We have had all the medical tests recommended to us and there is nothing wrong with either of us. What can we do now?**

If both of you have undergone tests that have revealed nothing, there may be simple reasons why you have not conceived yet. The most common reason is simply that it can take a long time – always far too long when you are waiting eagerly. Highly subtle psychological and physiological changes can make a difference here. For example, the slight shifts in pH levels – in both you and your partner – that can arise from continued yoga and relaxation practices, could help to lead you further down the road to conception.

**• What are the chances of success with IVF procedures?**

Only medical experts can advise you in your particular case. IVF procedures are increasingly successful.

**• I just can't relax. What am I doing wrong?**

Getting uptight about relaxing in order to conceive! It is better to learn to relax in order to reduce the stress in your life. This then creates an atmosphere where conception becomes more likely. Go on holiday with your partner and practise yoga together away from your daily routine. Make plans to simplify your lives when you get home so that you can enjoy more quality time together. Make yoga part of your life and use your positive affirmations each day. Most importantly, affirm your blessings with regard to what you already have in life.

**• I have a specific medical problem (such as having just one ovary) that makes conception difficult.**

A positive attitude is a great help in overcoming all kinds of obstacles, but we also have to cultivate an open, accepting disposition that will enable us to embrace our life equally well if conception remains elusive. Seek expert medical help and keep as healthy and relaxed as possible. Use regular yogic exercise, breathing, relaxation and meditation practices to keep all the systems of your body running as smoothly as possible.

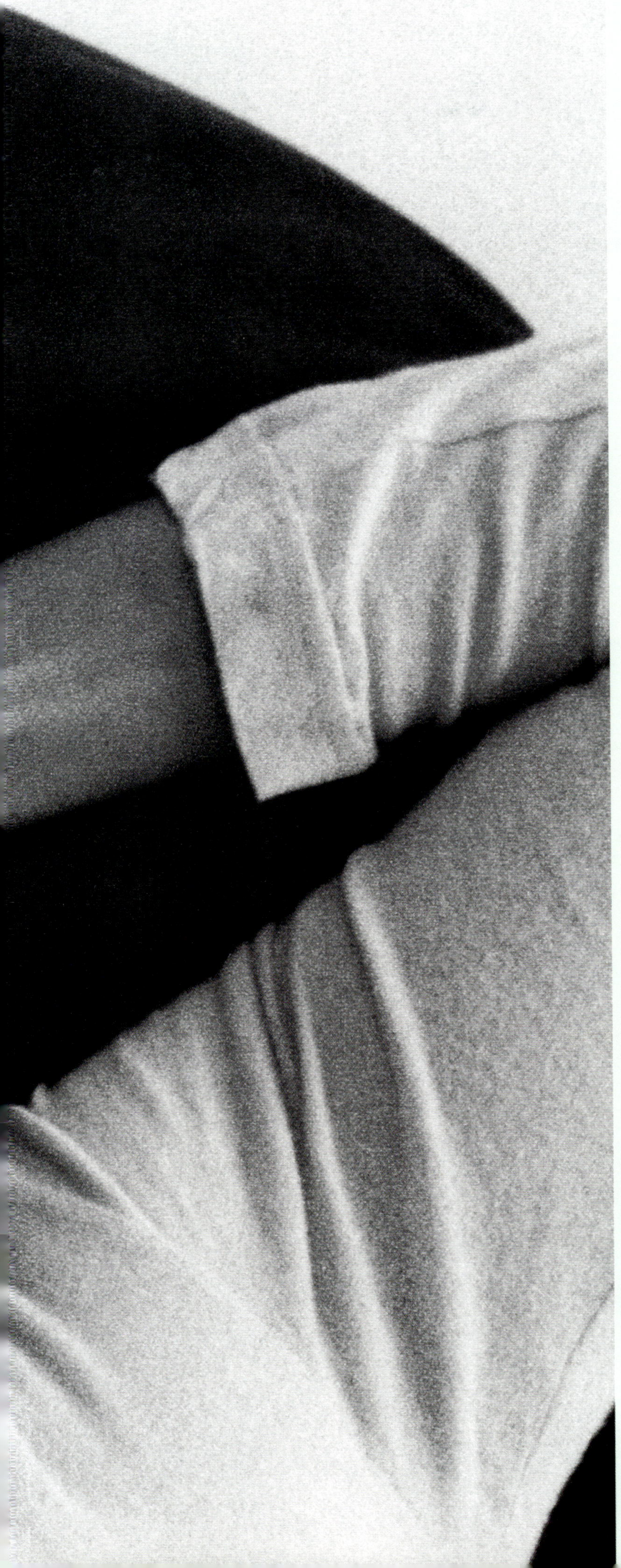

# yoga, aqua yoga and swimming for early pregnancy

From the moment of conception, Nature's first priority is the welfare of the baby growing in the womb, and your own needs take second place now. It is important to conserve your energy and to respond to your body's needs. Use relaxation in water to help it adjust, and gentle movements to stretch and tone your muscles.

# Make space in your life for your pregnancy





No doubt you already realize that you will have to re-arrange your priorities once your baby is born. However, the best time to start is right now. Making a baby requires a lot of energy, but our energy is limited, especially if we lead busy lives. That energy must come from somewhere and therefore, since Nature ensures that your baby comes first and gets all it needs to develop, it is vital that you conserve and boost your own energy levels. Yoga conserves energy by reducing stress through deep relaxation and boosts it by increasing your oxygen uptake through yogic deep breathing and movement.

## get the yoga habit now

Yoga will stand you in good stead right through your pregnancy, after your baby is born and for the rest of your life. You will soon be hooked on the sense of well-being that it brings. Your daily session can be quite short, as long as it is regular, and many yoga techniques can be incorporated into daily life. As you become more aware of your posture, emotions, thoughts and attitudes, you will want to adjust them, whatever you happen to be doing and wherever you are.

## learn to nurture yourself

Many women feel that they should hide their feelings, ignore their needs, always appear strong and independent and keep going, no matter what. But you must learn to stop, relax and nurture yourself. Only when you know what it feels like to be loved will you have the capacity to nurture the life in your womb and care for a tiny baby. Practise being vulnerable and learn to ask for help and support from your loved ones.

**CAUTION**
Whether or not you have practised yoga before, keep it very easy and simple for the first 14 weeks of your pregnancy. Focus on breathing and relaxation rather than movement.

## 12 Feet up the wall sequence

**This relaxing sequence rests tired legs and lower back, while stretching the muscles in the groin and preparing the muscles of the pelvic floor. Meanwhile, practise slow, deep breathing with awareness.**

△1 Sit with the legs along a wall. It is best to bend the inner knee, lean back on the hands and then forearms, and swivel your bottom round before raising the legs.

△ 2 Swivel your upper body round and straighten your legs against the wall – buttocks and legs should touch the wall. Place a cushion under your head.

△ 3 Place your hands under your head with elbows on the floor, to open up your chest. Breathe deeply for a few moments.

△ 4 Take your legs comfortably apart to release tightness in the pelvis and groin. Gently massage the inner thighs while breathing deeply.

◁ 5 Bend your knees and slide the soles of your feet down the wall, a comfortable width apart. Place your hands over your lower abdomen and become aware of your pelvic floor muscles. Draw in the muscles as you breathe in, and release the tension gently as you breathe out. Repeat several times.

## 13 Lying down stretches

**A similar exercise helps to relax the pelvic region for conception but it is just as effective here, where the point of focus is the lower back. The lumbar region of the spine, the sacrum and the coccyx should all relax against the floor – quite easy when the knees are bent and pulled gently toward the chest. If muscular tension prevents the lower spine from softening in this position, take long deep breaths out to relax more fully. The gentle movements will further ease your lower back and remove any stiffness or soreness.**

△ **1** Lie on your back with your spine long and chin down. Keeping your coccyx on the floor, take one bent knee in each hand. Bring your knees toward your chest then gently circle them out to the sides to massage your lower back against the floor. This is a great way to release backache. Repeat several times.

△ **2** Gently bring one knee toward the floor. As far as possible, make sure that both shoulders remain relaxed and your back stays flat against the floor. Keep your neck relaxed and breathe deeply.

△ **3** Breathe out as you roll on to one side, bringing your knees together. Relax in this position and breathe deeply. Breathe in to roll on to your back, raising first one knee and then the other, or both together if you can. Repeat on the other side.

## 14 The bridge pose

**This pose strengthens the leg muscles, especially the inner thighs, which helps you to support the extra weight of your baby as the pregnancy progresses. The Bridge Pose also stretches the muscles around the groin area, opens the chest and frees the diaphragm for deeper breathing. Alternate this exercise with the previous one so that you both relax and strengthen the lower spine and abdominal muscles. This will bring awareness and energy to the whole area.**

△ Place your feet flat on the floor near your buttocks, about hip-width apart. Stretch your arms alongside your body, palms down, for support. Breathe in and raise your pelvis off the floor. Breathe deeply a few times in this position. Slowly lower your buttocks to the floor on a long breath out. Repeat several times.

## 15 Deep relaxation with focused breathing

**Leave enough time so that you can end every yoga session with deep relaxation. It quickly dissolves any stress that may have built up, removing muscular tension and congestion and bringing new energy to all the body's systems.**

△ **1** Lie on your back with your spine long and chin down. Drape your legs over a beanbag or a pile of cushions, with knees bent out to the sides. Bring your heels close together and relax your feet.

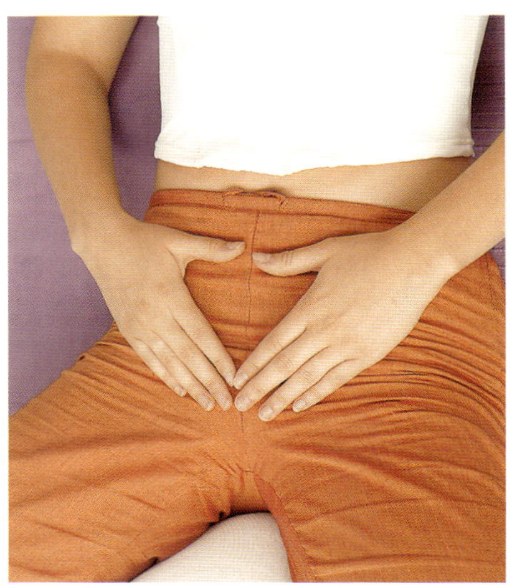

◁ **2** Place your palms over your lower abdomen, thumbs touching. Breathe deeply, and feel which is the best hand position to soothe you and bring nourishment to your baby. Close your eyes and relax.

# A strong, supple spine supports your baby

Good posture is especially important during pregnancy for the following reasons.

- It holds your womb, in which your baby lies, in its correct position in the lower abdomen. This makes your pregnancy a far more comfortable experience for both of you.
- It relieves backache and can avoid its onset.
- It creates more space in the chest and abdominal areas, which become increasingly crowded by the presence of the growing baby.
- It improves breathing, and therefore your energy levels, because it gives the diaphragm more room to move.
- It improves digestion, which cannot function properly if there is compression in the abdomen.
- It prevents congestion in the circulatory system to the womb, upon which your baby depends for all its nourishment.
- It streamlines your figure, however large or small the bump.
- It makes you feel great. Standing and walking tall express a positive outlook, whereas the general compression and congestion that result from poor posture can make your energy stagnate and your mood depressed.

Although changes to your figure may be hard to detect in the early days, especially in your first pregnancy, it is important to concentrate on your posture from the start, before any bad habits are established.

## 16 Dog pose

**This pose lengthens the spine and increases spinal awareness, as well as strengthening the muscles in the upper back, arms and hands. It also improves circulation and releases tension across the shoulders, and in the neck and face. Below are three variations on the Dog Pose. Try them all out and see which one suits you best.**

▷ **Pose 1** Hold on to a table, stool or radiator and step away from it until your spine and arms are stretched and horizontal to the floor, and your feet are hip-width apart. It helps initially if someone checks that your back is flat. Keep your head and neck horizontal, so that your ears are in line with your arms. Breathe deeply and bend your knees slightly if this helps you stretch further.

△ **Pose 2** Make a right angle by walking your hands forward (shoulder-width apart) with knees bent. Straighten your legs (feet hip-width apart) on a breath out, bringing your heels to the floor if you can. As you breathe in, stretch through the spine and arms. Hold the pose for a few breaths, breathing deeply.

△ **Pose 3** From the position shown in Pose 2, balance on one leg and raise the other. Keep the knee of the leg that is on the floor bent. Push down into your arms and hands. Now change legs to repeat on the other side.

## 17 Alignment of the spine

**Your posture can be improved simply by becoming aware and straightening up whenever you notice that you are drooping. The back of the body, being bonier than the front, has less sensation (fewer nerve endings), so it is quite difficult to be aware of the position of your spine. It helps to stand or sit against a surface such as a wall, so you can feel whether your muscles are holding your spine firmly upright or are slack. With practice, both awareness and posture will improve as you locate and strengthen the relevant muscles.**

△ **1** Stand with feet a short distance from the wall and hands behind your waist. Press against the wall with head, shoulders, waist and buttocks. Lengthen your neck, lowering your chin. Breathe in and stand as tall as you can. Hold this stretch and contact with the wall as you breathe out. Repeat a few times.

△ **2** Now bring your heels and calves against the wall and repeat the same stretch up as you breathe in, maintaining contact with the wall as you breathe out. Repeat.

△ **3** Bring your hands to your sides and press your waist against the wall as you stretch up, breathing in. Maintain contact with the wall as you breathe out. Repeat.

△ **4** Bend one knee and clasp both hands around your shin. Draw your thigh close to your chest as you breathe out, balancing on your straight leg. Release the pull on your shin as you breathe in and stretch up, maintaining contact with the wall. Repeat.

△ **5** Sit on a low stool with knees apart and feet firmly planted on the floor. Maintain contact with the wall with your head, shoulders, waist and buttocks as you breathe in and stretch up, then breathe out and hold the upward stretch.

△ **6** Once you have found and strengthened your spinal muscles, practise lifting up through your spine whenever you are standing or sitting.

# Easy standing poses

Now that you have learnt how to keep your spine aligned, and know how good that feels, you can maintain the alignment as you move gracefully through these sequences. They develop strength and suppleness, helping you to protect and nourish your growing baby as well as yourself. They also help to keep your feet firmly on the ground and remain steady as your body changes.

## 18 Grounding

**The joints and muscles around your hips, legs and feet take the weight of your whole body, and the muscles of the pelvis and pelvic floor carry the weight of your upper body and trunk. These important muscle groups can be strengthened and toned by the following grounding exercise, which allows your weight to pass smoothly through your legs and feet into the ground beneath you. It becomes ever more important to work with gravity rather than against it as your baby becomes heavier.**

△ **1** Stand with your feet apart and loosely bend your knees, making sure you maintain your upright posture through the spine.

△ **2** Bring your hands into Namaste, the prayer position, and press your palms firmly together with elbows out to the sides.

△ **3** Spread your hands wide, so that you keep your elbows bent and open up your chest area, all the time breathing in deeply.

◁ **4** Stretch your arms out to the sides and lower them, breathing out. Repeat steps 1 to 4 several times.

▷ **5** For a stronger version of this exercise, place one foot on a low chair and bend the other knee. Change legs after a few breaths and repeat with the other foot on the chair.

## 19 Standing stretches

**By stretching up from the hips and through the waist, these stretches create space for the diaphragm to contract downwards to a greater extent, so that you breathe more deeply. Twist and sway rhythmically as if you are dancing.**

◁ **1** Stand with knees loosely bent and stretch your arms overhead, first one side and then the other. Feel your ribs and waist opening and releasing.

▷ **2** Now bring your arms out at shoulder level and swing round from the waist, first to one side and then the other, without changing your leg or arm position. Repeat both movements.

## 20 Adapted easy triangle sequence

**This sequence works out your oblique abdominal muscles and your lumbar spine. Strong obliques help to prevent backache, hold your developing baby firmly and trim your figure.**

△ **1** Stand tall with feet wide and knees well bent. Place your hands on your hips and sway from side to side, tipping your pelvis up to the right as you sway to the right and up to the left as you sway to the left in a rhythmical movement. Keep your spine erect, coccyx tucked under and chest lifted. Repeat the sequence several times to loosen the hips and pelvis.

△ **2** Bend to your right side without tipping forward. Place your right hand along your leg and bring your left elbow back to open the left side of the waist and chest as you look upwards.

△ **3** Now stretch your left arm right up and back to open the left side of your body. Repeat the movement while bending to your left side. Repeat several times on each side.

# Greater challenges

An erect spine, an open chest and awareness of the position of your body and the flow of your energy are the fundamentals of yoga practice. Standing and sitting tall, at all times, will quickly improve your grace and posture and also help to prevent backache and digestive problems, while daily practice of deep breathing with awareness will soon make this your natural way to breathe. These simple practices are also the basis from which you can go on to develop more challenging yoga poses.

## 21 Adapted easy tree pose

**This is a balancing pose requiring good posture, steady deep breathing, stillness and focus. Start with the simpler versions of this pose and work up to the classical pose in your own time. All balancing poses create inner calm and poise as well as physical stillness. Standing tall and balanced becomes more difficult as the baby grows out to the front, so it is important to develop your balancing muscles from the beginning of your pregnancy in order to maintain your grace and poise throughout it.**

◁ **1** Stand with a wall on your right side. Stretch both arms to the sides at shoulder level. Rest your right hand against the wall for balance. Stand tall with chest open and coccyx tucked under. Bend your left knee and balance on your right foot. Now place your left sole against the inside of your right leg and bring your left knee to the side, opening up the left hip without compromising your erect posture. The aim is to get your knee out to the left so that you can push your sole high up against the right groin, without tilting your pelvis. Practise on one side then the other.

**CAUTION**
Make sure you keep your base foot straight and resist swaying to the side of your standing leg.

△ **2** Leave the wall and place a low stool in front of you. Place your left foot on the stool and bring your palms together in Namaste, the prayer position, in front of your sternum. Stand tall and gaze at a point in front of you, breathing steadily and deeply.

△ **3** Take your left foot off the stool and place the sole against your inner right leg. Use your left hand to help you find a good position for your foot, then return to the Namaste position and your steady gaze with deep breathing. Come out of the position smoothly.

△ **4** This is the classical pose. Place your heel against the groin with the knee out to the side. Focus on your breath and then join your palms together high above your head. Take a few good breaths while in this position, and then relax.

## 22 Pushing hands

**It is fun to practise yoga with a friend, so that you can help each other with your posture. Of course, you can also use a wall if you wish.**

▷ Stand tall, with arms outstretched and palms together. Each person takes a step forward with one leg (you can use either the same or the opposite leg to your partner). Keeping upright, with your hips facing forward, press your palms against those of your partner. Use comfortable pressure as you press, and, as you do so, breathe as deeply as you can and feel the involvement of your abdominal muscles. Change legs and repeat.

## 23 Classical cobbler's pose

**This seated position was traditionally used by cobblers and tailors, who needed to use both their hands and also hold things between their feet, and we can still benefit from it today. Many Western women have tight ligaments in the groin and pelvic area, through frequent sitting in a chair or car. It is important to stretch this whole area for ease in giving birth.**

**Practise sitting on the floor instead of lounging in an easy chair whenever you can – to watch TV, read or chat, for example – and this open position will soon become familiar and comfortable. Place cushions under your knees to begin with, until the groin ligaments stretch and relax naturally. Sit against a wall, or piece of solid furniture, until you can hold your spine erect without discomfort. Once this position feels easy and natural you can also use it to meditate on your baby or to practise deep breathing.**

**CAUTION**

Ligaments need to be stretched gradually and naturally without hurry or forcing. Ths is especially true during pregnancy, when special hormones gradually soften your ligaments so that they will stretch naturally to allow your baby to be born.

# relax and meditate with your baby





Focusing upon one thing, so that your heart and mind become peaceful and calm, takes you from deep relaxation into the meditative state. This yogic method is especially fulfilling when you are pregnant, as your baby can become the focus of your meditation. In addition, your baby will benefit enormously from your peaceful state and will relax with you.

This focus on your baby from the very beginning of his or her existence creates a close emotional bond between you even before birth – so that you and your baby are communicating and growing ever closer and more comfortable with each other right from conception. This is especially helpful if you are expecting your first baby.

## 24 Walking meditation

**It is important to take a break, with a change of activity and focus, when you have been sitting or doing mental work for a while. Stand up and stretch, then align your spine and go for a gentle walking meditation somewhere quiet, either indoors or outdoors. Your footsteps and breathing will gradually synchronize, taking you deep into yourself and into communion with your baby.**

◁ Stand tall and walk very slowly, with short, easy steps. Focus on your baby, placing your hands on your lower abdomen, over your womb. As you breathe in, lift your chest and open your heart space to receive the energy this brings. As you breathe out feel that you are giving this energy, and your love, to your baby. After a few moments, bring your attention slowly back to the outside world. Breathe deeply with a sigh or a yawn, stretch your arms overhead, look all around you and focus on the world outside yourself. Then return to daily life, fully refreshed and at peace.

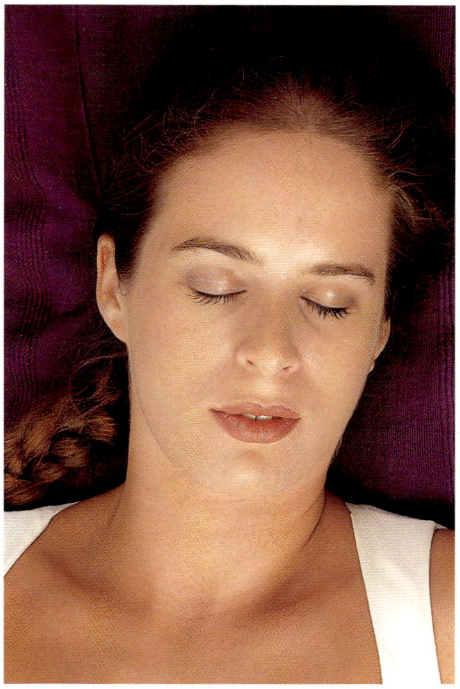

## 25 Deep relaxation, watching the flow of the breath

**It is easiest to relax completely when lying on your back, either with your feet up the wall or with cushions or a beanbag under your knees. If you plan to relax for more than 10 minutes you may want to cover yourself with a blanket or rug, as your body temperature may drop. Get comfortable and settled, close your eyes and breathe deeply and steadily for a few moments. Allow your mind to rest on the sensations of breathing.**

◁ Let your attention follow the passage of air in through your nose, deep into your lungs and out again through your nose in a rhythmic, soothing cycle. When you are ready to get up, breathe strongly and deeply before stretching through your whole body and, finally, opening your eyes.

"I am light with meditation..."

*Douglas Dunn*

# A sample practice for the early months

1

▷ Feet up the wall sequence (12)

2

△ Dog pose (16)

3

▷ Grounding (18)

4

◁ Triangle sequence (20)

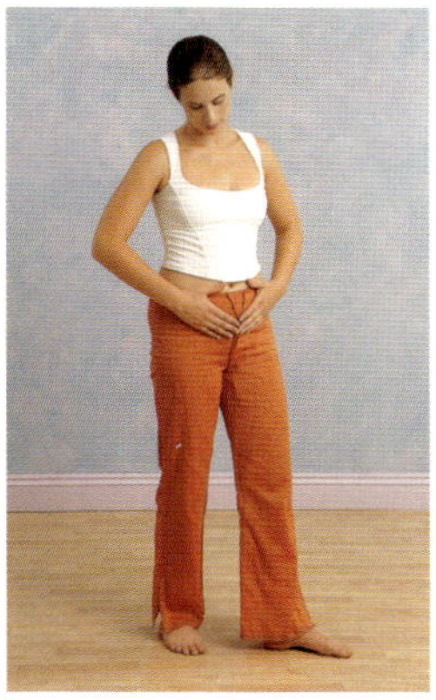

5

◁ Walking meditation (24)

6

△ Deep relaxation with focused breathing (15)



## Questions and answers

**• I suffer from severe nausea. Is there anything I can do about this?**
Nausea is a common problem while your hormonal system is adjusting to the requirements of pregnancy. It usually eases up after about 12 weeks and may be Nature's way of getting you to slow down until your pregnancy is firmly established. Practise relaxation with slow, gentle breathing, and avoid changing position too quickly. Many women find it helpful to sip milk or nibble dry biscuits, to give something for the stomach to work on between meals.

**• I get a lot of heartburn. What can I do apart from take medicine?**
Avoid rich or spicy foods and large meals. Keep putting bland food, such as a dry biscuit, into your stomach to absorb excess gastric juices. Watch your posture to avoid compression around the waist. Focus on the diaphragm and breathe deeply rather than in the upper chest only. Lean back from the waist with your palms pressed against your lumbar spine.

**• I feel sleepy, lethargic and tired most of the time. Any suggestions?**
This is Nature's way of getting you to rest, and the cure is to do so. Prioritize your activities and cut out the least essential ones to create more space in your life. Establishing a pregnancy takes up a great deal of energy but the good news is that you are likely to feel full of vitality once this early stage has passed.

**• Pregnancy is a totally new experience for me and I am really worried that I may miscarry.**
Breathe deeply and foster feelings of contentment and trust in Nature. Remember that your baby is becoming more firmly established in your body with every week that passes. Trust in the whole process, nurture your mind and body and enjoy regular relaxation practices – stresses of any kind will only increase any chance of miscarriage.

**• I feel anxious because I do not know how to cope with my pregnancy or if I'll be able to cope with my baby when he or she arrives.**
This problem arises because we can feel isolated in modern society. Many of us do not have an extended family on hand to support and advise us through the important stages in our lives, as would have been the case in past generations.

Help and reassurance are available, however. Join an antenatal group and make friends with other mothers-to-be – preferably in your neighbourhood, so you can easily get together to share experiences. Get to know women with babies and children and handle their babies, so that you will feel more confident when your own baby arrives. Joining a special prenatal yoga class or group gives women a regular opportunity to relax and become stronger and more confident. Above all, concentrate on breathing, relaxing – and trusting your inner wisdom.

# Aqua breathing

Breathing and relaxation in water are powerful tools to use for dealing with the emotional transformations of pregnancy. They create positive memories that the body can use efficiently in giving birth, and that babies may receive too. In the following exercises you are using not only your body but also your mind to control and expand your breathing in the water. Deeper, more expansive breathing has many benefits on the physiology as a whole and is of great importance in inducing confidence and calm. With practice, all the muscles of your pelvis become involved in your breathing, making it a powerful tool in labour.

## 26 Aqua breathing for non-swimmers

**Find the position that is most comfortable for you to breathe. At the same time, in preparation for exhaling in long dives, feel the water as an environment that surrounds and supports you. Nose clips are not recommended as aids to learning how to breathe under water, because they can place additional pressure on the sinuses. It is better to get used to inhaling through the nose as you lift your face out of the water and exhaling through both the nose and mouth underwater.**

△ **1** You may like simply standing in the water, against the pool wall, with a woggle to support you.

▷ **2** If the water is not too deep you can kneel, leaning on a woggle or holding it to stabilize you.

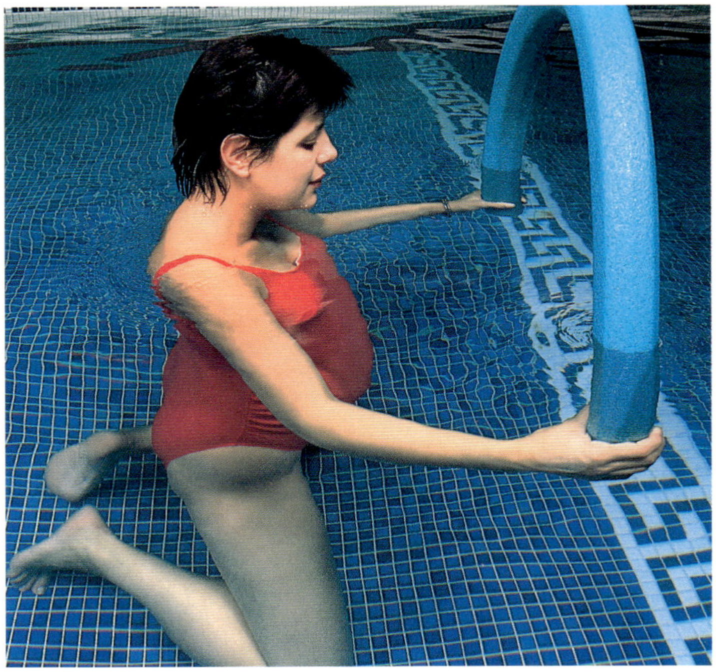

◁ **3** You can also float in an upright position, supported on a woggle.

▷ **4** Focusing on your breathing, extend your exhalation for twice the duration of your inhalation, counting to 2 when you inhale and 4 when you exhale, then to 3 and 6. Blow bubbles in the water if this makes it easier or more fun for you. You can also practise sinking to the bottom of the pool, which becomes increasingly difficult during pregnancy, slowly breathing out through your mouth.

## 27 Supported breathing stretches

**Two to four breathing stretches are a good preparation for floating relaxation at the end of your aqua yoga session. These stretches use floats or woggles for support. Try the different possibilities and choose the one that suits you best today. In a month's time your preferences and your skills may have changed. These stretches prepare you for the Breathing Dives with Relaxation (114) which are more comprehensive and effective.**

**If you dislike or cannot have your face in the water, inhale as you start and exhale as slowly as you can while you stretch forward without any movement of the arms or legs. The goal is to relax more and more as you reach the end of your forward movement and also the end of your out breath. If you are able to put your face in the water, you will notice not only an increase in the forward movement but also a better combination of stretch and relaxation. You may like to chant or hum a tune as you are breathing out in your forward movement.**

△ **1** Stand against the pool wall, holding a float or a woggle, and lower your body in the water. Pushing against the wall with your feet, knees bent, propel yourself forward with your arms extended, holding your float or woggle in front of you. You may find that your legs lower themselves in the water under you as you come to the end of your forward movement. Do not resist this, just relax as it happens and stand up when your feet touch the pool floor.

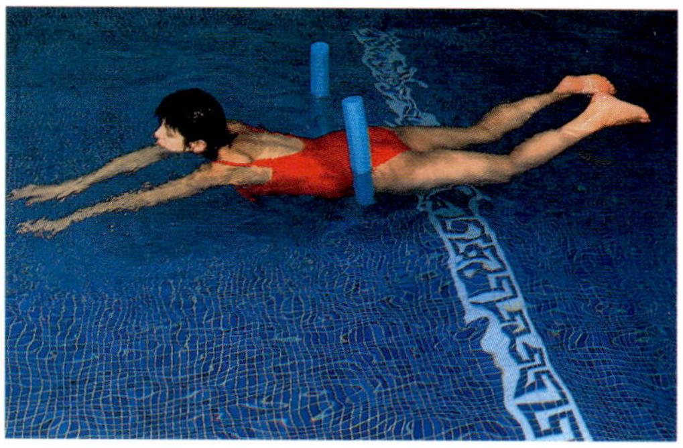

△ **2** You may prefer being supported by a woggle under your abdomen so that you can stretch your arms freely. You cannot be so streamlined as the woggle creates a transverse resistance, but your body can remain aligned until you run out of air in the stretch, without your legs going down.

△ **3** For a fully supported stretch, use two woggles, one under the abdomen and the other in front of you so that you can hold it with outstretched arms.

△ **4** If you are not a swimmer but you are reasonably water-confident and can go underwater, you can get the benefit of a dive with the support of a woggle under your abdomen. Inhale and push yourself gently off the wall to stretch, extending your arms forward and pointing them to the bottom of the pool in front of you. Blow out in the water and relax as you reach the end of your movement.

## 28 Submerged breathing

**If you are someone with a deep-seated, intrinsic fear of water, this exercise will be difficult at first, but most rewarding as you practise it.**

◁ **1** Extend your out breath under water as long as you can, until you feel you have to reach out to fill your lungs again with fresh air. This stimulates your breathing overall and makes you feel the power of breathing. Do not stay under water after pressure builds up in your head. If you hear a ringing sound in your ears, lift your head out of the water and take a breath immediately.

# spinal alignment and awareness in water





As the uterus becomes heavier and its weight pulls on the ligament of the pelvis in the third trimester of pregnancy, the lumbar curve in the spine tends to become more pronounced. To compensate for this, as your body seeks to maintain its balance, the thoracic curve can also become exaggerated, which may produce "waddling" in late pregnancy.

Aqua yoga exercises prioritize the lengthening of the lower back and simultaneous toning of the pelvic ligaments and leg muscles, which together ensure the correct progressive adjustment of the pelvis throughout pregnancy.

## The curvature of the spine in pregnancy

**Your growing baby affects the curves of your spine.**

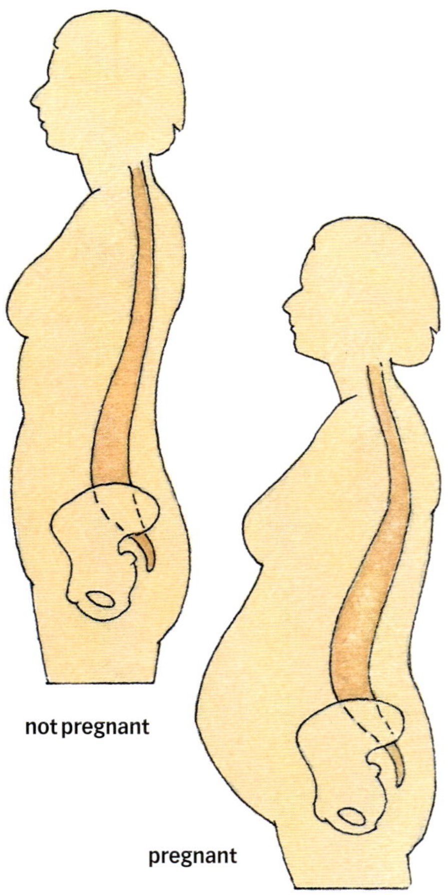


## 29 Free standing in the water

**Relaxed standing in the water at each stage of pregnancy will help with the mobility of the pelvis and free the lower back.**

△ **1** Free standing can be done facing the wall and holding the bar or edge, or facing the pool using a woggle under the arms for support. Stand with your legs apart, aware of your straight spine and the muscles of the pelvic floor.

△ **2** Bend your knees, keeping your back straight, and lower yourself in the water with a sideways zigzagging movement down and then up. Then bend and straighten your legs and shake your arms loose. This "loop" helps you gain awareness of your spinal muscles while you let all the superficial muscles "wobble".

## 30 Drops

**Easy to low squats will gently stretch the spine and are quite safe in the water. They allow women who are affected by pelvic pain to enjoy the benefits of easy squats with minimum risk and help them tone their pelvic ligaments.**

△ **1** First practise bending your knees outwards from a standing position with your legs apart, keeping your back straight. You can do this against the wall of the pool to help with alignment.

△ **2** As you flex your knees open, lower yourself in the water with a deep exhalation, keeping your back straight. Inhale as you return to a standing position. Do several small drops, lengthening the spine a little more each time.

# pelvic floor muscles



The pelvic floor, a deep "hammock" of muscles and fibrous tissues suspended between the coccyx at the back and the pubic bone at the front, supports your pelvic organs, the uterus, the bladder and part of the bowels. During pregnancy, the increase in weight of the uterus and the hormonal softening of the muscles weaken the pelvic floor, particularly around the three openings of the urethra, vagina and anus and their respective sphincters. The Pelvic Floor Lift and Release (31), below, involves the deep muscles in the lower back and pelvis.

## The muscles of the pelvic floor and perineum

**As the main support of the uterus, the pelvic floor muscles need constant toning and strengthening.**

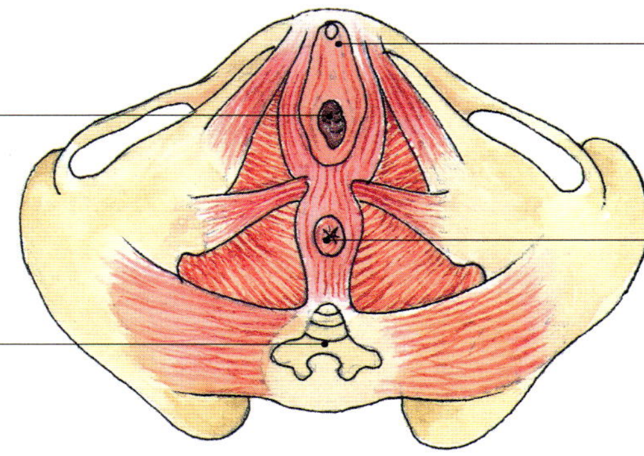


## 31 Pelvic floor lift and release

**It is important to gain familiarity with your pelvic floor muscles, which support your uterus and must remain toned yet able to relax to allow your baby to be born without tearing or needing an episiotomy. In yoga, breathing and exercise are combined to obtain optimal tone in these muscles. These exercises are particularly effective in water, giving you a firm, supple pelvic floor and preparing you psychologically for the physical motions of giving birth. The best way to protect your perineum is to learn to relax it fully, which requires learning to contract it first. The two actions go together and, coupled with breathing, they reinforce each other. They also contribute to the maintenance of a healthy vaginal tone throughout pregnancy, an easier return to sexual intercourse after the birth, and long-term pelvic health.**

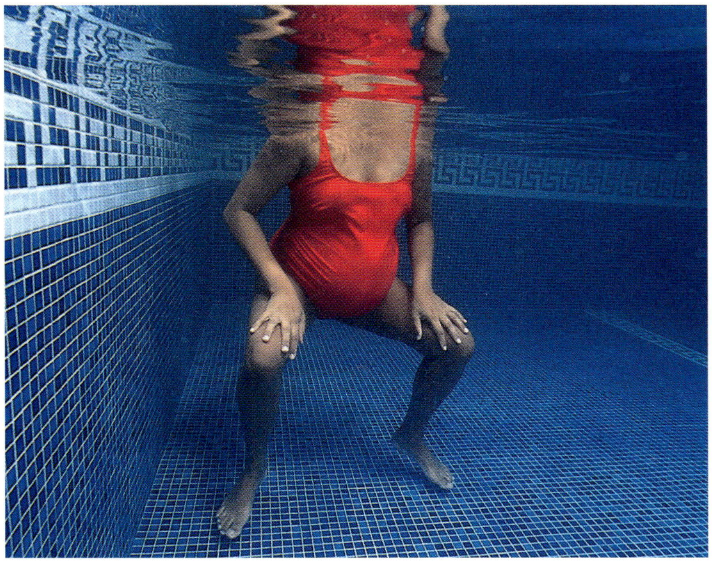

△ **1** Stand with your feet slightly apart. To locate your pelvic floor muscles, imagine that you are trying to stop yourself urinating in mid-flow (try this beforehand if necessary). Once you have found how to tighten the muscles, draw them in and up as you take a breath, involving your lower abdominal muscles as well. All this will become easier as you practise deep abdominal breathing in the water. Bend your knees outwards. As you breathe out, release all the muscles. Vocalizing your exhalation as "Aah" and making sure your lower jaw and neck are relaxed can help you feel this release even more. Repeat several times, concentrating on the feeling of the muscular action.

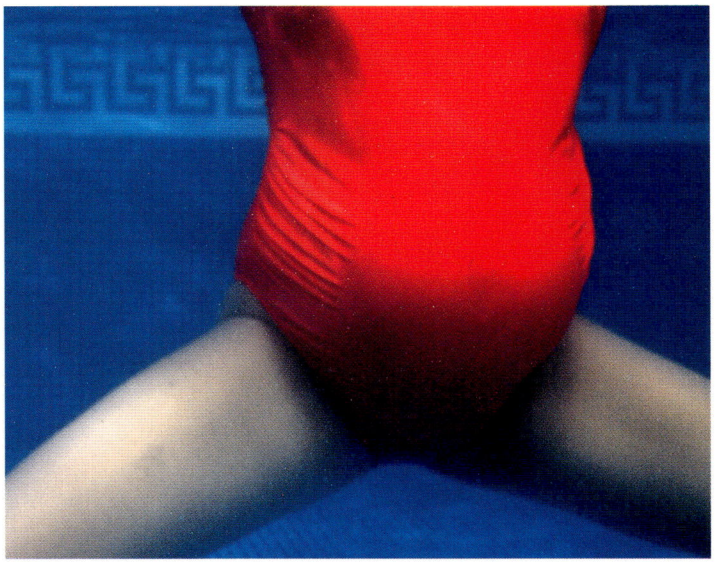

△ **2** Practise the same exercise in a semi-squat position. It is harder to draw the muscles up in this more open position, but also more powerful. You may find that you are also involving the muscles that hold the anus. These are useful when your baby is being born as as they are connected to your perineum and the birth is facilitated if they can be stretched and relaxed. With practice in this position you may come to feel separately the muscles that support the bladder. These are connected to the perineum at the front end, near your pubis.

# Opening the body **hip rolls** and **loops**





Rolling and looping hip movements will help to open the hips while lengthening the spine and strengthening the knee and ankle joints. These ample movements are much easier in the water and can be done at all stages of pregnancy, helping to prevent or relieve backache. They will also help you to find your rhythm in movement in preparation for labour. Make sure you breathe rhythmically while doing the rolls and loops, and enjoy the massaging action of the water on your body in these dynamic circling movements.

▷ **Before starting the rolls and loops, loosen your hips by bending one leg and then the other from a standing position with your legs wide apart, either against the wall or standing freely. If you are familiar with yoga, this is like the base of an Archer's pose in the water.**

## 32 Hip rolls and figures-of-eight

**Stand upright with your feet hip-width apart, supporting your hands and bent arms on the bar or pool edge. You can face the wall, which allows more traction in the loops, or face the pool, which helps you keep your back straight. In later pregnancy, rolls will relieve backache caused by uneven distribution of your weight, due to either your posture or the position of the baby.**

△ **1** Bend your knees and make a horizontal crescent movement with your hips from left and right. As you do so, find a good breathing rhythm that energizes you. Repeat the movement a few times, then extend the roll so that your hips are making a full circle. Circle your hips in both directions.

△ **2** Increase the intensity of the lower back stretch by opening your legs wider or extending your arms more to allow a wider circle. You can introduce a swing in the roll so that you are pulling more on the bar and bending your knees slightly further on the outer reaches of your circle.

△ **3** You can also use a woggle to support you when doing hip rolls, which gives you more freedom but is a less energetic movement. To make a figure-of-eight roll your hips from left front to right back and from right front to left back in a continuous curving motion that stretches your whole spine as you go.

## 33 Hip loop forward and back

**You can make this sinuous loop as small or as extreme as you wish. If you feel very energetic, you can make it more dynamic by positioning your feet wide apart and looping into a low squat. Paradoxically it may feel easiest to do this when you are in late pregnancy. Keep your head relaxed and be aware of the alignment of your spine throughout: your legs and arms are the bending stretchers in this exercise while your spinal and abdominal muscles are stretched and toned.**

△ **1** Stand upright with your feet apart, facing the pool wall, ideally holding on to a bar if there is one, or on to a woggle. Keeping your arms bent, inhale, bend your knees and let yourself drop as you exhale.

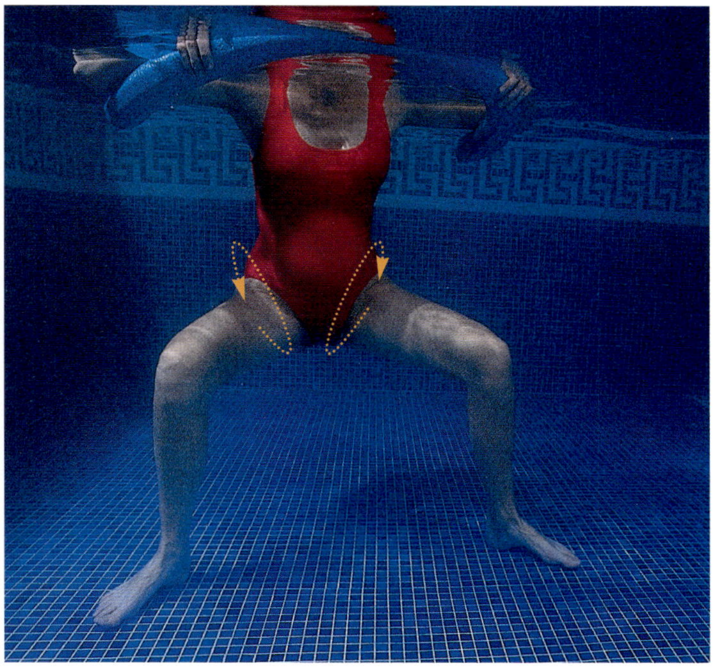

△ **2** Thrust your pelvis forward and straighten your legs as you come up, then, with your back extended, lean your trunk forward and bend your knees again to roll forward. Continue the movement as a loop, forward and back. You can then reverse the loop.

## 34 Hip wheel

**For the standing exercise, it does not matter whether you are facing the wall or the pool. Support your hands, with bent arms, on the bar, pool edge or a woggle. You can make the exercise more dynamic by having your feet further apart and therefore widening the wheel. You can also go into a deeper squat on the way down. Most of all, make sure you adopt a comfortable starting position that allows you to enjoy this hip wheel.**

△ **1** Begin with your feet wide apart. Bend your knees and swing your pelvis slowly from side to side in a vertical crescent, keeping your back very straight, finding a good breathing rhythm as you go down and then up.

△ **2** When you are comfortable with this swing, take your hips all the way round and make a vertical wheel, going down again on the other side, bending your knees as you go down, straightening them as you go up in a smooth, rhythmical movement, inhaling as you go up and exhaling as you go down.

# hip openers





Once you have loosened your lower back with rhythmical rolls and loops, you can proceed to further stretching of the ligaments and muscles in the pelvis, particularly those that control the hip movements. The hormones progesterone and relaxin that are produced in your pregnant body give you greater flexibility in your joints. This makes it possible to overstretch dangerously on dry land, but the risk is eliminated in water. Conversely, if you are normally stiff, water can help increase your flexibility.

## 35 Opening steps

**Stand upright in the pool, facing the wall or the pool and with your hands on the bar or pool edge. Keep your arms slightly bent. You can also support your arms on a woggle, facing the woggle or with your back to it. If you are facing the wall, you can wedge your feet at the base of the wall on the pool floor while doing ankle rotations, which may help to prevent swelling later in your pregnancy.**

△ **1** Stand with your feet apart, keeping your legs straight. Turn one foot out and rotate the ankle outwards in small circles. Extend your toes to the pool floor as your foot stretches fully in the circling movement. Repeat with the other foot. In late pregnancy, hold on to the side of the pool for balance or place your hands on a woggle in front of you.

△ **2** To increase the stretch, open your legs slightly wider and bend your knees, turning your feet out. You can also turn one foot in and one foot out at a time, moving sideways in steps that open your hips. There is something funny about this exercise, so enjoy it. Make sure you keep your upper body relaxed all the time as you bend down.

## 36 Russian squats

**You may be surprised at being able to do this exercise in water while you could not contemplate it on dry land even if you were not pregnant! It allows a deep squat while keeping your spine straight. During late pregnancy, both Russian squats and the open stretch that follows help the baby's head to engage in the pelvic outlet at the best possible angle, while you make the greatest possible use of gravity in preparation for labour. In a shallow pool, Russian squats can be practised from a kneeling position, with a short squat in between as you change legs.**

△ **1** Facing the wall or supporting yourself on a woggle, stand upright and let yourself drop in the water, keeping one leg bent while stretching the other into your heel in the fashion of Russian folk dancing. Keep your shoulders straight and your hips forward to elongate your spine.

△ **2** Jump up as you change legs so that you stretch alternate sides in a vigorous rhythm, keeping your back upright throughout the movement, lowering the base of your spine.

◁ **3** Once you have gained some experience stretching your leg with your heel on the floor, you can try to stretch it higher in the water. It is more strenuous, but your bent standing leg allows you to keep your back straight throughout the exercise, which is easier against the wall.

◁ **4** A variation of this exercise is to lift your leg straight in front of you in the water and bring it down bent, changing legs with a little jump. The resistance of the water makes this a more strenuous movement than it may seem at first sight.

## 37 Open stretch and pelvic swing

**For the open stretch you can face the wall or the pool, or use a woggle for support. The pelvic swing can only be done using a bar to support you. It is a very helpful exercise to prepare for the letting go that is required at the second stage of labour, when the head of the baby is ready to be born.**

△ **1** To do the open stretch, stand upright with your arms bent and your whole body relaxed, and let yourself drop on an exhalation while opening your bent legs wide. If you are facing the wall, it can help to wedge your feet against the base of it.

△ **2** To make this stretch even more open, drop further down, opening your bent legs wider. Breathe as deeply as possible while you stretch. Repeat several times, letting yourself drop slowly, stretching wide and coming back to the centre to a standing position between drops.

△ **3** For the pelvic swing, lower yourself in the water facing the wall and holding on to the bar, with your hands shoulder-width apart. Open your legs wide and bring them up so that you can wedge your feet on the pool wall with your knees slightly bent. Swing your pelvis back so that both your legs and arms stretch out, and then forward again close to the wall.

△ **4** To increase the stretch, bring your perineum as close to the water's surface as possible and swing further back. Find a rhythm that suits you and breathe as deeply as possible in a broad swing. The pelvic swing can be combined with a pelvic floor muscle exercise. Inhale and lift your pelvic floor muscles as you swing backwards and release them as you exhale in the forward swing.

△ **5** You can also do a pelvic swing using a woggle for support, either in front of you or behind you. Focus on your pelvic floor, exhaling and releasing all tension in a slow forward movement of the hips.

# Kneel open and swing





For these exercises, kneel down on the floor of the pool or, if the water is too deep for this, hang down from a support – the bar or a woggle – with your knees open and your legs loose. After stretching the base of the spine and opening the lower back with the hip openers, you are now stretching the muscles in the front of the body, particularly all the abdominal muscles. These exercises are toners for the thigh muscles as well as helping you to expand your abdominal breathing. The stretching of the lower back and abdominal muscles is combined in rhythmical movements, circling forward and back.

## 38 Kneel down and turn

**The closer to the wall that you are kneeling in this exercise, the greater the stretch will be and the straighter your back. It is also an ideal way to practise your pelvic floor lifts, drawing in your muscles as you inhale and relaxing them as you exhale.**

▷ **1** Holding the edge of the pool or a woggle, lower your knees wide open as far as you can, letting them rest on the pool floor if the depth of the water allows it. Breathe as deeply as possible in the whole abdominal area up to the diaphragm, keeping relaxed.

▷ **2** Lift one knee up and turn it out while placing your foot on the pool floor, opening the hip on that side. Keep your knee as straight above your foot as possible. Alternate right and left turns in a rhythm that suits you, taking time to breathe deeply and stretch fully.

## 39 Kneeling archer pose

**You can achieve this classic yoga pose even if you are new to yoga. It tones your buttocks and thighs and energizes you as you breathe in. If your pool is too deep to practise the kneeling pose, go directly to the standing archer pose.**

▷ **1** Begin in the kneeling position from the previous exercise, with one knee turned out. Keep your trunk upright as you turn your raised knee out and breathe into the stretch that is created. Repeat on the other side.

△ **2** As you feel stronger, you can practise the archer pose. Stand with your back to the pool wall and your legs wide apart. Bend one leg and turn out your hips and torso to face your front knee. Keep your back leg extended. Breathe deeply into the leg stretch. Your front knee should be directly above your foot. If you are experienced in yoga, you may be able to keep your back foot flat on the pool floor, but do not worry if your heel comes up to allow your hips to turn.

△ **3** As well as being done along the pool wall or holding a woggle to gain more stability, this pose can also be done free-standing in the pool, and in its full version it involves an extreme stretch. On your firm base, take a deep inhalation and extend both arms equally. Exhale in this stretch and breathe two more times as deeply as you can from the lower abdomen before bringing your arms down. Repeat on the other side.



## 40 Swing from kneeling to squatting and back again

**This exercise can be done either facing the wall or the pool and holding on to the bar or edge, or using a woggle as a support. This is a grounding, opening exercise that can be practised throughout pregnancy and facilitates an optimal position for your baby as birth approaches.**

◁ **1** Start by kneeling on the pool floor with your knees wide open, breathing deeply. Lower your spine and lift both knees at the same time, bringing your legs forward into a squat. Hold for a moment, then lower your knees again to go back to a kneeling position.

▷ **2** At first you can shift from kneeling to squatting very slowly. Once you are familiar with the exercise, you can do it in a dynamic fashion, jumping from kneeling into a squat and back into kneeling, inhaling as you jump and exhaling as you reach the kneeling and squatting positions.

# arms and shoulders

These exercises make use of the resistance of the water to tone the muscles of the upper body. During pregnancy, you may find that the outer part of your upper arms, like your thighs, are areas in which body fat may accumulate. Regular exercise will keep this to a healthy minimum and your arms will stay shapely. Aqua yoga tones the muscles that support your breasts through a mixture of held postures and rhythmical movements. Moving your arms under water is more energetic than it looks and strengthens your heart, which is essential to an active, healthy pregnancy. These exercises are designed to be a gradual and gentle training of your chest muscles to help your heart work harder as your baby grows, so that it can cope with the exertion of labour without reacting wildly. You can do them at your own pace, without strain, whatever your level of water skills. In a few minutes of moving your arms vigorously in water, you will not only feel stimulated but may wonder what was worrying you before you got into the pool.

## 41 Water sunwheels

**A graceful but very intense exercise that tones all the back muscles as well as the arms and shoulders.**

◁ **1** Standing in the water, bend your knees so that the water comes up to your neck. Move your arms forward and back, making figures-of-eight in the water, then open your arms and cross them in front of you with a sculling movement of your hands.

▷ **2** Extend your arms down in the water and stretch them outwards, pushing the water away from your body. Come back to the centre and repeat the movement, pushing away slightly higher towards the water's surface each time. Breathe deeply into the rhythm of the movement.

## 42 Arm twists

**While your hips and legs make an open base, these two arm twists tone your upper back muscles and open your chest. The more your arms are immersed below the surface of the water, the more effective the exercise will be. The second arm twist is asymmetrical and makes use of an energetic rhythm in the stretch.**

△ **1** Kneeling or standing with legs open wide and bent in the pool according to depth, clasp your hands behind your back, turning your shoulders out. Pull on your arms as much as possible, while breathing deeply, to move your shoulders right and left with an intense stretch in the pectoral muscles as well.

△ **2** If you are in a half-squat standing position, you may find it helpful to bend your legs alternately on each side as you stretch.

△ **3** Stand in the pool with your legs apart to make a strong base, bending your knees if necessary so that your arms can stretch in front of you just below the surface of the water.

◁ **4** Inhale and swing your shoulders to one side, stretching the arm on that side and letting the other one follow the movement in a relaxed way as you exhale. Allow your head to follow the spinal twist rather than to lead the movement.

▷ **5** Inhale and turn to the other side in a swinging movement. Your knee on the stretching side will tend to bend, increasing the movement on a stable base.

## 43 Standing and supported breaststroke

**The arm movement of breaststroke opens the chest and stretches the upper back and arms in a way that is ideal throughout your pregnancy. Even if you cannot swim breaststroke, practising the arm movement as an exercise has its own merit. It can prevent and cure heartburn in early and late pregnancy, as well as gradually making more space for the growing baby under the ribcage. It is also a good exercise to keep your breasts naturally supported as they grow larger and heavier. Three different versions are presented here.**

△ **1** Stand with your knees slightly bent if necessary so that the water comes up to your neck, or kneel if the water is shallow. Stretch your arms together in front of you, with the palms of your hands facing each other.

△ **2** Turn your hands out and open your arms in a wide circling movement, going as far back as possible before returning to stretch your arms again, and repeating the movement several times in your own rhythm. Inhale open, exhale back.

△ **3** If you find that you lack stability as the forward movement takes you off your base, you may want to use a woggle under your knees and stand in a semi-squat in the pool. This will give you a wide, supported base when stretching your arms.

△ **4** You can also make the same breaststroke arm movement lying in the water on your front supported by a woggle. Keeping your legs and head relaxed, repeat the arm motion described in step 1. Breathe in as you extend your arms.

# Adapted breaststroke swimming





Swimming is excellent for breath control, and adapted breaststroke in pregnancy encourages you to breathe using your diaphragm more effectively. Emphasis is put on the exhalation phase during the forward thrust, ideally with your face in the water. This ensures a smoother rhythm and eliminate any forced or jerky movements of the legs. The minimum amount of energy is used, while greater precision and a smoother movement is achieved.

If you wish to swim breaststroke without support, it is best to do so with your face in the water. Keeping your head above the water makes it impossible for you to open the pelvis in the way that makes breaststroke valuable during pregnancy. It also places strain on the muscles at the base of the neck.

If you learnt to swim breaststroke a long time ago and never explored how to breathe, now is your opportunity to do so, at the same time acquiring a more precise and efficient technique with a fully aligned spine.

△ **You can check the breaststroke leg action at the bar first. If you learnt how to swim this stroke as a child, the triple action of opening your knees, stretching your legs open and bringing your knees under your body again will return to you easily. Feel the effect of this movement on your pregnant body and explore the rhythm that suits you best as you focus on your breathing at the same time.**

## 44 Water-boatwoman

**This exercise resembles the action of the insects called water-boatmen on the surface of ponds. The resistance of the water to your whole body is decreased to an absolute minimum. Ideally you should hardly move forward at all, while you feel more and more spread out on the surface of the water in a floating movement in which your hips open wider and wider.**

△ **1** Propel your body with a very wide breaststroke leg movement while your upper body remains relaxed, supported on floats. Your pelvis is open, your buttocks raised and your supported arms open. Raise your knees as much as possible, to achieve a very wide circle close to the surface. This can also be done with floats under each arm for support.

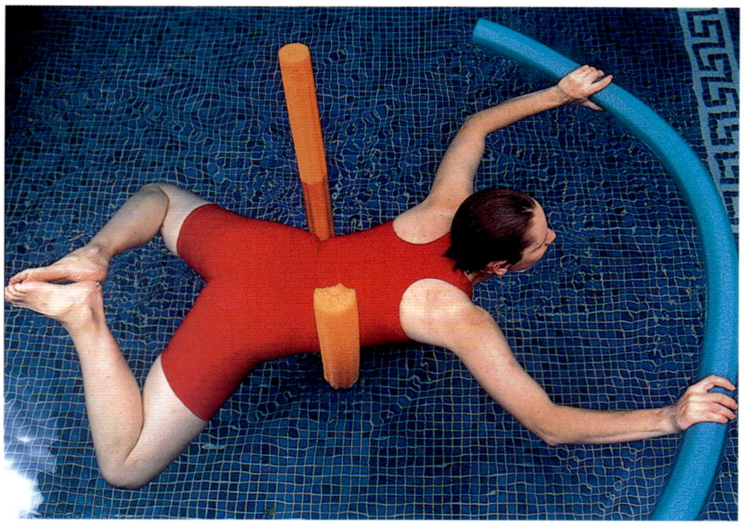

△ **2** Using two woggles as supports helps you align your upper body along the surface of the water while you focus on the leg movement. From a nearly static "water-boatwoman", you can extend your legs more, propelling yourself in the water with a strong yet flowing movement, avoiding the uneven action of the legs that can make breaststroke swimming uncomfortable.

## 45 Aqua yoga breaststroke

**Once you have achieved a smooth circling of the legs with your arms supported in the "water-boatwoman" exercise, you are ready to synchronize the arm and leg movements of breaststroke. Most of the propulsion comes from the legs but the emphasis is on the lateral stretch rather than on a forward motion. The arm movement opens the chest in a way that helps to expand your breathing and uplift your spirit.If you have been swimming competition-style breaststroke before pregnancy, the challenge now is to lengthen your whole spine along the surface of the water rather than raising your upper back out of the water as you inhale and propel yourself. Start swimming very slowly and consider it as a different stroke – one for stretch rather than speed. It is an extended exhalation in the stretch that will enable you to discover the "yoga of swimming": minimum expenditure of energy with a fulfilling rhythm in an increasingly efficient stroke.**

△ **1** If you find it a challenge at first to keep your back extended close to the surface of the water, place a woggle under your arms for additional support. With your shoulders and neck relaxed, focus on synchronizing your breathing with a broad, regular movement of your arms and legs. Allow a long, gliding stretch before bringing your arms back and bending your knees open to propel yourself forward again, extending both your breathing cycle and your movement at the same time.

▷ **2** Stand with your back against the pool wall. Bend your knees and extend your arms forward, inhaling as you propel yourself away from the pool wall. Take two long strokes with your mouth or your whole face in the water, inhaling on the second stroke. Aim to stretch the front of your body as much as possible, extending the gliding forward thrust of each stroke as far as you can.

▷ **3** Raise your head and inhale again as you bring your arms back at the end of the second stroke. The most effective head position is with the waterline about mid-forehead, raising the head just enough to inhale – through the nose or more often through the mouth – and then exhale under the surface. Aim at a smooth forward movement in which there is virtually no gap between your arm stretch and your arm pull, your in breath and your out breath.

# Adapted backstroke





This stroke is ideal if you do not like putting your face in the water. Non-swimmers can be supported with woggles or floats. In late pregnancy it is useful if you feel you stretch best on your back in land-based exercise, as it is inadvisable to lie on your back after about 30 weeks. Supported aqua yoga backstroke is an essential aquacise during pregnancy, opening the pelvis and toning the muscles that support the baby and are used in childbirth.

As in breaststroke, the aim during pregnancy is to improve relaxation in the swimming movement so that the energy expended is reduced and a greater stretch is achieved in a steady, slow rhythm of deep breathing. This in turn leads to further relaxed stretching and greater efficiency of movement and breathing combined.

Whether you are using your arms or not, when swimming on your back, check that you remain as streamlined as possible. Let the water support your head and back together, getting into your stroke from the pleasure of floating.

Even if you are not a backstroke swimmer, you can still enjoy unsupported swimming on your back. Try using your arms and hands to keep your upper body on the surface of the water with a sculling action under water, while your legs and feet propel you just as when you were supported by the floats. If you find yourself sitting and sinking rather than taking off on your back, don't get discouraged. Part of becoming a mother is giving up being an overachiever; take it easy and welcome successes and setbacks as an ongoing process.

## symmetrical backstroke

Once you can move freely in the water on your back, you can practise an open, symmetrical stroke known in swimming circles as the "English backstroke". This is an excellent stroke for pregnancy although it has fallen into disuse due to the greater effectiveness of the back crawl.

In this stroke, propulsion through the water is created through the movement of your arms and hands and your legs and feet in a symmetrical, synchronized stretching and circling. Inhale as you open your arms as widely as possible behind you and at the same time open your knees as in the supported backstroke. Exhale as you bring your arms back to the centre. Make this a wide, flowing movement.

Although it is energetic, there is no need for huge splashes. Try to keep your body close to the water surface. At first, there is a tendency to sink the pelvis and heave your arms back instead of lifting them in a smooth movement. Then you may feel that the rhythm of the stroke propels you without the need to raise your body up and backwards in the overarm action.

## back crawl

If you can, swim backstroke with an alternating arm pull. This is known as back crawl. Keep a good balance and fluent action to maintain the balance of your body through the stroke. This will help you to elongate your back muscles in your early to mid pregnancy. It is important to position your head so that your ears are in the water and your neck feels relaxed. Your arms should move freely over the side and then along your body with a relaxed stretch. Keep your leg-kicks light and just below the surface of the water. In late pregnancy, it may become more difficult to preserve your balance as your body rolls with the alternate arm action. In that case, focus on the Backstroke Leg Circles (47) until you can resume the back crawl again after the birth.

## 46 Back rowing

**This exercise uses the resistance of the water to tone arm and shoulder muscles as well as the muscles that support the breasts. The blood flow to and from these muscles is increased and the lymph nodes in the armpits, which may be very sensitive during pregnancy, are better drained.**

**Back rowing also improves your capacity to relax and it is a good exercise to practice if you have only a short time in the pool and are feeling agitated and stressed when you arrive.**

△ **1** With your feet under the bar or resting on a woggle, lift your arms back over your head, opening them wide in a circling movement.

## 47 Backstroke leg circles

**The propulsion created by your legs and feet pushes the water behind you in this stroke, with a vigorous yet harmonious circling movement of the hips and knees, while the upper body is supported on floats or woggles. At first, give priority to your leg movement and do not worry if you find yourself half sitting in the water. As you become familiar with the exercise, stretch your back as much as you can along the surface of the water.**

▷ **1** Your pelvis should be open, your knees turned out (not tucked up), your chest open and your head relaxed, with your chin tucked in. Breathe out as you pull your legs in towards your body and inhale as you open them out again.

◁ **2** To relax and stretch your legs at the same time after practising your backstroke leg circles, alternately extend one leg while bending the other, using a relaxed kicking movement just under the surface of the water with your ankles relaxed.

▷ **3** If you have practised backstroke leg circles or back rowing as a main component of your session, always relax in a floating position afterwards. Use woggles or floats to align your whole body on the surface of the water, with your legs stretched open. Breathe deeply into your abdomen, allowing your heartbeat to return to normal, then enjoy a relaxing floating stretch for a few seconds.

# freestyle swimming





Crawl is suitable during pregnancy if you are a good swimmer and this is your stroke of choice. Also, if you are expecting your third baby (or more) and you still feel stretched from your previous pregnancy, the crawl can tone your abdominal muscles before you begin stretching again, particularly in early and mid-pregnancy. How well strokes serve you during your pregnancy depends on how much you can incorporate your breathing into the stroke cycle. In late pregnancy, when you are preparing to give birth, it is best to give priority to breaststroke and basic backstroke in your practice. The butterfly stroke is only appropriate in early to mid pregnancy if it is your favourite stroke. Dolphin Dives (49) are suitable throughout pregnancy.

## 48 Front and back crawl

**Keeping a good balance is important in the crawl when you are pregnant. Controlling your breathing pattern and improving your rhythm helps you adjust your balance as you grow larger each month so that you do not develop lateral body movements or excessive rolling from side to side. Swim with a continuous, flowing action, keeping your head and neck relaxed as you turn to breathe.**

◁ **1** Stretch as much as possible on the surface of the water, steamlining your body and keeping your legs and ankles relaxed as you kick. Avoid making a splash with your feet; your movement is more efficient if they remain just below the surface, without actually breaking it, at all times.

▷ **2** In the alternate overarm action of the back crawl, a relaxed stretching of each arm in turn along the ear is very pleasant in mid to late pregnancy as it extends the whole body better and more safely than could be achieved lying down. Keep the flutter kick relaxed, knees straight but not tense, with the movement coming mainly from the ankles. Ideally your chin would be tucked in but in this relaxed version, just make sure that your head is not extending back. If you are able to see the edge of the pool, or, even better, your feet, you will be streamlined enough to enjoy breathing freely in the stroke, experiencing a balanced, relaxed, pleasurable stretch in your own rhythm.

## 49 Dolphin dives (1)

**The butterfly stroke is the basis for Dolphin Dives and requires the most physical strength of all swimming strokes.It carries the risk of exaggerating the lumbar curve of your spine – even more so as your uterus grows. If you are a keen swimmer and it is your favourite stroke, you can continue to enjoy swimming it in early to mid pregnancy, but do not attempt it otherwise. Dolphin Dives are different. They are a safe, adapted version of the butterfly and protect your lower back. The combined action of breath and movement make it a streamlined stretch, effective and easy to practise in a pool where the water is shoulder deep. Dolphin Dives single out and accentuate the diving and emerging actions in the butterfly stroke but do not need the strength or skill to propel the body through the leg and back movement. You can also vary the depths of your dives, from just below the surface to the bottom of the pool. With little expenditure of energy, you can exercise all the muscles of your back in just a few minutes of dives.**

◁ **1** Standing in the water, extend your arms in front of you and, rounding your back, flex your legs and jump to dive. Either trail your extended legs as you move down and up or use the flipper leg motion of the butterfly stroke to propel you.

▽ **2** Take your arms back slowly to your sides as your body follows the trajectory of the dive down then back up to the surface. In a shallow pool you can stretch along the pool floor before coming back up, all in one long breath. As you come up, open your arms out to the side, then extend them in front of you and take another dive.

# yoga and aqua yoga for mid-term pregnancy

Your pregnancy is now firmly established and you should be feeling full of vigour and joy, especially if you have been practising yoga and aqua yoga regularly. It is time to focus on building up strength and stamina, on making space to "breathe for two" and on creating and maintaining the best possible alignment of the spine at all times. Most of all – time to enjoy your pregnancy.

# breathing for two





You are likely to be feeling much more energetic during this middle stage, so enjoy your vitality – many of the yoga routines designed for these months are lively, invigorating, almost dance-like. They get your breathing and circulation working optimally and the vigorous arm movements and upward stretches, plus deep breathing, help blood circulate through the abdominal organs and bring fresh, nourishing blood to your baby via the placenta.

You will find at this stage that your balance changes as your abdomen enlarges, so it is important to take your centre of gravity downward, while keeping your spine stretched up and your chest open. This upright, graceful stance will make you feel elegant and confident and also allows more space to be created around the diaphragm, which needs to find room to contract downward so that you are able to breathe really deeply and fully.

"Oneness of breath and mind... this is called Yoga, integration."

*Maitri Upanishad 25*

## 50 Sunwheel stretch

**This exercise really focuses on upper body stretches to open the chest and loosen the shoulders. The movements wake up the whole of the upper spine and dissolve tightness in the neck, shoulders and arms – this is particularly helpful if you spend a lot of time sitting at a desk or driving a car. These movements also create more space in the abdomen, so that your digestive system has room to function and your baby has room to grow.**

▷ **1** Sit with knees a comfortable width apart and feet firmly planted on the floor. Tuck your coccyx under so that your pelvis is level – imagine that the pelvis is a bowl of water and you don't want to spill any of it. Stretch up through your spine from the base to the crown, with your neck long and shoulders relaxed and down. Breathe in deeply to open and lift the chest. Hold the lift as you breathe out, drawing your shoulder blades together with arms relaxed and then pushing the palms down toward the floor with fingers spread wide, to end with straight arms. Repeat, pushing down against imaginary resistance with each breath out and relaxing your hands as you breathe in.

△ **2** Repeat, but this time start with your elbows bent and hands pointing up as you breathe in – this is so that you create a greater push downward as you breathe out. Make your movements graceful and rhythmical, rather like a seated dance.

△ **3** Then, on each breath out, push strongly away from you to the sides, with your palms at shoulder level (the picture shows mid-push; you finish the push with straight arms). Engage the muscles around your spine and the back of your waist as you push. Relax as you breathe in. Repeat rhythmically.

△ **4** On an out breath, stretch your palms to the sides with arms raised as high as you can, engaging your upper arms and back muscles. Finally, repeat the arm movements in reverse order, moving down until your arms are beside you. Repeat the whole sequence several times.

## 51 Swing high, swing low

**This movement should be done rhythmically and with enthusiasm. It loosens up all the joints from your heels to your fingertips and blows away the cobwebs from your mind.**

◁ **1** Stand with feet comfortably apart and knees well bent, and rotate your upper body from side to side, making sure your arms are loose and relaxed. Keep your spine upright, your hips and legs steady and your centre of gravity low.

◁ **2** Now stretch your arms right up to the right and clap your hands. Then sink into the previous position before stretching up to the left to clap your hands. Keep breathing deeply and vigorously as you alternately sink and relax then stretch to each side in turn.



## 52 Centring down

**Getting your legs, rather than your lower back, to support your increasing weight and bulk is probably the most important postural adjustment that you can make during your pregnancy because it will save you from backache. Your womb is situated in the lower abdomen, which is held in place by the spine at the back, the pelvic girdle below and the hips on each side, so it has nowhere to expand as your baby grows except upward and forward. Any upward growth is constrained by your digestive organs and diaphragm, so most of the bulk has to move forward. This extra weight should flow downward through strong and well-toned legs, restoring your vital balance and centre of gravity.**

△ **1** Stand with legs a comfortable width apart, feet firmly planted and knees loose. Stretch your spine upwards, taking your weight downwards through your legs. Press your palms together at throat height with elbows out to the sides. Breathe in and expand the lungs at the back by opening your back ribs more.

△ **2** As you breathe out stretch your arms forward and bend deeply at the knees. Hold a moment, then breathe in again. Repeat often.

# Yoga in with movement





When you are pregnant it is better to move through a variety of yogic positions, in a type of yogic dance, than to hold each position separately. This encourages deeper breathing, which is important as your breath provides oxygen for your baby's metabolism as well as your own. The yogic dance creates more flexibility in all your joints, making you feel loose and limber despite the added weight and bulk of your growing baby. Moving the spine rhythmically in all directions takes pressure off the lower back and strengthens all the muscles that hold the spine in alignment. Moving with knees well bent ensures that you avoid arching your back and that your spine and pelvis remain perfectly aligned. Your shoulders and neck should remain relaxed throughout.

## 53 Pat on the back

**This free and rhythmic swinging movement loosens the tensions that so readily gather around the upper spine and shoulders after sitting. It also eases stresses in the joints of the hands and arms.**

△ **1** Stand tall, with knees very loose and coccyx tucked under. Swing your upper body from the shoulders, letting your arms and hands hang freely. Swing from one side to the other, but face to the front – your head and hips do not move.

△ **2** Repeat this relaxed swinging movement, but this time bend your elbows so that you bring one hand right up and slightly over your shoulder, as though almost patting yourself on the back, and the other arm around to the back of your waist.

## 54 Ball of energy (1)

**Imagine that you are playing with a huge, soft, invisible ball of energy. You create it by rubbing your palms briskly together, rather like rubbing two sticks together to create a flame. Then separate your hands a little before bringing them closer together in a pumping or kneading movement to enlarge your energy ball. Use your imagination and sense of touch, feeling that you are actually plumping up the ball of energy, tossing it from one hand to the other and holding it lightly between your fingertips as it grows and grows.**

△ **1** Keeping your knees well bent and spine stretched, bend forward with your ball of energy, holding it lightly between your open palms.

△ **2** Now toss the invisible ball of energy to the side, twisting your body in a wide movement, but without moving your feet at all.

△ **3** Catch the ball above your head, with both arms. Keep your arms and your legs slightly bent, and feel that you are centred around the navel area.

△ **4** Compress your ball, then roll it across your body, first on one side then on the other, twisting your body in a wide movement, from a strong base.

△ **5** Now expand the ball of energy, holding it with your arms wide to the sides and opening your chest. Your base should be strong, with knees slightly bent.

△ **6** Be inventive and lively as you continue to play with the ball, stretching and moving in all directions. When you have done enough, hold it between your palms and gently squeeze it until it gets smaller and smaller and disappears between your joined palms.

# Gentle twists and shoulder stretches

Vigorous exercise with arm movements and deep, natural breathing is a good way of keeping healthy, strong and supple while you are carrying your baby. It gets your circulation going, makes you feel great and relieves any strain, tension and tiredness that may have been building up in your neck and shoulders. It also exercises the muscles of the trunk and spine. These kinds of invigorating movements require both concentration and focus. They are most effective if you keep your knees bent throughout.

## 55 Thunder claps

**These positions work the muscles across the chest and upper spine to lift the sternum and open the chest for deeper breathing, as well as opening and rotating the shoulder joints and strengthening the arms to relieve stiffness and tension. The pectoral muscles across the upper chest can become shortened if you slouch forward, especially when sitting at a desk or table and leaning on your elbows. Let the vigorous rhythm of this exercise do the stretching for you, even if you can't clap behind your back at first. You will soon loosen up with frequent practice and enjoy the feeling of openness in the chest.**

◁ **1** Stand tall through your spine, but with knees well bent and feet more than hip-width apart. Stretch your arms out to the front and clap your hands at shoulder level, reaching forward to open the back of the shoulders without moving the spine.

◁ **2** Now take your hands behind you and as high up as you can, to open the shoulder joints at the front and stretch the pectoral muscles across the upper chest. Bring your palms together to clap, straightening your arms if you can.

## 56 Disco twist

**This is a rhythmic, twisting movement done with feet wide and knees well bent. Get into the swing of it, following your natural rhythm, and really get your breath and bloodstream moving. Stop as soon as you feel out of breath and rest in the starting position before moving on to the next exercise.**

◁ **1** Stand with knees springy and loose and feet comfortably apart, arms relaxed.

◁ **2** Lift your chest and twist your upper body to the left, and also swing your arms and hands to the left. Bend your knees a little more to dip to the left, lift up again and twist to the right and repeat. Keep your coccyx tucked under, your spine upright and your legs springy as you twist from one side to the other.

## 57 Crossovers

**These wide, sweeping movements combine stretching with a bending and twisting of the trunk. They require mental focus and deep, rhythmical breathing, and will fill you with energy, so practise them regularly. Circle your arms boldly, as though they have flags attached and you want to be seen from a distance. Crossovers require good co-ordination and are best done naturally and vigorously, without too much thought.**

**Start out by doing the sequence as a plain twist-and-stretch, feeling the lengthening in each side of your body as you alternate arms. Then build up to a much more fluid, wider circling movement, by stretching up higher, bending lower at the knees and twisting more deeply. Eventually, you should feel that as soon as you reach the maximum stretch on one arm, the other arm is sinking down to create another circle overlapping the previous one.**

△ **1** Stand with knees springy and loose and feet a comfortable width apart – as you did in Step 1 of the Disco Twist (56).

△ **2** Slowly twist the upper body to the left as you raise your right arm in front of you and stretch it up high. Look up at it.

△ **3** Start to twist to the right as you begin lowering your right arm in a circle behind you. Keep the chest open and your knees well bent. At the same time start to take your left arm in front of you.

△ **4** When your left arm is stretched right up, look at your left hand. Try to make as straight a line as possible from your back heel to the very tip of the middle finger of your stretched hand.

△ **5** Lower your left arm behind you as you start to twist to the left, and bring your right arm through to the front and across your body, ready to raise it again to complete the double circle. Repeat several times.

# The three movements of the pelvis

Flexibility in the pelvis is natural in young children, and also in adults who live in traditional societies without the comforts and technology that we take for granted. But our sophisticated, Western way of life inhibits this flexibility, from schooldays on. We don't squat down to wash clothes or prepare food. Instead, we spend most of our waking hours in one form of chair or another while we chat, read, use the computer, and even while travelling. In order to regain our innate grace and suppleness, and to maintain it throughout our lives, we need to relearn the natural ways of holding and moving our bodies. Flexibility in the spine, hips and pelvis is especially important during pregnancy, as it alleviates many common discomforts, such as backache, sciatica and cramps, and also prepares the body for active, easy birthing.

"How long will you keep expecting answers from outside? Just go inside."

*Frederick Leboyer*

## 58 Seated pelvic rolls

**Your lower abdominal muscles and the long transverse abdominal muscles (at the sides of the trunk) need to be strong and active, or they fail to play their part in supporting the weight of the body and leave your lower back muscles to carry the whole load. This exercise is a good way of strengthening both these sets of muscles.**

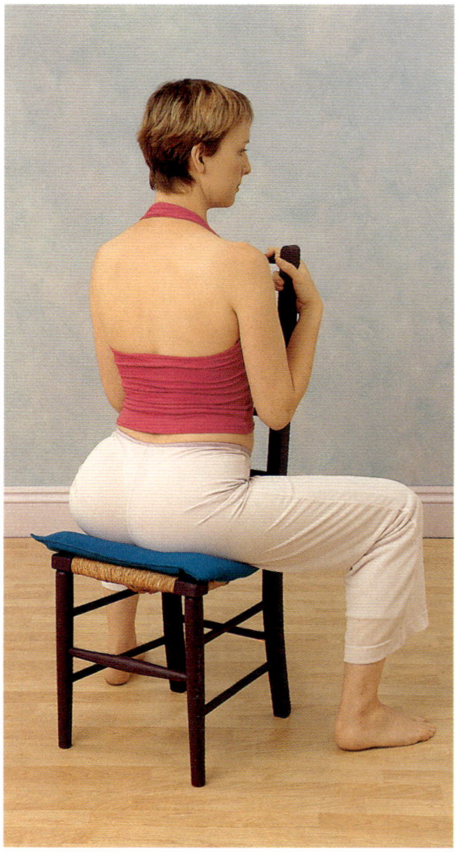

△ **1** Sit squarely in a sturdy, upright chair, facing the back of the chair. Place your sitting bones near the front of the seat and hold on to the back of the chair for support. Arch your lower back strongly, lowering the front rim of your pelvis forward and bringing your abdomen closer to the chair. Feel the muscles of your spine contracting strongly as the abdominal muscles relax.

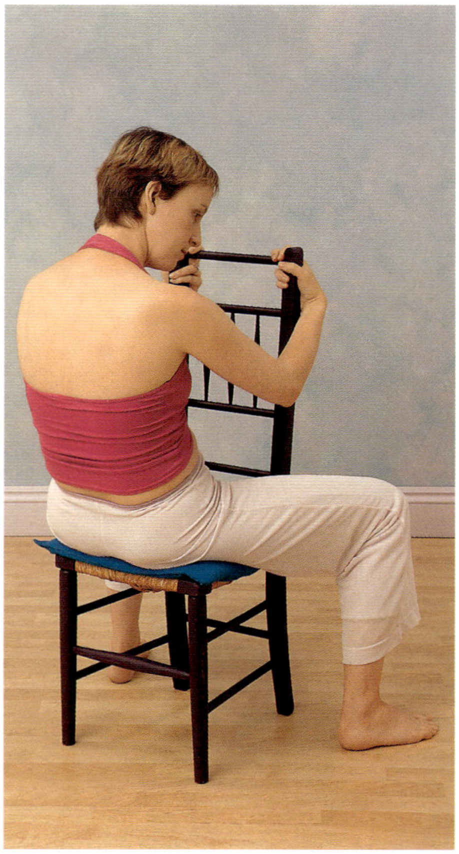

△ **2** Reverse this movement by tilting your pelvis back to lift the front rim of the pelvis. Stretch and relax your lower spine. The lower abdominal muscles are now contracting strongly.

△ **3** Now contract the long muscles on your right side, while consciously relaxing and stretching the ones on the left. This will lift your right hip up toward your right ribs, so that you are sitting on one side of the lower pelvis (your left sitting bone). Repeat this on the other side. Gradually combine these movements into a flowing, clockwise roll. Then repeat in an anti-clockwise direction.

## 59 Standing pelvic roll

**This is a stronger, standing version of Seated Pelvic Rolls (58). It can be practised easily in any spare moment. If the abdomen feels distended and crowded by the growing baby, a few pelvic rolls can quickly create more space and relieve uncomfortable pressure. Placing your hands on your hips helps you to focus on the pelvic girdle and become more aware of its range of movement.**

△ **1** Stand with feet apart and knees well bent and springy. Place your hands on the front of your hip bones. Keep your whole spine stretched up from the base and through your neck and shoulders to the crown. Tilt your pelvis up on the left side so that you contract the transverse abdominal muscles on the left side and relax them on the right side. Don't move above the waist.

△ **2** Now drop your pelvis on the left side and tilt it up on the right side. Practise these two movements until they are smooth and flowing.

△ **3** Stand up straight again and roll the rim of the pelvis forward and upward, tucking your coccyx under and lengthening and relaxing through your lower spine. Avoid clenching your buttocks, as you allow the lower abdominal muscles to stretch with the forward movement.

△ **4** Tilt the rim of your pelvis down and back to arch your lower back. These four movements make up the pelvic roll. Continue round clockwise – left hip up, pelvic rim up, right hip up, pelvic rim down – in a smooth, rolling movement. Finish with the same number of anti-clockwise rolls.

## 60 Jump for joy

**This is an exuberant movement, celebrating the lightness and grace in your legs and hips. Feel yourself bursting with energy and full of the joys of life as you open your hips and chest wide, affirming your trust in a world that welcomes the baby that you are now carrying within you. You can even include a light jump in the air if you feel like it.**

△ **1** Stand on your right leg, keeping your right knee relaxed. As you raise your left knee in front of you to hip height, bring your elbows high and wide, with the backs of your hands above your face.

△ **2** Open your left hip to swing your left knee to the side at hip height, flinging your arms wide, still at shoulder height. Step down on to your left side and bring your right knee up to repeat on the other side. Keep your arms circling round.

# Gaining strength and stamina





The following movements have isometric qualities: that is, one set of muscles contracts strongly to push against a second set that are resisting the push. The result, with practice, is that both sets of muscles get stronger by pushing against each other. There is also a centring and stabilizing effect, as the two-way push ripples throughout the whole body. Each strong pushing movement should be balanced by a letting-go pose, so that muscular strength is built up rather than muscular tension. Isometric exercise helps posture, breathing and spinal alignment. It builds strength symmetrically, which is especially important during pregnancy.

## 61 Swing and release

**In this vigorous exercise, the palms are pressed firmly together to strengthen the muscles of the hands and arms, and especially the muscles that lie each side of the upper spine. Strength here makes it easy to maintain a good upright posture through the spine and neck, so that the circulation of the blood and the messages passing along the nervous system can flow freely through the neck and trunk. Raising the arms while pressing the hands together strengthens the muscles at the sides of the body and lifts the sternum for deeper breathing.**

◁ **1** Stand with your feet a comfortable width apart and your knees bent but relaxed and loose. Bring your palms together and bend forward from the hips so that your fingertips touch the floor. Breathe out in this position.

△ **2** Stretch your arms forward, pushing the palms hard against each other and engaging the muscles of your upper back for lifting. Breathe in strongly, raising your head, arms and trunk up and to the right side, twisting the spine to the right from the waist upward. Hold this position for a few seconds, pressing your palms together and feeling your muscles engaging all along your arms and upper spine.

△ **3** On a strong breath out through the mouth in a "Hah" sound, drop back to your starting position with your knees well bent. Keep your hands together and strong, like a knife slicing through bread. Let go of all effort as you breathe in and out to relax in the starting position, before breathing in again strongly to repeat the upward stretch and pushing movements to the left side. Repeat a few times.

## 62 Push and release

**Here, two different isometric pushing movements are counterbalanced by the same open and surrendering pose. This is an important principle in everyday life as well as in yoga practice. We should always relax between activities in order to dissolve any physical, emotional or mental tensions before they can take a hold. In this way we build up our strength and stamina rather than depleting our reserves.**

△ **1** Stand with your spine erect, coccyx tucked under, pelvis level and knees well bent. Clasp your hands at chest level and push one hand hard against the other for two strong breaths in and out.

△ **2** Breathe in, then, with a voiced-out breath "Aaah", open your arms to the side in a surrendering gesture. Keep the chest open and the back straight. Rest in this position and take a deep breath, relaxing the facial muscles.

△ **3** Bring your arms straight out in front of you and make fists. Push your fists forward, opening and stretching in your back and maintaining balance by using your lower abdominal and front thigh muscles. Then relax as before in the surrender position. Repeat these movements several times.



## 63 Hip openers in pairs

**Two people exercising together can have good fun, but you will also help each other to develop strength and stamina and to improve muscle tone. Be careful to judge your partner's strength and balance – it is easier to work with a partner who is roughly the same height and weight as you are. Some of these positions can also be practised on your own, by using a wall to lean against or a strong counter to pull on.**

▷ **1** Stand facing each other with feet planted firmly, quite wide apart, and knees loosely bent. Take hold of each other's forearms with a firm grip. Both partners then bend forward at the waist. Adjust your position so that each partner makes a right angle with their legs and trunk. Once settled, start to pull away from each other. Stretch the base of your spine and make space in the lumbar region, wriggling your hips from side to side.

◁ **2** Face to face and gripping each other's forearms, both partners lift their left knees out to the side, opening up the hip joints. This mutual support helps you to keep your balance and also allows you to extend the raised knee further out and back than you could on your own.

▷ **3** After extending the raised knees as far back as possible, both partners land their left foot softly on the floor behind them. Raise the left leg again for another round and repeat a few times. Now change legs to repeat on the other side.

# kneeling stretches



Some kneeling positions enable you to build up strength and stamina (to help you carry your baby without getting tired), and kneeling stretches can prevent and ease low back pain. At the same time, kneeling exercises focus upon the birthing muscles, especially important if this is your first baby, as these muscles will not have been used before. Getting used to a kneeling position for your stretches is an important part of preparing for labour, since many women prefer this position in childbirth.

## 64 Cat pose

**The Cat Pose is traditionally used to loosen all the joints before going into classical yogic seated poses. A simpler version, called the "kitten roll" here, is included as a warm-up. Avoid sagging at the waist by holding your middle spine firmly in line, like a table top, as you move through the rolls.**

▷ **1** Kneel on your yoga mat with knees about hip-width apart, so that there is plenty of room for your baby. Place cushions under your knees, if you like. Sit back on your heels and, without lifting your buttocks, stretch your arms out in front, about shoulder-width apart. Crawl forward with your fingers while anchoring your buttocks on to your heels. Feel the stretch through your spine and breathe slowly into this stretch to loosen any tension in your back, hips or shoulders.

△ **2** For the "kitten roll", sit back on your heels before breathing in to bring your weight forward on to your elbows. Lift your shoulders as you breathe out to arch your spine and tuck your coccyx under before rolling back on to your heels. Repeat the roll several times, and as you do so, focus your attention on feeling the stretch at the back of your waist.

△ **3** For the "cat roll", bring your weight forward on to spread palms as you breathe in, so that your shoulders are directly above your wrists, your arms are straight but not locked at the elbow and your back is flat like a table top. This is the classic Cat Pose. Breathe out to arch and stretch your spine before sitting back on your heels, again, trying not to move your hands. Breathe in to repeat the rolling movement.

## 65 Hip and knee circles

**These circles are practised while in the Cat Pose (64). They loosen tightness in the hip joints, can relieve cramps in the groin and increase the circulation of blood around the abdomen and pelvis.**

▷ Place yourself in the Cat Pose (64), with your weight evenly distributed and your back and head held firmly in line. Raise your right knee from the floor, keeping it bent at a right angle, and move it around in small circles parallel to the floor so that you are rotating the hip joint. After circling clockwise and anti-clockwise, repeat this sequence of movements on the left side.

## 66 Shoulder and elbow circles

**These circles are great for relieving tension in the neck and shoulders, stretching the pectoral muscles and opening the chest for deeper breathing. Both Hip and Knee Circles (65) and this exercise provide the same benefits as swimming movements.**

△ **1** Place yourself in the Cat Pose (64) and then sit back on your heels. Keeping your weight evenly balanced, and your spine and head firmly in line, stretch your right arm out in front of you.

△ **2** Bend your right elbow and bring your arm up and back in a circle, turning your head and opening the right side of your chest and your right shoulder. Lift the elbow as high as you can before stretching the arm to the front again. Repeat on the left.

## 67 Tiger stretch and relax (1)

**This is one of the best ways to relieve lower backache and sciatica. This can sometimes become a problem as your pregnancy advances and the weight of your baby presses on the sciatic nerve as it emerges from the lower spine and carries on down your leg. You will need to balance firmly on strong wrists and hands as you raise your leg parallel to the floor.**

△ **1** Place yourself in the Cat Pose (64) with spine stretched and firm, especially at the waist. Slowly raise your right leg behind you until it is parallel to the floor, neither higher nor lower. Stretch right through your leg and into your toes, and kick away any tension or pressure.

△ **2** Let your leg sink limply to the floor and relax it completely. Maintain your balance and the strength in your spine, but drop your right hip. Shake your leg loosely from hip to toes to release cramps or pressure on the sciatic nerve. Then readjust your position and do the same movements with the left leg.

## 68 Manual back stretch

**As your baby grows it becomes ever more important to relax frequently and to ease away tiredness and tension. A partner or friend can work wonders, simply by gently helping your spine to stretch as you lie comfortably draped over a beanbag or pillows, either on your bed or on the floor. Your helper does not need to be an expert, just intuitive and happy to be guided by you to discover the position where you can relax and breathe most deeply.**

▷ Your helper needs to be in a firm, comfortable position, where they do not strain their own back. He or she extends their hands so their fingers trace light pressure either side of your spine as you breathe out. They release pressure on each in breath. Your partner should avoid direct pressure on the spine and check what feels best for you. The aim is to reduce compression and create space and comfort through a gradual deepening of the breath.

# Your birthing muscles





A sphincter is a ring-shaped muscle that acts like a valve by squeezing tightly around the bottom of a tube to keep the contents in. If you want to release the contents, you simply relax the sphincter muscle, or you can get it to push the contents out by controlling the flow with rhythmic pulses. Women have three "tubes" that are either sphincters or are sphincter-like. These open at the base of the body – an area often called the pelvic floor – through the perineum (a mass of muscle that stretches right across the base of the body and holds the abdomen's contents in place.) Each of these openings is controlled by strong muscles, which are:

- The anal tube at the end of the digestive system, which opens to release waste matter. It is found near the base of the spine, at the back of the pelvic floor.
- The urethra – the tube leading from the bladder. This is found close to the pubic bone, at the front of the pelvic floor.
- The muscles each side of the vagina, which can contract and release around the cervix. The cervix thins out during labour to become the birth canal and let your baby descend through the vagina. Squeezing the vaginal muscles – "pulling up inside" – helps you locate and feel your cervix.

With regular practice, you can learn to contract or relax these muscles at will. This will help you throughout pregnancy (when your baby is pressing down against the pelvic floor), during the birth (to help control the baby's movement down through the birth canal), and after the birth (to restore perineal muscle tone as quickly as possible, thus avoiding many common postnatal problems).

## THE BIRTHING MUSCLES

### The pelvic area at around mid-term

**Note how the baby presses against the internal organs shown**

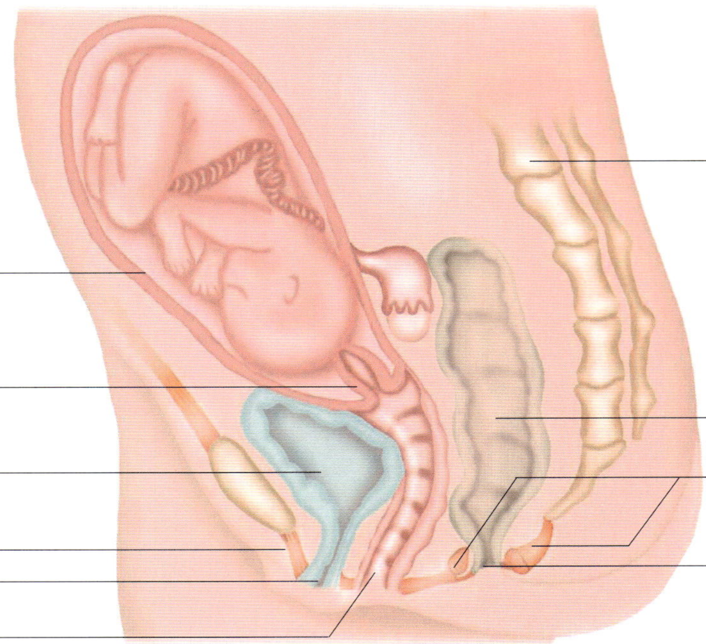


### The perineum

(seen from below)

**The red, striated areas are muscle**

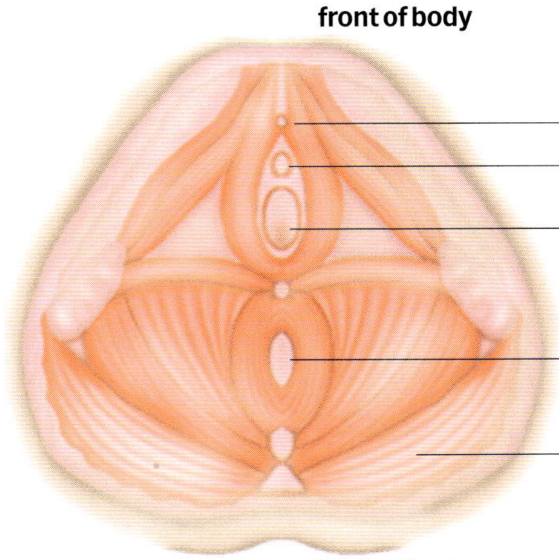


### exercising the birthing muscles

Yogic philosophy maintains that energy follows thought. So focusing on muscle groups that we usually ignore helps to bring movement to the area and encourages awareness, which leads in turn to control of those muscles. Using the breath intensifies the muscular action. Yogic actions are never mechanical because you are using your breath and awareness simultaneously with the contraction and relaxation of the muscles. By connecting breath with muscular action you are toning, in a unique way, the muscles of the perineum, including those that attach it to the pelvis at the front and the lower spine at the back.

Begin your birthing muscle workout with the anal sphincter, contracting and releasing it in turn. Focus on how this feels, so that you learn to draw in the anus on a breath in and slowly release it on a breath out. Now focus on the sphincter of the urethra, squeezing it in and relaxing it in small, rapid movements. Finally, focus on the vaginal muscles, squeezing them tightly to draw your pelvic floor up and in. You will find that the lower abdomen is also drawn up and inward. These are the "birthing muscles" that you want to strengthen.

## 69 Pelvic floor stretches

**In this modification of the Cat Pose (64) your weight is distributed through your knees and elbows, leaving your lower back and pelvis weightless, released from the constraints of gravity that usually restrict flexibility in this area.**

◁ **1** Kneel in the Cat Pose (64), with your knees spread wide enough to accommodate your baby as you lean forward on to your elbows. Place your head on a cushion if it is more comfortable. Distribute your weight evenly between your elbows and your knees, so that your head and neck are comfortable and your coccyx is raised as high as possible. Focus upon your pelvic floor, then exercise the three main birthing "sphincters" one by one, as explained on the opposite page.

◁ **2** Alternate the kneeling position with this pelvic lift, which uses different sets of inner muscles. Lie on your back with your buttocks on a cushion to raise the pelvis. Keep your knees bent, with feet apart and firmly planted on the floor. Place your hands over your baby to feel the movement as you squeeze the whole pelvic floor in and up. Hold the squeeze for a few breaths to strengthen these muscles, then let go and relax completely. Repeat several times.

## 70 Supported pelvic floor lift

**Your baby needs space to pass down through the vagina. This space is created naturally, as hormones are released during pregnancy to loosen the ligaments that hold your bones in place. This allows your pelvic opening to widen naturally. You can help by relaxing your hip and leg muscles in a wide-legged seated position, reclining comfortably against a beanbag or other support. Do not force yourself, just breathe gently in this position. Once the muscles around the groin have gently relaxed, the ligaments can stretch. In addition, the more relaxed you are the easier it is to practise strengthening the inner muscles of the perineum and vagina.**

△ **1** Sit with your legs as wide apart as is comfortable for you. Make sure that your spine is well supported, especially at the base. Flex your ankles and stretch through your legs. Lean back and relax in this position. The muscles around the groin area should be especially relaxed, to allow the ligaments to stretch.

△ **2** Now clasp your hands in front of you at chest height, breathing in as you press your palms firmly together, and at the same time contract the muscles of the perineum and vagina. Hold this contraction for a breath or two, and then relax completely before repeating.

# seated stretches





These easy stretches can be done at any time, sitting on a chair or on the floor with your back upright and legs uncrossed. The more you practise, the more flexible and relaxed your whole body will become. If you have to spend hours in front of a computer or driving, for example, try to stretch regularly. You should, of course, be working your inner muscles in the lower abdominal and pelvic area while seated throughout the day. One of the skills that comes with regular yoga practice is the ability to work one area of the body quite strongly while keeping all the other parts completely relaxed.

## 71 Neck rolls

**Tension is apt to build up around the neck and shoulders when you sit and concentrate for any length of time, whether travelling or working at a desk. You can prevent this build-up by being aware of your posture, and by stopping for a short break whenever you can.**

▷ Sit erect on an upright chair, maintaining the stretch through your spine as you relax your arms and shoulders. Sit with knees wide and feet planted firmly on the floor, resting your hands comfortably on your thighs. Relax your neck muscles and bring your chin forward, lengthening the back of your neck, then round to your right shoulder. Bring your chin forward again then round to your left shoulder. Repeat gently, with relaxed breathing.

## 72 Chest expander

**This energizing exercise strengthens the muscles that hold your upper spine in place, so it is excellent for improving your posture, as well as increasing your lung capacity for deeper breathing. Try it when you are feeling mentally tired.**

△ **1** Sit upright, with knees wide and feet firmly planted on the floor. Raise your elbows to shoulder height. As you breathe out press your forearms and palms together in front of your face.

△ **2** As you breathe in take your elbows high and back, squeezing your shoulder blades together, lifting your sternum and stretching your pectoral muscles across your upper chest. Bring your elbows forward again. Repeat several times.

## 73 Seated side stretch

**This exercise prevents and alleviates heartburn. It opens the sides of the body to make more room in the abdomen for better functioning of the diaphragm and the digestive organs. It also gives your developing baby more room to move around.**

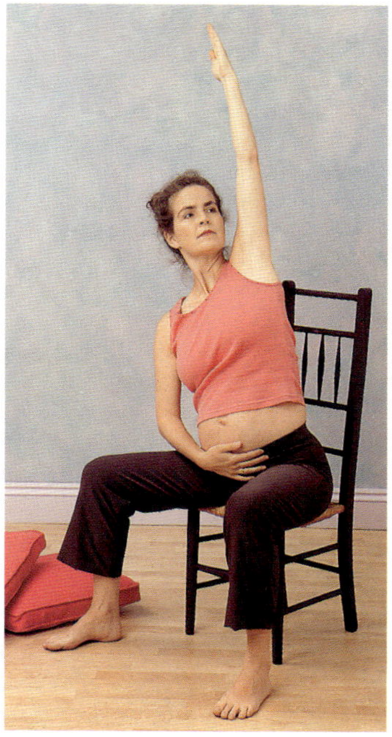

◁ **1** Sit on a firm chair with knees wide and feet on the floor. Bring your left arm out to the side and up overhead, stretching your whole left side. Resting your right elbow on your right thigh, turn your head to look up at your outstretched hand and breathe deeply into the stretched side, holding the position. Repeat on the other side.

▷ **2** For a stronger stretch, place your right ankle on your left thigh then raise your right arm. Hold your foot with your left hand, your ankle flexed and in line as you drop your right knee to the side. Stretch your right arm up. Hold, breathing deeply into the stretched side. Repeat on the other side.

## 74 Seated stretches in pairs

**This lively sequence is fun to do and really gets your energy flowing and blood circulation moving. If you are different heights, then the shorter partner can sit on a cushion to even things out.**

△ **1** Sit back to back with legs crossed and spines pulled upward. Lean on each other just enough to increase awareness of the position of your spines, so that you can both adjust your alignment. Breathe deeply and notice how you start to breathe together.

△ **2** Face each other with right legs straight and left knees bent (left feet against right thighs). Sit up tall with your palms pressed against your partner's palms. Circle your hands out to the sides and in again. Change legs and repeat.

△ **3** Keep in the same position, but this time both partners use isometric pressure on each other's palms to rotate the trunk, twisting first to one side and then the other. Look over your shoulder to take the twist through your upper spine and neck.

△ **4** Sit back to back with your legs crossed or knees comfortably bent. Link arms and rock back and forth, so that one partner folds forward as the other stretches backward. Keep your spines in contact while rocking.

△ **5** Hold each other's hands, then stretch your arms out to the sides and up overhead to maintain a stretch in the sides of your trunk. Go gently and learn to sense what the other person needs – no force, pulling or pushing.

# lying down stretches





When you are tired - or after your standing, kneeling and sitting exercises – you can lie down to relax and also stretch, so that you are still gaining strength and flexibility while the floor supports the weight of your baby. You will feel much more renewed and refreshed after these kinds of gentle movements than if you were simply to collapse in a heap in front of the television. Remember to keep a large cushion handy beside you – for total relaxation after you have completed the stretches.

## 75 Side loosener

**In these movements, the lower side of the trunk (the side that is lying against the floor) is gently stretched and the upper side is strongly contracted. You need to avoid overbalancing on to your back as you raise your upper leg, as this will reduce the contraction of the transverse abdominal muscles.**

**CAUTION**
It is safe to lie on your back for the first 30 or so weeks of pregnancy, provided you feel comfortable. After this time, always recline or lie on your side for both stretching and relaxing. This avoids pressure on the main blood vessels to and from the uterus.

△ **1** Lie on your left side with your left knee bent (your other leg is more outstretched but still relaxed) and your left arm outstretched under your head. Place your right hand on the floor in front of you to help you maintain your balance. Lean forward as you raise your bent right knee and bring it toward your elbow.

△ **2** Make gentle circles with the right knee, opening up your right groin and leg to extend your right leg slightly behind you. Do not over-stretch yourself. Return to your starting position with your right knee bent and repeat the circling movement. If you are skipping step 3, roll on to your right side and repeat with the left leg.

△ **3** This is an optional extra step. Only do this if it feels comfortable and enjoyable. If you have been circling the right leg, then stretch this leg straight up, with your ankle flexed, to open the right hip. Press forward into your right hand to avoid rolling backwards. Hold the stretch, feeling the muscles in your right side contract.

△ **4** At the end of a series of leg-stretches, relax for a few moments, placing the cushion between your knees to take the pressure off your lower abdomen.

## 76 Pelvic lift

**In this position, you contract and strengthen the muscles around the base of your spine and make space at the front of your body. It is an excellent position for focusing on breathing deeply because you use all your abdominal muscles while the chest muscles are held open and immobile. It is also an excellent position for pulling your inner muscles in and up to strengthen the pelvic floor muscles in relation to the muscles of the abdomen and back.**

◁ **1** Lie on your back on the floor, with your head on a cushion if this feels more comfortable. Bend your knees and plant your feet on the floor more than hip-width apart. Turn your toes slightly inward to engage the muscles of the inner thighs and groin area. Place your arms alongside your body with the palms down. Now breathe in.

◁ **2** Breathe out as you lift your pelvis from the floor, engaging your perineal muscles and tucking your coccyx under to extend your lower back. Breathe in, continuing to lift your pelvis by contracting the muscles behind your waist and in your upper back. Breathe deeply in this position, focusing on your diaphragm muscle. Then lower your spine slowly to the floor, vertebra by vertebra from the neck downward. Rest and repeat several times.

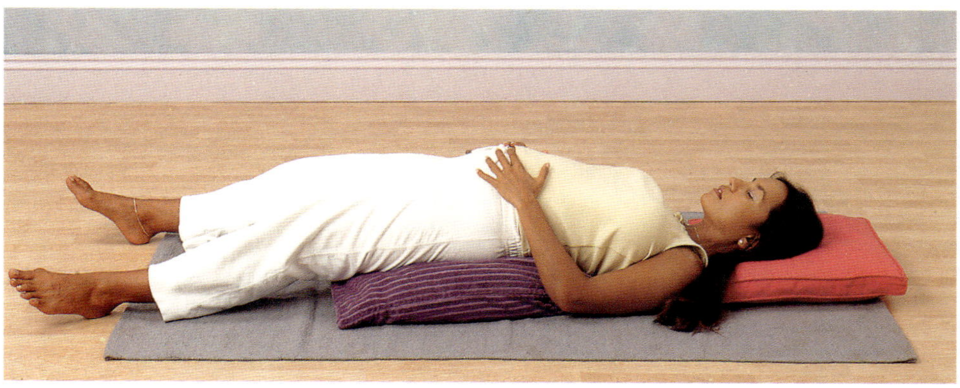

◁ **3** Lie on your back with a cushion under the small of your back. Stretch your legs out at least hip-width apart and place your hands around your baby. Close your eyes and relax deeply for a few minutes.

## 77 Double cycling

**This isometric exercise strengthens the muscles in your feet, legs, hips and pelvis as you push your feet against those of your partner.**

▷ Lie on your back on the floor, supporting your upper body on your elbows and forearms. Place your soles against your partner's soles and push against them as though riding a bicycle. For each person, one leg pushes forward against your partner as the other leg is being pushed back by your partner.

# Changing positions in pregnancy





As the weight in your abdomen increases, it becomes more tiring to do certain everyday movements, such as rising from a chair or getting out of bed in the morning. This is inevitable, but there is no need to struggle if you learn some simple steps, preferably before you need them. As your baby grows in your womb (and also after the birth), you will be glad of your strong leg and arm muscles, as well as your strong back. Here's how to make these movements gracefully and easily.

## 78 Standing from sitting

**It is more difficult to haul yourself out of a chair if you are slumped or sprawled backwards. Let your muscles hold your body firmly, so that gravity becomes your friend rather than your enemy. Of course, it is also easier to rise lightly from a firm, upright chair than a soft, low sofa, so choose carefully where you sit as well as how.**

◁ **1** First sit up straight, so that your weight passes in a straight line from your head, through your neck and into your spine. Place your feet apart and firmly planted on the floor, ready to receive your weight. Raise your elbows to lift up through your spine and chest. Keep the stretch.

◁ **2** Lean forward with your back straight and place your hands on your thighs. The thighs are among the strongest muscles in your body, designed for weight-bearing, so use them fully to protect your lower back. Press hard on your thighs with your arms.

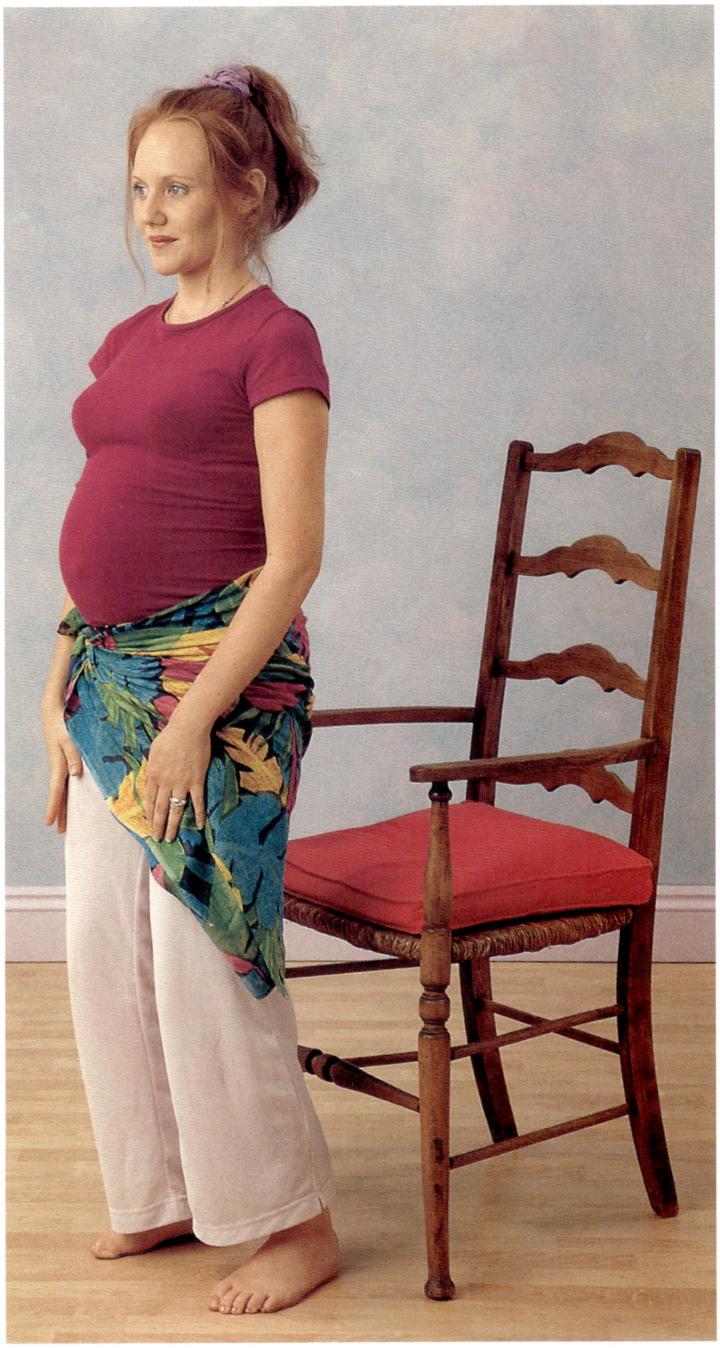

△ **3** Now rise gracefully and realign your spine before moving away from the chair.

## 79 Rolling out of bed

**To begin this movement, make sure that you are lying facing the edge of the bed. You may like to rest or sleep with a cushion between your bent knees as this takes the pressure off your lower back and frees sensitive nerves in your back (particularly the sciatic nerve).**

▷ **1** Lie on your side near the edge of the bed. You should have your lower elbow bent and your chest open – the ideal sleeping position for later pregnancy.

△ **2** To get up, roll more on to your front. Bring your top hand and your top knee over to the edge of the bed.

△ **3** Put your weight on your top hand, lifting your upper body, and slide your top leg over the edge of the bed to place your foot firmly on the floor. Raise your buttocks and rise out of bed.

## 80 Standing from lying

**This technique will serve you well every time you get off your yoga mat after doing floor stretches or deep relaxation.**

△ **1** Bend both knees and place your feet on the floor. Bring your right elbow to your left knee at about waist level.

△ **2** Roll on to your left hip, leaning on your bent left leg, and support your upper body on your right hand. Bring the left hand up to shoulder level too.

△ **3** Move on to all fours in the Cat Pose (64) and turn your toes under.

△ **4** Walk your hands back toward your knees. Your knees will then come up from the floor as your weight shifts back, so that you are in a squatting position, with your heels as low as possible.

▷ **5** Engage your thigh muscles and stand up slowly.

# Some subtle yoga movements





Now for something totally different. You have discovered how effectively yoga helps you to strengthen your body and increase your awareness, and how you can use these benefits in your everyday life. Well, in yoga there are also certain positions that look – and are – simple to do, yet they create very subtle internal adjustments and strengthen groups of muscles that we are not usually aware of. These can bring huge benefits once you have explored, practised and become thoroughly familiar with them. These exercises require a calm, focused approach; in turn, they foster inner strength and self-confidence.

## 81 Gentle perineal stretch

**This simple exercise should be done as often as possible from mid-pregnancy onwards, as it stretches all the muscles that make up the pelvic floor. It also strengthens, relaxes and brings awareness to the whole perineal area, which is the area through which your baby passes to be born. If the perineum is flexible, strong and lively, it helps you to give birth actively and with greater ease. You will be able to take your foot further out to the side as you gradually loosen up with practice.**

△ **1** From the Cat Pose (64), bring your left foot forward, placing it as far to the left of your hands as you can comfortably manage. Lean forward and breathe in deeply, keeping your spine stretched.

△ **2** Breathe out as you sit back on your right heel without moving your left foot. This stretches the perineal muscles. Repeat several times, then change sides and repeat.

## 82 Rib stretch with Namaste hand mudra

**This powerful exercise helps you to open your lungs more fully and to breathe more deeply by stretching between the ribs, especially at the back where your ribs are attached to your spine. It brings increased awareness to your back and is also an isometric exercise that strengthens your arms and upper spinal muscles. A mudra is a gesture with a spiritual as well as a physical expression. Adding the Namaste Hand Mudra focuses your scattered thoughts and centres your vital energies. It should be practised frequently for greater posture awareness, increased vitality and a focused mind. In late pregnancy, this exercise helps to create more space in the chest for your lungs to expand as your baby develops below the diaphragm.**

△ **1** Stand with your feet hip-width apart and knees loosely bent. Stretch the spine and drop the shoulders. Raise your elbows to the sides at shoulder height and press your palms hard together as you breathe in slowly and deeply. Feel your sternum rise and your ribs open at the back.

△ **2** Now, breathe out slowly as you bring your hands down, with palms still joined. Relax your chest completely. Pause and rest with the breath out, then repeat the sequence twice more. When you have finished, rest for a moment and observe how you feel deep inside.

## 83 Sectional breathing with mudras

**You will probably be surprised to discover that your breathing changes according to the position of your hands in these subtle hand mudras. Ensure that the first three types of breathing come easily to you before you join them together in the complete yogic breath. Allow a minute or two of rest before and after this practice to gain maximum benefit.**

◁ **1** Sit up straight with your chest lifted to make room for your breathing muscles to move freely. Place your hands at your lower abdomen with fingers pointing toward each other. Join the tips of your index fingers and thumbs together to create a closed circuit of energy. Breathe in deeply and feel your abdomen expand as your diaphragm contracts downward. This is called "lower breathing" and gives you energy. Breathe out and repeat.

◁ **2** Now change your hand position, so that your fingers are curled into your palms and your thumbs are free. Breathe in deeply and feel your sternum lift and your ribs move out to the sides. This is called "middle breathing" and it also gives you energy. It comes to your rescue when your growing baby makes it difficult for your diaphragm to contract downward fully. Breathe out and repeat.

◁ **3** Change your hand position again, so that your thumbs are enclosed within your curled fingers. Breathe in deeply and feel how your upper chest is now moving much more freely. This is called "upper breathing" and is very useful if you have indigestion. Breathe out and repeat. You may also need this during labour, so start practising now.

◁ **4** With your thumbs and fingers curled into your palms, press your knuckles together with the fingers of each hand back to back. Turn your palms upward, with your hands in front of you. Open your chest and breathe in fully, from the bottom of your lungs to the top. Breathe out fully and repeat several times. This is full yogic breathing, excellent for recharging your energy and integrating mind, body and spirit in the here and now.

# balancing activity with relaxation

Our energy is called forth by stimulation, motivation, desire or need, which is the urge that gets us going every morning. Then we enjoy the experience of doing things and of being energetic, busy and involved. When this energy begins to ebb, we need to call it back within ourselves for recharging, so that we rest, relax and renew ourselves at every level by "just being".

If we are to maintain our zest for life, this cycle should be repeated throughout the day, until we finally wind down for our sleep at night. It is a rhythm as natural as breathing and it continues throughout life. Yet, somehow, in our modern society, we have become addicted to just one phase of the cycle – the active phase – at the expense of the passive phase. We seem unable to respond to the need for rest even when we feel tired and depleted.

Yoga teaches us how to balance activity with rest, doing with being. It teaches us when and how to relax, and to respond to our body's signals that it is time for a short break. Deep relaxation does not take long and is less a question of time than of attitude. This vital life skill is one of yoga's most valuable gifts. First we become aware of the rhythm of the breath and realize that each breath in is a muscular exertion; each breath out is the release that follows. Then we learn to apply this rhythm to all our activities – both mental and physical. We gradually learn to relax and release the toxins and tensions of living as they arise. It is their build-up that causes stress, congestion and poor functioning of body and mind.

With any relaxation practices, the most vital first step is to make yourself really comfortable, with support just where you need it, so that you can let all your muscles relax and your mind sink into repose.

## 84 Take your focus inward

**"Time out" breaks work best when you have something gentle and non-stressful to focus on. Here are three useful suggestions.**

◁ **1** It can be very soothing to just sit quietly and turn inward, becoming aware of your growing baby. Try focusing on your own gentle breathing or on feeling your baby's life and movement inside you.

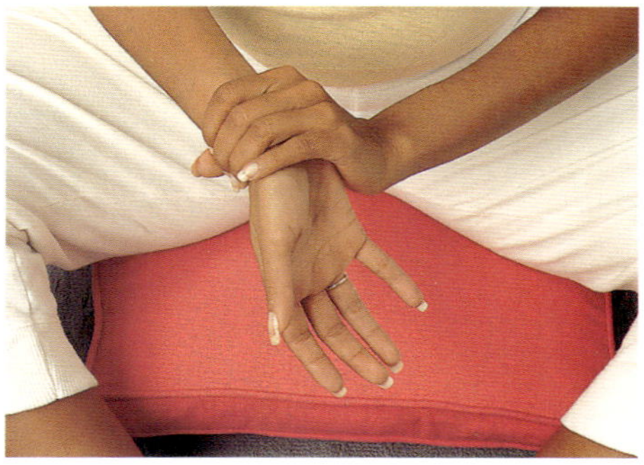

△ **2** Gently massaging your wrists and all the little joints in your hands releases tension and helps to balance the nervous system and pelvic area.

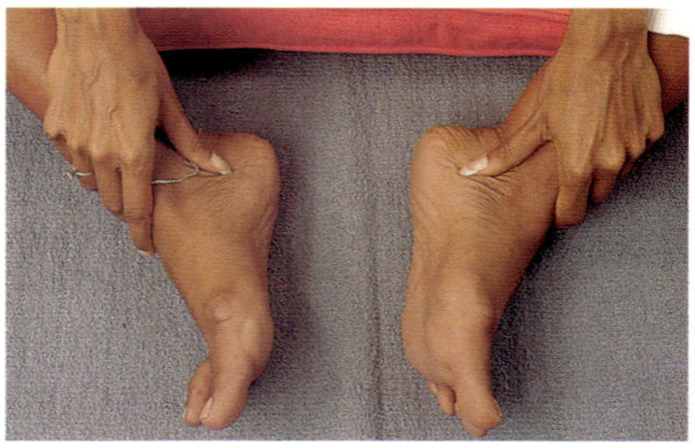

△ **3** The same principle applies to massaging your inner ankles. This is the reflex area for your womb and massaging gently helps tone and strengthen.

## 85 Focus on your baby

**By now your baby is probably moving around vigorously, alternating between periods of sleep and activity, and growing into a real person. Get to know this person who is coming into your life. Enjoy the communication of loving touch between you.**

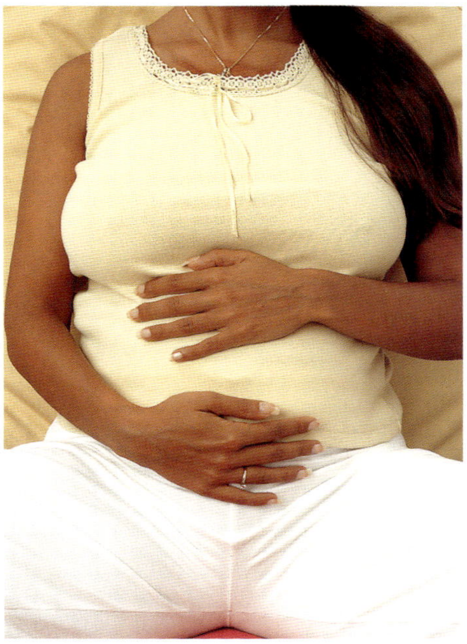

△ **1** Delight in noticing how your baby responds to the massaging movement of your loving hands.

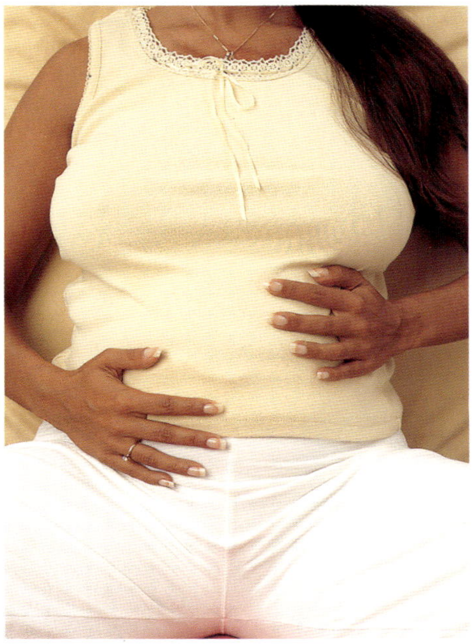

△ **2** Take time to explore your baby's contours. Are those heels? Is that a head?

## 86 Focus on yourself

**Being pregnant, and focusing on your baby, does not make you any less of a person yourself. Relax for your own well-being, too.**

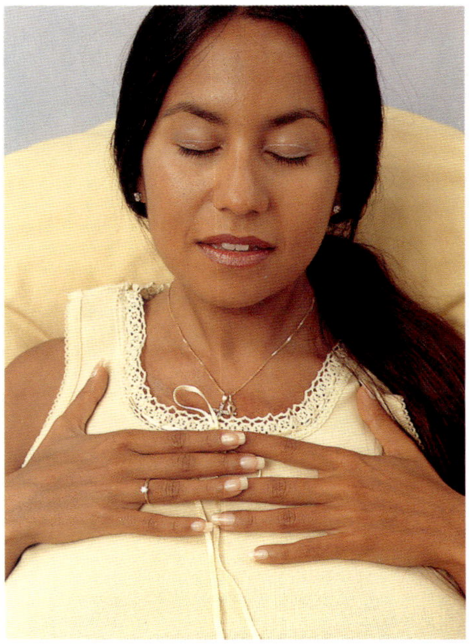

△ Feel your breathing and your own glowing heart centre radiating outward. Just be.

## 87 Relax with your partner

**Both of you should celebrate the experience of your pregnancy. Invest time in getting to know this new person who is coming into your lives. Touch and talk to your baby together.**

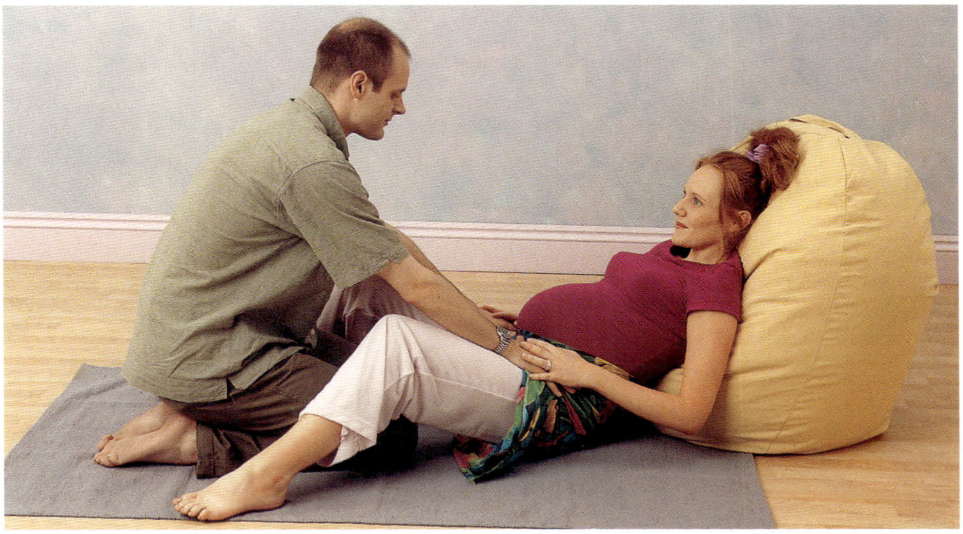

▷ **1** Relax while your partner explores your baby's movements. By placing his hands right under the base of your uterus (thumbs on pubis, fingers extended out toward the hip bones), he can give you a strong resistance that deepens your breathing while relaxing – excellent preparation for breathing through contractions without over-tensing muscles.

▷ **2** In joint relaxation with your partner, you can both place your hands on the baby. This quiet communication through touch generates harmony between the three of you – now and into the future.

# deep relaxation

Deep relaxation is an essential part of your yoga practice. It may come at the end of a daily yoga exercise and breathing session, if you have time, or you may find it more convenient to divide your yoga session into two parts. You may like to practise yoga exercises with short rests for breathing and relaxation in the morning, then add an extra half-hour slot for breathing and deep relaxation at another time of the day when you will not be disturbed. The more regular your practice, the better the results.

## 88 Modified positions for deep relaxation

**As your baby grows, lying on your back will no longer be comfortable and, as it can restrict circulation, it is not a good idea. The classical yoga relaxation position needs to be modified from about 30 weeks onwards. You can bend your knees or place a cushion or blankets under your hips, lie on your side or lean forward over a beanbag. You can even relax deeply while sitting up, as long as you are well supported and your legs are not hanging down. Below are six alternatives for you to try.**

**CAUTION**
Those with high blood pressure should not rest with arms raised above their head – it makes the heart work harder. It is fine to raise arms while exercising, as the blood is already moving briskly.

△ Place a firm cushion under the head, to lengthen the neck and stop the chin jutting up, and a soft one under waist and hips to ease the lower spine. With bent elbows, wrap your palms around the abdomen to keep contact with your baby.

△ Bend your knees out to the sides and bring the soles of your feet together. Place plenty of soft padding under the thighs and knees. This makes more space in the lower abdomen for your baby.

△ Place a beanbag under your legs and a cushion under the hips. Your raised legs improve blood flow to the heart and reduce swelling and aching in the legs; raised hips ease the lower back. This position also helps to turn a breech baby.

◁ Kneel down with knees wide, to allow plenty of room for your baby. Lean forward over a beanbag and rest your head in your arms. This is a very relaxing pose. The whole spine is gently stretched by the raised arms, the pelvis and hips are open, and the beanbag is taking the weight of the baby.

▷ Push the beanbag against a wall for extra support and recline against it so that you are as comfortable as possible. Sit with your knees bent and out to the sides and add cushions underneath to open up your hips.

△ Lie on one side with a cushion between your knees and one under your head. Lying on your left side is a popular position as pregnancy advances, as it encourages the best presentation of the baby for birth.

# A sample mid-term practice

1

▷ Swing and release (61)

2

▽ Supported pelvic floor lift (70)

3

△ Pelvic floor stretches (69)

4

◁ Sectional breathing with mudras (83)

5

△ Modified positions for deep relaxation (88)

"The secret life stirs within me
O my darling, I can hear your
heartbeats."

*Indian birth song*



## Questions and answers

**• I get a lot of backache, especially in my lower back.**
This is usually because of tightness (caused by tension) in the muscles of the lower back as well as weakness in the lower abdominal and pelvic floor muscles. Practise the movements suggested in this chapter to strengthen these groups of muscles so that they can help to support your spine and keep your trunk in good alignment.

**• I get pain in my groin or pelvis, which seems to be caused by pressure or constriction.**
This can be due to muscular weakness or imbalance causing poor posture and undue pressure from the growing baby in the pelvic area. Practise abdominal strengthening, as well as upper spine and arm movements that lift your chest and pull the weight of your baby upwards. When resting, keep your legs up and your hips raised, to ease any pressure.

**• The pressure of the baby on my bladder wakes me up at night and I have to keep getting up.**
Avoid drinking at bedtime, and sleep on your side with a pillow between your knees to take the pressure off your bladder.

**• My joints feel so loose that I am afraid they will not support my increasing weight.**
Hormones are released during pregnancy that soften the ligaments that hold your joints in place. This is to prepare the pelvic area to open and let your baby pass through the birth canal. Avoid overstretching in any position, especially in those joints that bear the body's weight, namely your hips, pelvis, lower back and knees.

**• I can't get a really good night's sleep, and this is making me feel so tired all of the time.**
This lack of sleep can be due to all kinds of things – such as pressure on your bladder, indigestion, or swelling and puffiness in your legs. Exercises that will help to ease these conditions are given throughout this chapter. It may also help to play your relaxation tape in bed, just before you go to sleep. When you wake in the night, focus on your breathing, commune with your baby and repeat the "seed-thoughts" and affirmations that we talked about in the introduction. Provided that your mind is profoundly relaxed and peaceful you should not be deprived of the rest that you need, even if you are not actually asleep.

# Aqua yoga poses

On dry land, stretching in yoga is achieved against gravity in standing, sitting and kneeling, prone and supine poses called "asanas". Together with deep breathing, they are the hallmark of yoga as a unique form of exercise. Water allows a greater freedom of movement and facilitates relaxation in the stretch itself. While in theory most yoga poses can be adapted to be practised in water, some lend themselves to aquatic versions better than others.

During pregnancy, poses that open the hips and stretch the whole body are particularly valuable. Three classic asanas are presented here in their aquatic versions, and can be practised throughout pregnancy. Since only a small proportion of pregnant women can float, relax and stretch at the same time, you will probably need to use a supporting woggle or float to align your spine in the stretch and get the maximum benefit from floating poses.

Take your time to get into each of these three poses and enjoy them as you breathe fully in the stretch. If you are a swimmer, what is asked from the body here may be quite new to you. If you practised yoga before you were pregnant, the aquatic adaptation of these three poses may help you adapt other asanas which you particularly enjoy on dry land, first in standing and then in floating versions. Start from bent knees to enjoy a fuller stretch.

## 89 Warrior balance

**Although the Warrior Poses (227, 251) and water may seem contradictory, the aquatic versions offer a strengthening and energizing stretch just like the land-based classic postures. Water facilitates a sound grounding at the bottom of the pool without strain. Rather than raising the arms up, they are extended on the surface of the water, to allow an intense stretching of the inner leg muscles in the balance that follows the Warrior Pose taking off to float forward.**

△ **1** Stand in the pool, inhale and take a wide step forward, bending your front leg so that your knee is above your heel and keeping your back leg extended, front foot solidly on the pool floor and turning out slightly to open the hips. Extend your arms in front of you, palms facing each other, and feel an intense stretch on the side of your back leg as you exhale. Even if you already practise yoga, it may be difficult to keep your back heel on the pool floor. Stretch from the base of your toes, extending the back of your knees. Take a few breaths in this pose, finding more extension in your middle back with each exhalation.

△ **2** While you inhale, stretch your front leg as you shift your weight forward on to it and raise your back leg slowly into a balance as you exhale. The buoyancy of the water transforms this balance instantly into a long relaxed floating stretch, as your body extends forward with the movement and the two legs join together.

△ **3** Your body is now streamlined from the toes to the fingertips. Repeat this balance with the other leg and practise it a few times until you become familiar with the co-ordination of the movement and the breathing.(You may hold a float in the pose to achieve a full floating stretch at first.)

## 90 Floating tree pose

**The Tree Pose (see 21) is a classic yoga posture. One leg is bent, with the foot resting on the inside of the other leg in order to achieve an energizing yet calming alignment of the whole body. The arms extend over the head and ideally the hands are joined, palms facing each other, while the head remains in line with the spine. The aquatic version of this pose is best done with the support of a woggle or foam board in pregnancy, to allow a perfect alignment of the hips with the shoulders and legs in the water. A woggle or board under the base of the buttocks helps stabilize the pose, which only very good swimmers who practise yoga might sustain without support. In this pose, you stretch, relax and breathe deeply all in one. Two alternative ways of getting into the pose are presented.**





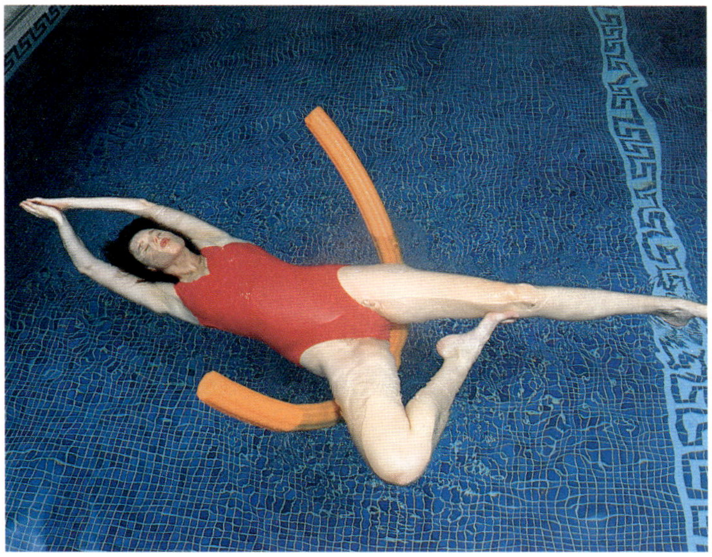

△ **1** Start by standing in the pool, holding the woggle behind your back. Lower it and lie down on your back with the woggle comfortably under you. Stretch your arms back over your head, palms together, and bend one leg, bringing your foot as high as you can go along the other leg without disturbing the alignment of your body.

△ **2** Alternatively, you can bend your leg first, holding on to the ends of the woggle and checking your alignment, before you stretch back and extend your arms above your head. Make sure your head is perfectly aligned in the pose.

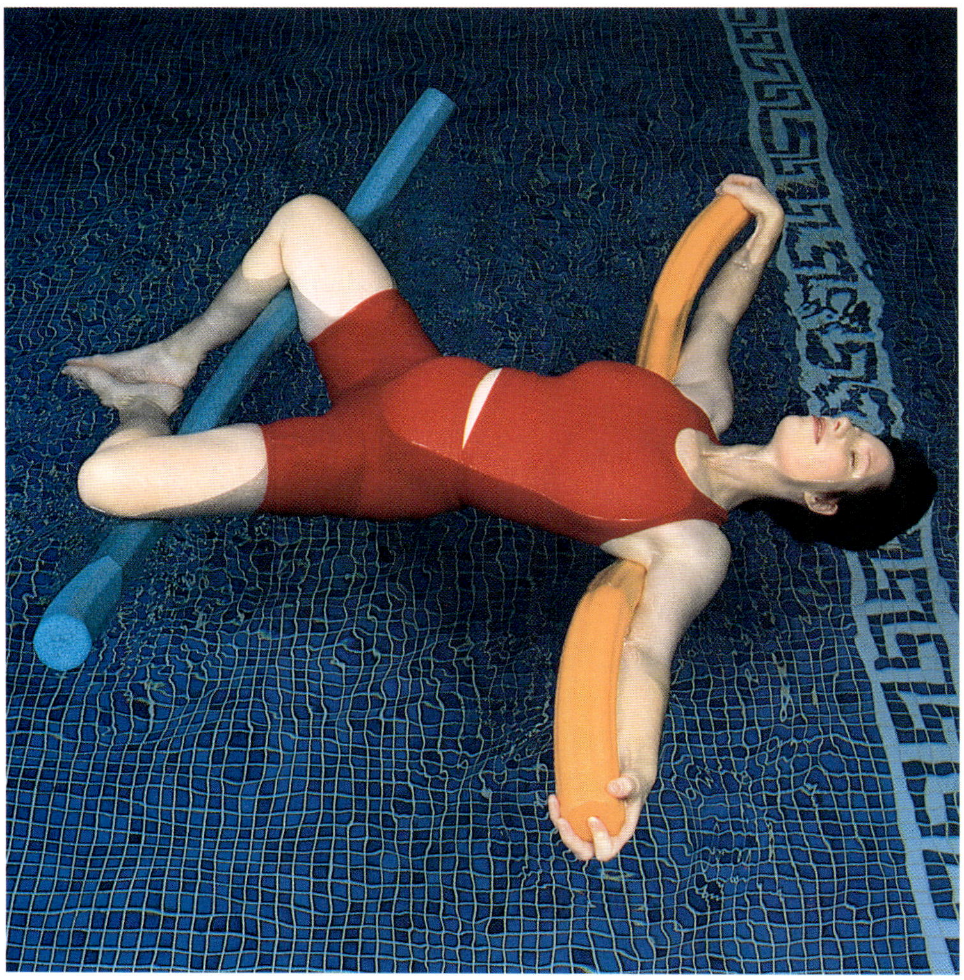

## 91 Floating butterfly pose

**This is a restful, relaxing pose in which your pelvis is maximally open while your feet are joined, soles together. It is a good opportunity to enjoy the full benefits of classical yoga in the water, as this pose is reputed to be a panacea for women's health. Even if you float easily, having a woggle or board to support you will enable you to stretch and relax more in the pose. You can practise it throughout pregnancy, drawing a calm energy from it. Practise opening your legs wide and stretching them while you lie on your back in the water with your arms resting on a woggle in order to relax in the stretch, before you attempt the pose.**

◁ **1** With a woggle supporting you behind your back and under your arms, stand facing a bar or a second woggle in front of you. Lower yourself in the water and place your bent legs over the bar or woggle, bringing the soles of your feet together and opening your knees wide. Stretch back, close to the surface of the water, resting your arms over the woggle on both sides. Let yourself completely relax in this supported floating pose and breathe deeply into your lower abdomen.

# Dynamic stretches





This set of simple exercises is designed mainly for swimmers, or at least for those who are confident in water. They are aimed at strengthening and lengthening the muscles that are used in swimming. The exercises are quite demanding and are intended for active, reasonably fit women who enjoy being in water. In these exercises, the resistance of the water against your body helps you deploy greater strength in the movement, yet with much greater freedom than in land-based yoga.

## 92 Full back stretch

**In this rhythmic sequence, the whole body is stretched using simultaneous and alternate extensions and bends of the arms and legs. It is best done in a pool equipped with a bar along the side. You can do the symmetrical stretch holding on to a woggle but this does not give you as much resistance against which to stretch and bend your arms. You may launch yourself from the supported stretch into the floating one, either by pushing yourself off the pool wall or by letting go of the woggle and stretching back into a floating position. At first, while you are exploring your full stretch, you may find it helpful to keep your arm and leg slightly flexed for the asymmetrical stretch. Later, when this exercise is familiar to you, try to extend both arm and leg as fully as possible.**

△ **1** Start with the supported, symmetrical stretch, even if you are a swimmer. Hold on to a woggle or the bar, breathe in and, as you breathe out, stretch out your arms and legs, extending your legs straight out together.

△ **2** Bend your legs and arms simultaneously on an in breath and extend them on the next out breath, getting into a steady energetic rhythm. This is quite tiring and you need to be careful not to exceed your optimal quota.

△ **3** Now open your legs as wide as possible and find a similar rhythmic movement in which you stretch further on each out breath while keeping the whole sequence very relaxed. Some women find the version with legs open easier than the previous one, but both are equally demanding.

△ **4** For the asymmetrical stretch, float on your back with your arms along your body and your legs straight. You may use a woggle if you need support but try doing without one in this particular exercise as it can hamper your movement.

△ **5** As you inhale, open your left leg to the side and stretch your right arm behind you simultaneously. Stretch further as you breathe out.

△ **6** Bring your stretched arm and leg back to the centre as you breathe in again and immediately extend your other arm and leg in the same way as you breathe out. Continue to stretch alternating sides steadily with full cycles of your breath.

## 93 Back bend stretch

**This sequence takes you from a back stretch to an open squat and back to the wall on your front. It can be as slow and relaxed or as fast and vigorous as you wish. Even in the vigorous mode, the mid-point of the sequence is totally relaxed as the body changes direction. This exercise tones the whole body and also improves your co-ordination. It is satisfying for the body and mind to experience a sense of loop in the sequence. If you are a confident swimmer, you may start your back stretch under water and return to the wall in a front stretch from your squatting position, pushing yourself from the pool floor to the pool wall. Skilled turns of freestyle swimmers against the wall can be seen as a closer, more rapid and advanced variation of this back bend, using the wall in the rotation phase rather than at the beginning of the sequence.**

△ **1** Stand facing the pool wall and lower your body into the water by bending your legs. Inhale and push against the base of the wall with one leg, propelling yourself into the pool with a vigorous, yet relaxed, back stretch as you breathe out.

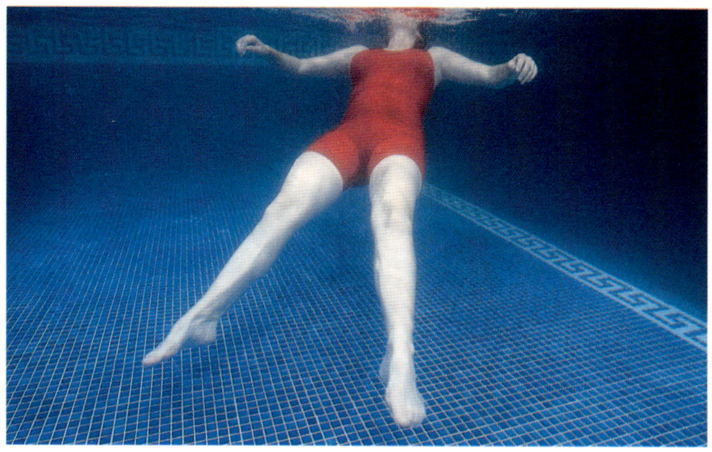

△ **2** Relax completely on the next flow of breath, letting your body lower itself again into the water.

△ **3** Breathe in again and open your legs wide, with a vigorous movement.

△ **4** As you breathe out, bend your knees and rotate forward so that you find yourself close to a kneeling position in the water, facing the pool wall. You are now ready to start this exercise all over again.

# Energetic stretches





Aqua yoga helps you to stretch vigorously and relax fully at the same time. Both stretching and relaxing are your best allies in preparing for the birth of your baby.

These energetic stretches invite you to combine both movement and complete relaxation. This corresponds not only to the essence of yoga but to the ways of many water animals, particularly water turtles and water mammals. Relaxed stretches both on the surface and under water will suit those who feel most at ease in water and enjoy going under the surface.

Simply do these stretches to your own rhythm. Pay close attention to the liberating and peaceful feelings of gliding relaxation and amphibian stretching which they will induce in you. The vigorous start of the Water Turtle (94) helps launch you with momentum into the submerged pose, while the Relaxed Roll Stretch (95) gives you a unique freedom of movement coupled with your own breathing rhythm. Make the most of these stretches: the water helps you enjoy the pleasurable feeling of your pregnant body in a way that would be impossible on dry land.

## 94 Water turtle

**To start this sequence, in which the pose resembles that of a swimming water turtle, stand in the pool with your legs wide apart, your back straight and your arms along your body; breathe deeply.**

△ **1** On an in breath, lift your bent legs as high as you can and rest your hands on your knees as you exhale. Shift your weight forward on the next in breath.

△ **2** Release your hands as you exhale, so that you find yourself in the water turtle pose. Sink slowly and land with your legs apart on the pool floor. Repeat the exercise a few times, paying attention to your breathing cycle.

△ **3** If you find your water turtle sinking too rapidly or your body tensing as you try to reach your knees with your hands, try using a woggle under your arms. Instead of landing on the pool floor after taking your hands off your knees, you may choose to stretch forward along the surface of the water and touch your knees again from this position, opening and closing alternately as you swim like a turtle.

△ **4** If you are ready for a greater challenge, start from the wall, with your bent knees open, feet flat on the wall and your buttocks as close to the wall as possible. A vigorous breaststroke movement of your arms will keep you against the wall and make you breathe deeply in an intense open stretch.

△ **5** You can then push your legs from the wall and stretch your arms wide before relaxing and letting yourself go down towards the bottom of the pool like a water turtle. Stand up again when you are ready. This exercise is strenuous and repeating it twice is sufficient in one session.

## 95 Relaxed roll stretch

**This swimming stretch will be very enjoyable for women who like moving in the water without using the particular skills of any given stroke. It is a free, flowing movement that can be done right up to the time of birth, making the most of water as a weight-free environment in which the constraints of late pregnancy can be forgotten for a while. Under water, the feeling of freedom is even greater. Although this exercise can also be done along the surface, it is difficult to roll sideways without putting your face in the water and those for whom this is not possible should not attempt it.**

◁ **1** Stand with your back to the pool wall and knees bent. Lower your body and after taking a breath, push yourself off the wall with one foot, extending the arm on the same side. This is a relaxed stretch of your whole side.

▷ **2** As you move away from the wall, blow out and, stretching your other arm back over your head in an overarm movement, roll on to your back, taking air again as you stretch. You can "roll-stretch" in this way a few times without getting tired if you keep your body relaxed in the movement.

# Aqua yoga together





Aqua yoga, like yoga, is designed as an individual pursuit. However, it does not always have to be a solitary form of exercise. It can be done with friends both before and after birth. Here are a few examples of how friends and birth partners can help each other to stretch in aqua yoga, to their mutual benefit. Practising aqua yoga with a friend can considerably increase your confidence if you rely on the use of floats and woggles when you move away from the pool wall. It can also strengthen the non-verbal communication between birth partners that will be invaluable during labour.

If you have a toddler or small child who cannot quite swim yet, you can also involve him or her in part of your aqua yoga practice, holding on to you in the water.

Practising aqua yoga with your partner helps to strengthen the bonds between you through this transformative time. Being in water facilitates the inevitably complex process of regression, adjustment and growth that the arrival of a new baby triggers in most families.

You can practise all the exercises in this book with a companion and find innovative ways of synchronizing and co-ordinating them. Here are just a few examples of what you can do.

## 96 Leg circles on the back

**In this exercise, friends take turn to stretch each other. The pregnant woman, supported by one or two floats under each arm, is stretched on her back by either a standing or a swimming helper, who moves her legs in wide circles. If you are not totally water-confident, it is best to start with the standing version. You need more space to do the swimming version, as both you and your helper move in the water with your bodies extended.**

△ **1** Get into a stable supported position on your back in the water before your helper takes hold of your feet. This is a passive exercise where the movement is done for you. Let go and enjoy it completely, focusing on breathing as deeply as possible.

△ **2** Your helper starts circling your legs as wide as possible, bending the knees and stretching the legs in a wide breaststroke movement.

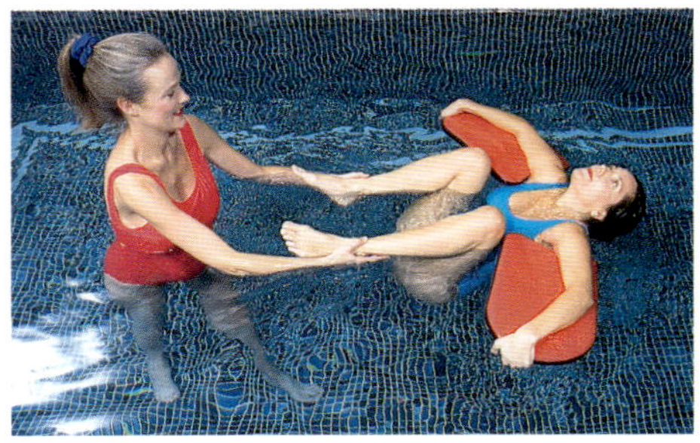

△ **3** Guide your helper if necessary to find the steady, slow, smooth rhythm that suits you best. If the helper also breathes fully at the same time, this can be an equally good exercise of the arms and shoulders.

△ **4** If your helper is also pregnant she can use a woggle to gain as much from the swimming version of the exercise as you. Your starting position is as before, but the helper is more immersed, with the woggle in place, standing with bent knees so that her arm movement is on the surface of the water in line with your leg circling. Once a suitable rhythm has been found, the helper can take off, synchronizing a slow breaststroke with the outward stretching of your legs.

△ **5** A further variation of this exercise is a joint breaststroke leg movement in which the two of you hold a woggle on either side, so that you exert a resistance against each other as you stretch together.

## 97 Joint floating stretch

**Stretching side by side with a friend can be a very enjoyable shared experience. Joint floating stretches and relaxation can deepen non-verbal communication between friends and promote friendship, enhancing the individual experience of each woman in a non-competitive, relaxing way. Drifting along may bring friends close together and apart again.**

◁ **1** Use a woggle each to support the tops of your thighs, protect your lower back in a full stretch and ease your floating. Extend your arms back over your head on an inhalation. As you exhale, bend one knee and bring your foot against the inner side of the other leg, which remains extended on the surface of the water. Breathe fully as you continue stretching and relaxing at the same time, enjoying both the stillness and the extension of your body, which is pure yoga. Change legs and repeat on the other side. To end this exercise, bring your arms to the side and along your body and lower your pelvis in the water into a half-sitting position so that you can remove your woggle easily and stand up. You can also extend your bent leg and get into a floating relaxation directly from this stretch.

## 98 Involve your toddler

**A woggle under your arms, at the front or at the back, will give you enough extra buoyancy not to mind having a toddler hanging on to you while you are doing aqua yoga exercises. A couple of stretches are shown here to inspire you but, with the exception of the stretch-bends and swings, most of the exercises in this book can be done with a toddler in tow. It helps if he or she is water-confident and does not mind going under occasionally.**

▷ **1** Try a full stretch, propelling your body forward with either a frog kick or by pushing your feet off the floor.

◁ **2** Your toddler can sit on you while you are lying back, supporting yourself on one or two woggles. This gives you the freedom to stretch your legs wide and then bend them, which opens your pelvis. Circle your legs if you can: you might not be able to extend your body as much as if you were on your own but you may share a lot of fun with your child.

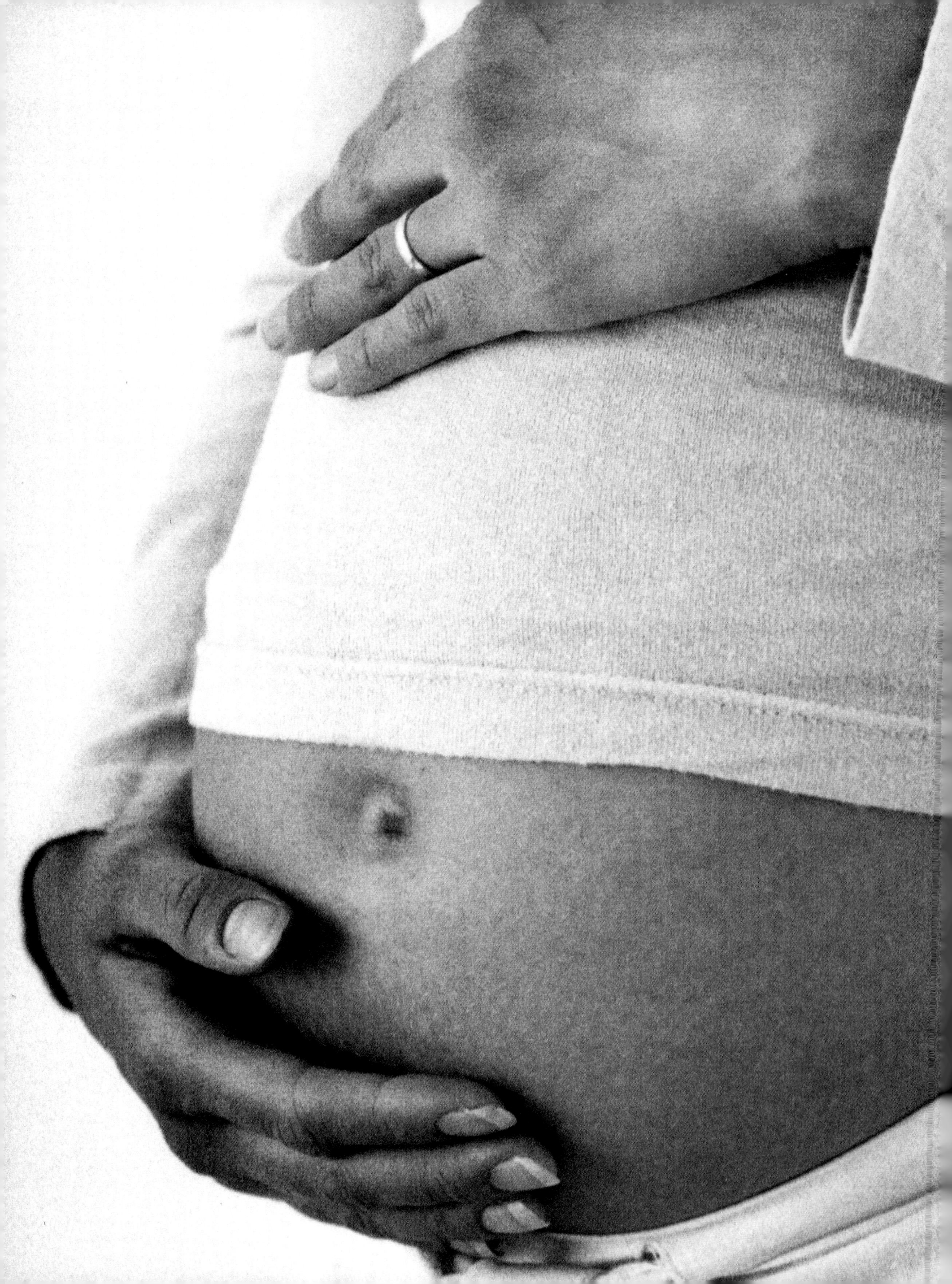

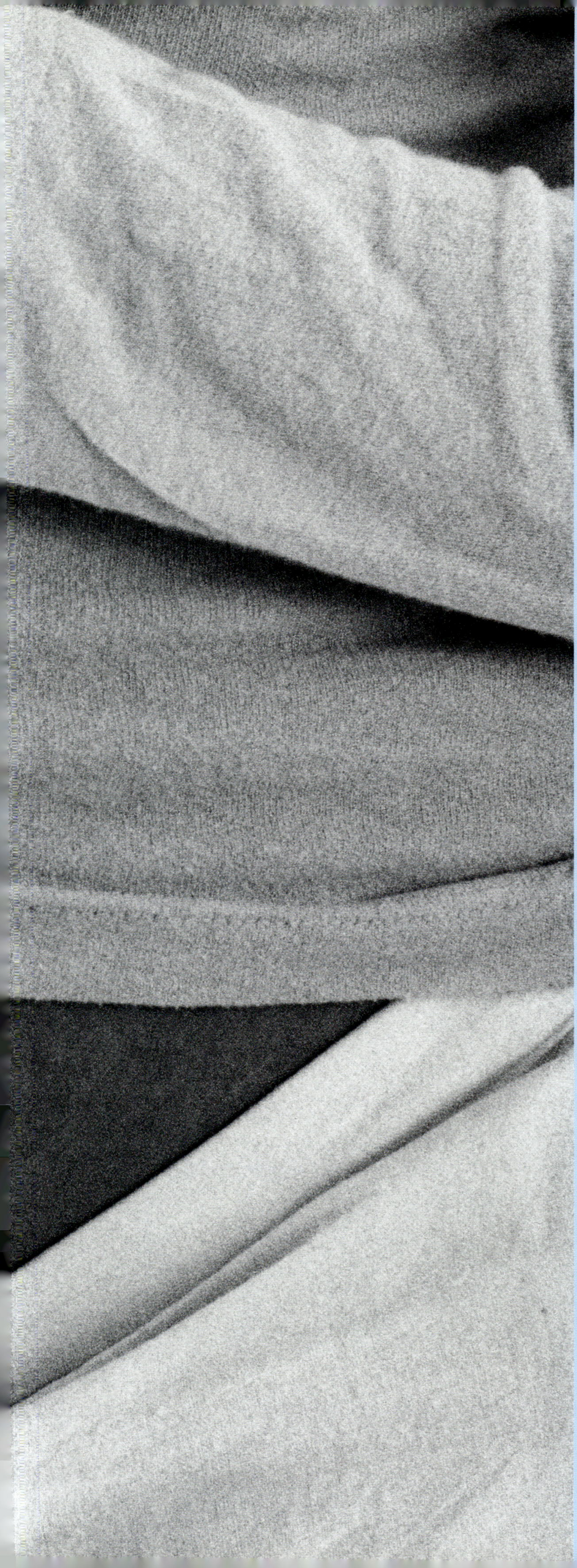

# yoga and aqua yoga for late pregnancy

During the last few weeks of pregnancy your priorities will be to keep yourself as fit and comfortable as possible, and to practise all the yoga and aqua yoga techniques that can help you during the birthing process. These prepare you physically, mentally and spiritually for labour. However your birthing may unfold, yoga will help you to feel centred and empowered.

# Yoga in late pregnancy

Your baby will be growing rapidly by now, so your yogic priorities need to change. First, you will need to protect your back much more by ensuring that your pelvic and leg muscles are able to carry the extra weight properly. Your focus will be on building power in these supporting muscles. This means paying more attention to centring and grounding exercises, and always remembering to keep your knees well bent in any of the standing poses and movements. Cushions and beanbags should be used to support your back at all times, to enable you to rest more deeply during relaxation. Second, you will need to make more space for your baby, your breathing and your digestive organs. Finally, you will be focusing specifically on increasing the tone in your birthing muscles – in other words, the muscles of your lower back, abdominal area and pelvic floor.

## 99 Centring into the earth

**This exercise combines both power and release. Imagine that you are hauling yourself up a ladder, one arm at a time, and then climbing down again as you support your weight with your arms. Your legs should be well bent to support your weight. Feel a line of strength developing along a vertical axis between earth and sky, passing through your body.**

△ **1** You are going to climb up your metaphorical ladder. Stand with knees bent and spine loose. Now, stretch first one arm overhead and then the other, as though you were climbing a rope ladder without using your feet. Squeeze your fingers tightly to hold on to the ropes. When you get to the top, spend a few moments just hanging from both arms, alternately squeezing and releasing your hands.

△ **2** To climb down again, imagine you are going down a fireman's pole. All the strength is in your arms as you lower your weight one hand over the other down the pole. Slide down several times, bending your knees and grounding strongly along the vertical axis. These exercises can be done anytime, anywhere.

## 100 Supported side stretches

**You need to practise side bending while sitting and resting your spine against a soft but firm support – here we show a beanbag placed against a wall, which is ideal.**

▷ **1** Sit, leaning against a beanbag or a pile of cushions, with your legs stretched out in front of you and comfortably apart. Bring your hands behind your head with your elbows wide and pressed back to open your chest and stretch the sides of your body – you can breathe much more deeply in this position. Relax as you breathe and lengthen the breath out.

△ **2** Still leaning against the beanbag, tilt your upper trunk to one side as you breathe out. Breathe in to straighten up and then tilt to the other side as you breathe out again. Repeat a few times.

△ **3** Now, open your arms wide and stretch overhead, breathing deeply. This stretch really eases pressure in the lower body.

△ **4** Keep one arm overhead and take the other forearm on to your thigh for support, then tilt to the side on a breath out. Breathe in to straighten up and out to bend to the other side.

## 101 Hugging rest

**This resting pose is ideal for late pregnancy. You may also find it comfortable for deep relaxation. The beanbag (or pile of cushions) supports your abdomen, spine and head. Spread your arms wide to lift and create more space in your chest.**

◁ Kneel down, facing the beanbag, with your knees spread wide to accommodate your baby. Now rest the front of your body and the side of your face against the softness of the beanbag and give it a big hug. Breathe deeply and relax completely.

# Light on your feet, light at heart





To say that you are light and full of vitality may sound like a counsel of perfection when you are carrying around a baby that is almost ready to be born. It is, however, largely an attitude of both mind and heart. At this stage of your pregnancy it is very helpful to think "strong" and "graceful" simply to be in harmony with the pull of gravity and to lighten your spirits. Strong standing poses with graceful stretching movements will make sure that you stay full of joyful energy and in great shape.

## 102 Ball of energy (2)

**This is a repeat of Ball of Energy (54), which was introduced earlier in your pregnancy. It is included here to remind you that it is a wonderful workout that lifts your spirits, and is just as useful for this late stage. Keep your legs strong and your knees well bent to protect your lower back as you stretch and bend your upper body in all directions.**

**CAUTION**
Do only what you feel comfortable and happy with, at your own pace and without strain. Take plenty of rest between sequences.

◁ **1** Take hold of your ball of energy in your hands. Take time to feel its weight and dimensions. Once you have its measure, start to play. Roll the ball between your hands, working your arms and shoulders.

◁ **2** Now roll your imaginary ball out to one side, twisting in your upper body as you do so.

◁ **3** Bounce your ball on the floor, bending forward and relaxing your neck. Remember to keep your legs strong but relaxed and knees bent.

◁ **4** Toss the ball in the air, opening your chest and arching your upper back. Continue to improvise in whatever way you like – the idea is to be creative and have fun, as well as exercise your body.

## 103 Dynamic hip opener and stretch

**This is a fluid, dancing movement, expressing feelings of well-being and exuberance, lifting the spirits and opening the heart as well as lifting the upper body and opening the hips. It is excellent for creating lift in the upper body by stretching the arms up, which removes pressure around the diaphragm, and creating more space in the lower abdomen by opening up the hip joints.**

△ **1** As you breathe in, raise one leg to the side with the knee well bent and the hip open. At the same time, stretch up your arms and lift your sternum.

△ **2** As you breathe out, gracefully lower your arms and bent leg. Then begin again with the other leg. Repeat these two movements rhythmically, so that they merge into one fluid dance movement.

△ **Sometimes you may need a little help to make your yoga more fun. Enjoy these unscheduled moments.**

"Delight in yourself, in the meditative movement and the dance you are creating... this yoga is truly a dance..."

*Janine Parvati Baker*

# Stretches for a strong lower back and abdominal muscles





Think of yourself as an athlete in training who needs to build up power in specific groups of muscles for the task in hand, in this case giving birth. The muscles you will be using for childbirth are those in your lower back (for support and pushing against), your abdomen (to push the baby down the birth canal), your perineum and pelvic floor (for elasticity and control) and your breathing muscles (to make sure you stay energized throughout). You do not need complicated or expensive equipment in order to strengthen these particular muscle groups – you can find the props you need around your own home.

## 104 Kitchen yoga

**Isometric exercises help to strengthen muscle groups, and a good way to do this is to push or pull against an immovable object to create resistance. For these exercises, do make sure that what you are pushing and pulling against really is immovable.**

◁ **2** Bring your feet in line as you stand facing a ledge or shelf. Get a good grip with your fingers and, as you breathe out, pull down hard, bending your knees and sinking into a half squat. Hang there, breathing deeply and stretching through your trunk and arms as you work the muscles in your legs.

◁ **3** Stand in front of a counter top with one leg forward and the other back. Lean forward, bending your knees, and place your forearms on the edge of the counter with your forehead on top. Now, push down to open your chest and upper trunk, taking the push through your back heel as you lengthen your lower back. Hold, then repeat with the other leg back.

△ **1** Stand in front of a wall unit (or a wall). Place one foot well in front of the other, with the front knee well bent. Lean forward and place your palms on the unit at head height. Adjust your position so that you are the right distance away to push hard. Breathe in deeply and push, taking the force down through your back leg. Involve all your abdominal muscles on the breath out as you maintain the push. Swap legs and repeat.

## 105 Stretch and squat with chair

**Use a steady, upright chair to both stretch and squat down, as both positions will help to open up in the groin and stretch the pelvic floor. Keep your spine horizontal and your heels on the floor. To make the chair even steadier, push it against a wall.**

◁ **1** Stand in front of the chair with feet apart and toes turning outward, so that your knees will bend over your feet at the same angle. Bend forward and hold the sides of the chair seat, keeping your back stretched and horizontal.

◁ **2** Squat down, bending your elbows to keep your back as flat as possible. Focus on stretching the inner thighs, the groin and the pelvic floor in preparation for giving birth. Breathe through this stretch, exhaling as you go down. Repeat frequently.



## 106 Perineal stretch with chair

**Use a chair to help you when practising the Gentle Perineal Stretch (81) at this stage. For comfort, place a cushion under the shin and foot that you are going to sit on. This exercise will really help you to prepare your body for birthing. Finding the position in which your perineum is most relaxed and you can move your pelvic floor muscles easily is most important for this exercise – you might even get some kicks from your baby.**

◁ Move from the Stretch and Squat with Chair (105) posture to a wide kneeling position, resting one knee on a cushion. Place the other foot out to the side of the chair. Now, holding on to the chair, press down and stretch through the whole perineal area on an out breath. Change legs and repeat the stretch. Practise frequently.

## 107 Relaxation throughout the day

**Never miss an opportunity to relax, alone or in company. If you can relax the muscles that are carrying your baby at every opportunity, it will greatly enhance your feeling of fitness and well-being. Keep a beanbag handy for those blissful moments.**

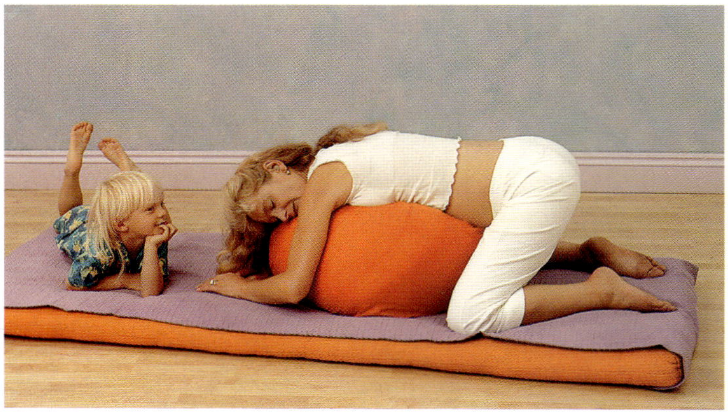

△ Kneel in front of a beanbag and flop over it to conduct weighty conversations with your toddler.

△ If someone can be gently massaging your thighs meanwhile, then so much the better. Relaxed enjoyment is the key.

# Yoga movements for tone and energy

All these standing and walking movements help to create space in your abdomen and between your hips so that your baby has more opportunity to move around and get settled in a good position ready for the journey down the birth canal. So wriggle around as much as you can. In addition, shifting your weight from one leg to another, either in standing or walking poses, helps to prevent or ease varicose veins and swelling caused by an uneven distribution of your body weight.

## 108 Upper torso circles

**These stretches lift your chest up and away from your abdomen, relieving pressure on your abdominal organs and giving your baby more room to change position. They help to diminish the effects of wind or gas in your digestive system and alleviate heartburn in the last few weeks of your pregnancy.**

△ 1 Stand with feet wide and knees well bent. Stretch your arms overhead with hands clasped and palms facing the ceiling. Breathe in and stretch up some more.

△ 2 Make large clockwise circles with your clasped hands as though you were swinging a rope around above your head. After some clockwise circles, repeat the movements anti-clockwise. Engage the muscles at the sides of your body as you circle your upper torso and shoulders.

## 109 Pink panther strides

**These exaggerated strides open the hips and pelvis, as well as the chest for deeper breathing. They work the muscles at the sides of the abdomen and spine. You will have to concentrate to make sure that you use the right combination of legs and arms at the right time.**

◁ **1** Start off in a centred, firmly based standing pose with feet together. Now stride forward boldly with your left leg, swing your left arm forward and your right arm back. Freeze in this position.

▷**2** Making a big stride, bring your right foot forward along with your right arm, taking your left arm back. Holding in between, repeat these alternating strides. Now change to left leg forward, right arm forward and right leg forward, left arm forward, and repeat for a few strides. Then swap over again to left-left and so on.

## 110 Hip drops

**This is another name for the famous "Charlie Chaplin walk". Hip Drops can be practised either standing on one spot or striding forward. This walk will ease pressure in your hips, pelvis and lower back and encourage your baby to join in and get moving. Try to get the rhythm of "strong then limp" in each hip as you wobble forward in an aimless sort of way with a silly grin on your face. This isn't as odd as it sounds – a tight jaw can be a sign of a tight pelvis. Your midwife may even ask you to drop your lower jaw during labour to relax your pelvis.**

△ **1** Turn your feet out. Stand on your left foot with left leg strong. Drop your right hip, letting your right leg dangle loosely. Swing your limp right leg forward.

△ **2** Stand on your right foot with right leg strong, dropping your left hip and letting your left leg dangle loosely. Repeat.

# Helping your baby move into position





You will find that your baby is sensitive to your moods, shares your enjoyment and joins in with all your activities. So the more that you dance around and stretch, and open and tone your body, the better he, she or they will like it. Your centre of gravity lies deep within your pelvis. The opening up of your hips and pelvic area, plus all the activity, will encourage your baby to find the very best position to be in as birth approaches. Putting aside time each day for a few minutes of energetic yoga dance, followed by perineal breathing, is the perfect way to prepare for labour with your baby. Don't forget that all these rotating, twisting and opening movements of the hips should be done with knees bent.

## 111 Knee circles

**This is a balancing exercise that shakes out your hips and legs as you get into a knee-swinging stride. It is a loosening and strengthening movement, good for the circulation and for lifting your mood. If you feel wary about trusting your balance, place one hand against a wall for support. These knee circles should be done smoothly and lightly. Keep arms, shoulders and neck relaxed. The raised leg is also kept as loose as possible throughout.**

▷ **1** Stand on your right leg, with arms spread to the sides at shoulder level for balance and your spine erect. Now swing your left knee up in front of you as high as is comfortable.

△ **2** Bring your left knee to the side to open your left hip and so make more room in the abdomen and pelvis.

△ **3** Now, swing it round behind you and kick back strongly with your left foot. Finally, swing your knee forward, straightening your left leg and placing your left foot firmly on the floor. Repeat with the right knee.

## 112 Standing twist

**This is a good position either on its own, to ease tension in the neck and shoulders, or as a counter-pose to the strong sideways stretch of the Knee Circles (111). Breathe deeply and twist through the whole torso.**

△ Place your right foot on a low stool or chair, making sure that your thigh is parallel to the floor. Raise your arms and open your elbows so that your chest feels open. Place your palms behind your head with neck strong and straight. Breathe in. As you breathe out, twist your head and shoulders to the right. Your upper chest will follow, but your lower body is kept steady by the bent leg. Repeat the twist to the left, with your left foot on the stool.

## 113 Seated perineal stretch

**Now that your baby has grown so much, a low stool and several cushions are useful props for this modified version of the Gentle Perineal Stretch (81). Place one cushion on the stool and the others under your dropped knee as required. Remember throughout that it is the breathing that creates all of the action when you are stretching the yogic way – otherwise nothing happens, or you simply stretch a little in the groin area.**

△ **1** Sit on a cushion astride a low stool, with your knees wide and feet firmly planted on the floor in front. Stretch up through your spine by pressing your palms against your spread thighs.

△ **2** Pressing down firmly into your right foot, drop your left knee back and down on to the pile of waiting cushions, to stretch through the left groin and the perineum. Clasp your hands, breathing in as you push the palms away from you in a forward stretch, taking your weight through your strong right leg. Stretch further as you breathe out and lift through the spine as you breathe in several times. Change legs and repeat.



# A sample practice for late pregnancy

1 △ **Centring into the earth (99)**

2 ▽ **Upper torso circles (108)**

3 △ **Perineal stretch with chair (106)**

4 ▽ **Hugging rest (101)**

# The breath of life

When you practise this diving exercise, your body comes to terms with unspoken fears such as running out of oxygen, drowning, failing or exhaustion. These are the same fears that you are likely to experience in labour during long contractions. Use the aqua breathing to find a way to relax while in the grip of these deep-seated fears. It can transform the frightening experience and is an extremely useful aid during labour.

Gaining further and easier forward movement in your long dive is not just an inspiration for your labour, but is an actual practice for your body, a physical training to help you to deal with these sensations in a positive way. Bodies learn fast and yours will reward you for this practice.

All women who have done this exercise in pregnancy use it in a positive way during their labour. For many, it has transformed their experience of giving birth.

## 114 Breathing dives with relaxation

**Breathing dives can be done on the surface or underwater, or using a combination of both. Underwater dives are more effective, not only because the body is freer in the water but also because the mind enters another world. In a few seconds, a different state of consciousness can be reached. It can also be left behind easily as the body re-emerges into the activity of the pool. Start relaxing as soon as you emerge.**

**It helps to do this exercise with a partner, who can give you a little push when you are learning to release more movement from your relaxed stretch, or just cheer as you go further and further each time and finally cross the pool. Once you have found the way to continue your initial movement effortlessly, relax as you extend your exhalation to the maximum of your breathing capacity. The distances between your starting and finishing points will surprise you.**

◁ **1** Start in a semi-squat position against the pool wall, ready to propel yourself forward by pushing your feet against the wall.

▽ **2** Take a breath and, with a strong push from your feet at the base of the wall, stretch as much as you can in a long dive.

△ **3** Streamline your body as much as possible to diminish the resistance of the water as you push forward, relying on kinetic energy to take you as far as possible. The more you relax in a streamlined stretch, the less additional resistance is created and the further you reach.

△ **4** The challenge is to learn to relax more as you feel the urge to raise your head and breathe. Relax your whole body. You may find yourself sinking, or going to one side, even going into a full circle. Let it happen. Register your feelings. Do not struggle, but when you cannot let go any longer, surface and breathe deeply.

◁ **5** If you find that your legs start sinking as soon as your head and shoulders emerge from the water, place a woggle under your arms. Often it gives you just the support you need to avoid tensing up and to fully enjoy deepening your breathing as you stretch.

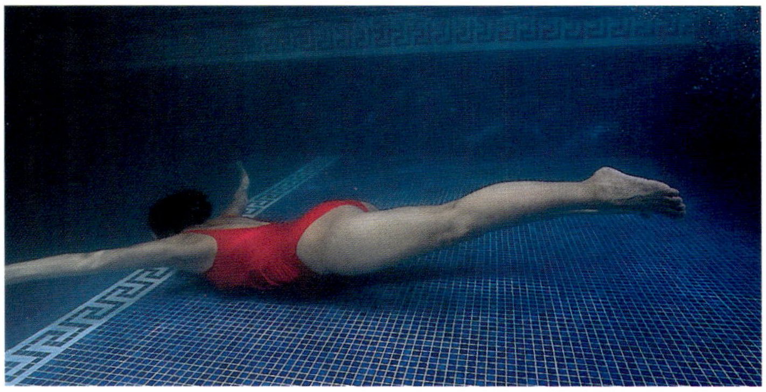

△ **6** As you feel more comfortable in your breathing dives and are able to extend them and relax in them, you can stretch close to the bottom of the pool in a deeper dive. In doing so you become even more at one with the waterworld of fairy tales and myths for a moment, with all its creative potential. Many pregnant women experience this as an environment in which they can feel freer.

▷ **7** Some women feel more comfortable taking dives with their arms running along their bodies rather than outstretched. If you have a tendency to high blood pressure and try to avoid raising your arms on dry land, this version may also be more appropriate for you. It is important to keep your neck and head relaxed in the forward movement.

# Floating relaxation

If you have already tried the adapted swimming strokes described earlier in this book, you will have found that when you use the breath fully in swimming and make your movement as economical as possible, you become more relaxed. Within a very short time, you have forgotten the concerns, and even anxieties, that are inevitable as you go through pregnancy. By the time you get out of the pool, many preoccupations will have been reduced to a manageable scale. Anxiety is the greatest unacknowledged discomfort that prevents most women from enjoying their pregnancies fully. Relaxing in water is both the best prevention and cure and can be achieved easily.

◁ In the same way that relaxation integrates and draws together the benefits of stretching in land-based yoga postures, floating relaxation is essential to the practice of aqua yoga. Floating relaxation can be practised on your own or with a partner. Except for very experienced swimmers who can relax in water without support, it is best done with floats, woggles or human hands to help you float effortlessly.

## the benefits of relaxation

Floating is an extremely powerful form of relaxation. Relaxation encompasses your body, mind and emotions. Its physiological effects include a lower heart rate and blood pressure, a lower respiratory rate, lower blood cortizone level and the production of theta and alpha brainwaves. As these brainwave patterns are produced, emotions – from yesterday or many years back – can be triggered by sensory or mental stimuli to surface in the psyche.

The floating relaxation recommended here is gentle and safe. During pregnancy it can nevertheless result in the release of pent-up emotions, either positive or negative, and have a cathartic effect. For this reason it is important to follow the instructions carefully and, particularly in the last few weeks of pregnancy, it is preferable to relax in water with someone else, ideally the person who will be with you during labour.

Floating relaxation is an effective way to learn to relax quickly during pregnancy if you have not practised relaxation before. The more you practise, the more effective it becomes, as the relaxed body sends signals to the brain which in turn sends more signals of relaxation to the body. If you are familiar with yoga, you will find that floating will deepen your experience and also enrich your yogic relaxation. In the water, it is easy to access quite rapidly levels of relaxation that are normally reached through the apprenticeship of "withdrawing the senses" (pratyahara) in yoga practice. Having practised floating relaxation during pregnancy, you will derive great benefit from it during labour and later on, as you gain the ability to centre yourself instantly, either to draw upon your inner resources or to let yourself go into deep sleep after being woken up by your baby. Relaxation in water also enhances the rise in endorphin levels during the latter part of pregnancy, producing a sense of well-being and suppressing undue anxiety.

### Theta brainwaves

**Theta brainwaves are produced in deep relaxation or when we are absorbed in daydreaming. Brainwave patterns have been detected in foetuses as early as the fifth week. By the time the baby is born, brainwaves are mostly theta or delta (daydreaming or sleeping) until they change gradually into the normal beta rhythm that indicates a greater focus on the external world. Floating relaxation may induce theta waves in a pregnant woman's brain and in turn allow her baby to produce more theta waves. Its regular practice may continue to have a calming effect on the baby in the first year.**

## supported relaxation

Although greater buoyancy is released as the supported woman relaxes more deeply, the action of supporting requires some strength. Particularly when two pregnant women are helping each other, you should take time to ensure that supporting is as beneficial as being supported. It is a good idea to take turns to experience the two roles and to learn to relax as a supporter as well. Ideally, both are complementary in the experience. Allow approximately 5 minutes of relaxation at first, 5–10 minutes when you have gained experience.

## 115 Relaxation with a partner

**It is beneficial to practise floating relaxation with a pregnant friend as regularly as possible throughout pregnancy, ideally once a week. In late pregnancy, your labour partner, whether the father-to-be or someone else, can also begin to support you in the water as a way to deepen the unspoken communication that may prove to be most valuable to you at the time of birth. If two pregnant women are partners in the floating relaxation, they may find that their respective babies are involved too, and sometimes show it by their simultaneous movement in the womb.**

**It is best to swim a little after floating relaxation before getting out of the pool. If you are not a swimmer, do a few drops at the bar or practise your favourite swings or rolls. In late pregnancy be very careful if you have to drive away from the pool. Take time to allow your body to come back to active mode. After having a shower, practise Alternate Nostril Breathing (4) for a couple of minutes. Ideally, sit down and have a healthy drink and snack before leaving.**

△ **1** The position of the supporting person is very important. As the supporter, you should stand with your knees slightly bent so that your back is straight and your body is relaxed with a solid base. You will be supporting the relaxing woman with your arms, yet the source of the support will be your lower back. Once the supporter is in a strong open standing position, the relaxing woman lowers her body so that she is nearly sitting in the water. If the supporter is right-handed, the relaxing woman should sit sideways with her legs to the right, as the strong hand of the supporter will be under her lower back taking most of the weight. If the supporter is left-handed, the pregnant woman faces the left of the supporter.

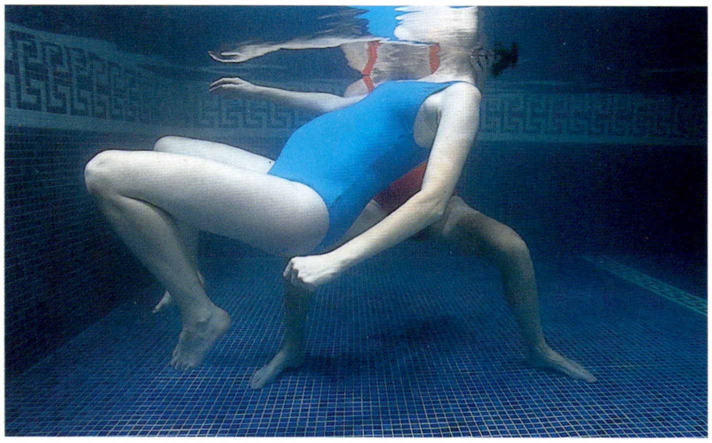

△ **2** Adjust your positions so that support can be given firmly with the strong hand under the lower back and the other hand at the base of the neck. With hands in place, the supporter assists the relaxing woman to swivel into a lying position as effortlessly as possible. There is always a point that feels right and most comfortable for both of you, at which stage the relaxation can begin.

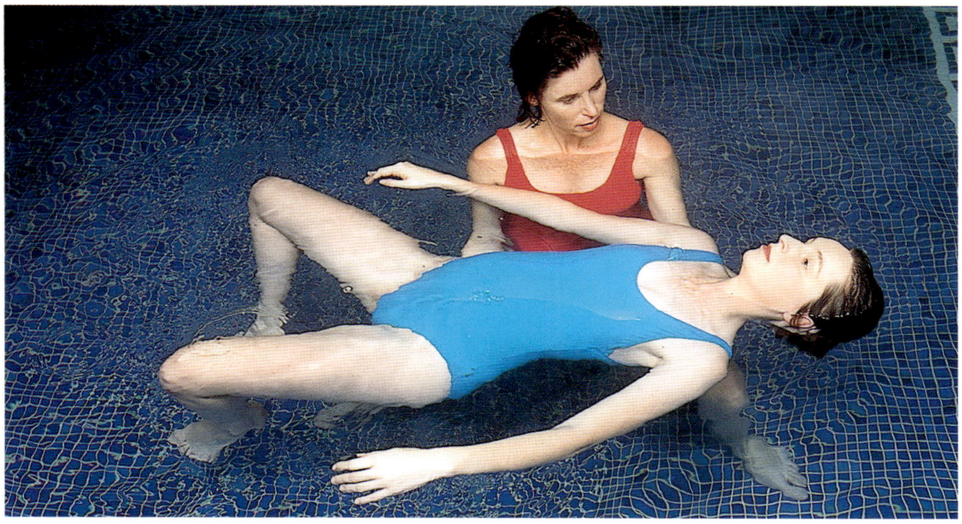

△ **3** If you are the supporter, check that the pregnant woman's body is level just below the surface, with her legs hanging loosely or floating. At first, rocking her body from side to side can help her start relaxing, while her eyes are still open. Encourage her to exhale consciously several times to achieve a state of deep relaxation. She can then close her eyes. Check that her ears are in the water so that only her face is emerging. From then on, you as the supporter will relax too, yet keeping a watch on the pregnant woman. If she shows discomfort and stirs, lower your hand under her back immediately to bring her back to a standing position; if you experience discomfort or feel tense in holding her, do the same, as any tension will inevitably be communicated to her.

△ **4** The floating woman will need 2–5 minutes to get her body back in focus, sometimes longer in late pregnancy. The supporting partner can keep the hand under the base of the neck in place to help her do this at her own pace.

# Just you and your baby





Self-supporting floating relaxation can be a time of exceptional intimacy with your baby, in which you experience each other without any external stimuli and with less of the usual train of thought that keeps the mind engaged in all the activities of the day. It allows you to reach a deeper state in which superficial worries and anxieties have no hold. The sheer magic of the little being growing inside becomes more congenial and can be experienced in the present moment just as it is. This experience may facilitate bonding at the time of birth.

## drifting

As you relax you may find yourself drifting in the pool, sometimes even a considerable distance from your point of departure. If you are relaxed, you will not hurt yourself if you hit the pool wall while you drift, although it may bring you out of your relaxation in an untimely way.

With practice you will learn to control your drifting by relaxing more deeply: the deeper your relaxation, the less you will move. This is another reason why it is better to relax with a friend at first if you can, as he or she can gently look after you while you relax. There is no timekeeping when you are on your own and some women have spent half an hour floating while feeling that barely a couple of minutes had passed.

## relaxation and release

If you connect with past traumas or painful memories while you are practising floating relaxation on your own, try to talk about your experience with someone you trust. This will help you decide whether you need to seek further help to address the experience in a positive way.

In Ayurveda, the ancient medical system associated with yoga, pregnancy is seen as the greatest purifying process the human physiology can experience. Deep relaxation during pregnancy allows the possible resolution of difficult past experiences, particularly miscarriages and pregnancy terminations, which can compromise the full enjoyment of pregnancy for many women. In the intimately comforting environment that water provides, floating relaxation is a gentle yet very effective way of letting go of past experiences and simply being with this growing baby or babies in the fullness of the present moment.

### Be safe

**Self-supporting floating relaxation should be practised with a lifeguard on site, or at least with someone watching at all times.**

## using supports

If you do not have access to woggles, use one or two floats under each arm. It is possible that your legs will sink down as you relax. You may use another float under your feet, though it can be difficult to hold it in place, or let your legs dangle down in the water.

You will find relaxing easier and more comfortable with woggles than with floats and there are various ways you can use them. Experiment to find the way that suits you best and allows you to close your eyes and relax deeply. If you are not water-confident and need more support to feel safe while floating, a second woggle can be added to one placed under the arms.

### 116 With one woggle under the knees, holding on

**Many women like the sense of control that this position gives them as they can let go and relax in their own time. If they are interrupted they have only to lower their bodies into the water, keeping the ends of the woggle in their hands. Others find holding the woggle a constraint that limits the depth of their relaxation in the water.**

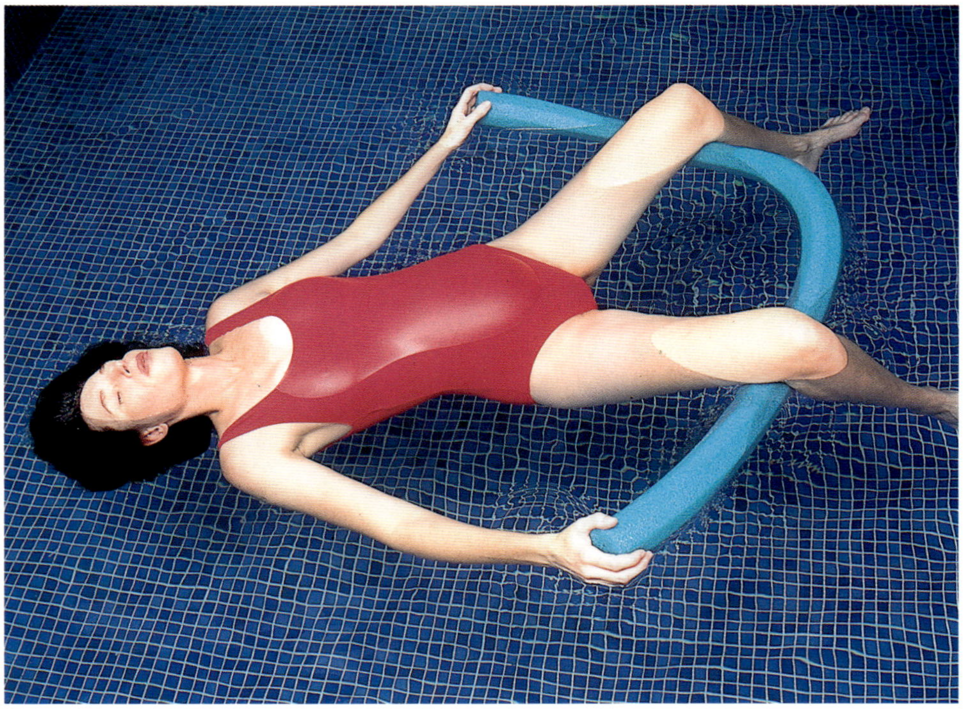

△ Stand in the pool with the woggle behind your back, holding its ends. Lower yourself into a sitting position and bring the woggle under your thighs. Stretch back so that your whole trunk can be on the surface of the water. Open your knees slightly and find a comfortable position in which you can be most relaxed, extending your legs only to the point where your arms are not stretching to hold the woggle. Once you have found this balance, let go and close your eyes, keeping your ears in the water and your face above the surface.

## 117 With two woggles, holding on

**You can use an additional woggle under your shoulders and arms as you hold your main supporting woggle under your bent knees. This gives you complete support, yet still some control as you hold the woggles at their junction. It also gives extra support to your neck and creates a comforting ring in which you can be less easily disturbed in a public pool.**

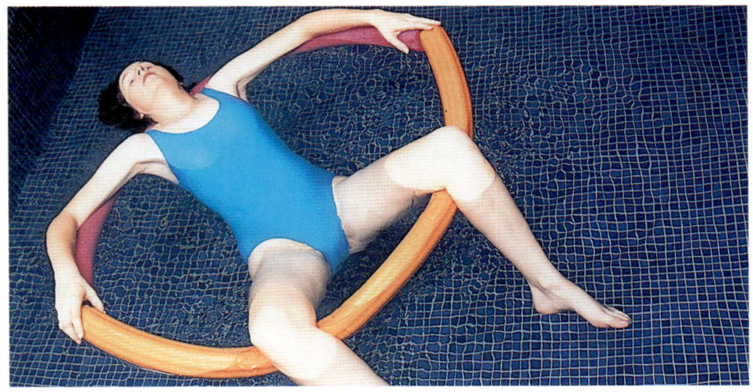

▷ Have the second woggle under your arms so that when you lower your body to pass the first woggle under your knees, it stays in place for you to spread your arms on and then join the two woggles together.

## 118 With one woggle under the knees, letting go

**If possible allow space around you when you start relaxing or be prepared for the risk of being interrupted. Remember that it is not advisable to practise floating relaxation on your own in a pool without a lifeguard on duty.**

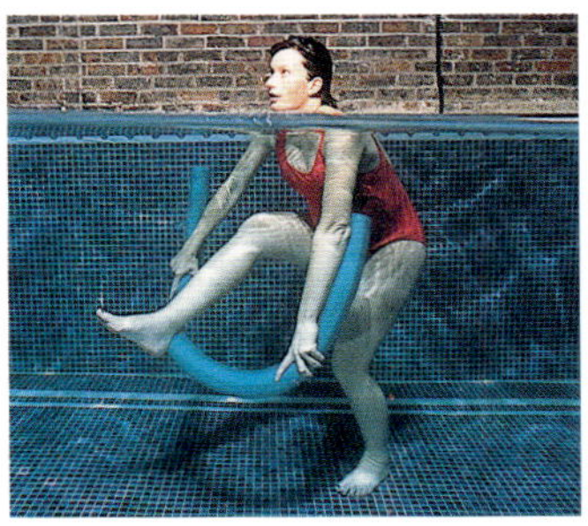

△ **1** Stand in the water holding a woggle in front of you and lower it in the water. Bend one leg and lift it so that you can pass the woggle under it.

△ **2** Lift your leg higher as you lower your body in the water, which makes it easy to bring your other leg on top of the woggle.

◁ **3** Now you can release your hands and lean back, with the woggle in place under your ankles, looking at your feet on the surface of the pool. At this stage, you may be in a reclined position, half sitting in the water.

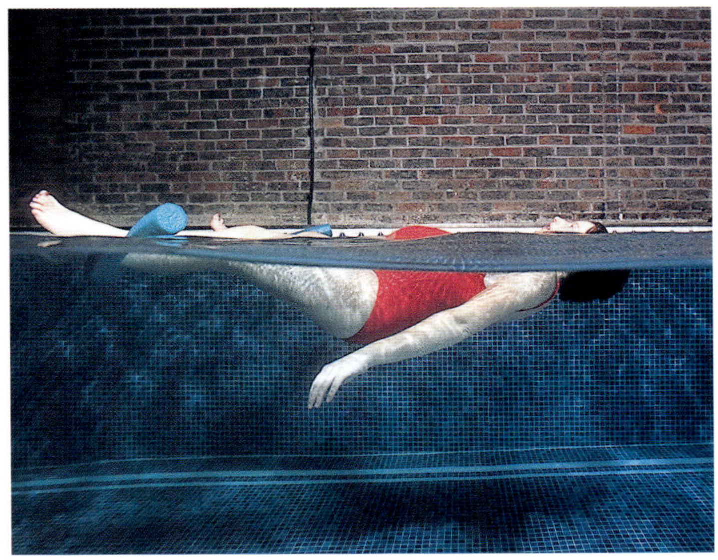

△ **4** Take a breath and as you exhale, stretch back and let go more so that just your face is out of the water. You can now start relaxing deeply, closing your eyes. Let your ears submerge and, if comfortable, lower your head so that just your nose and eyes are above the surface. Close your eyes and roll your whole body gently. You are now ready to relax deeply.

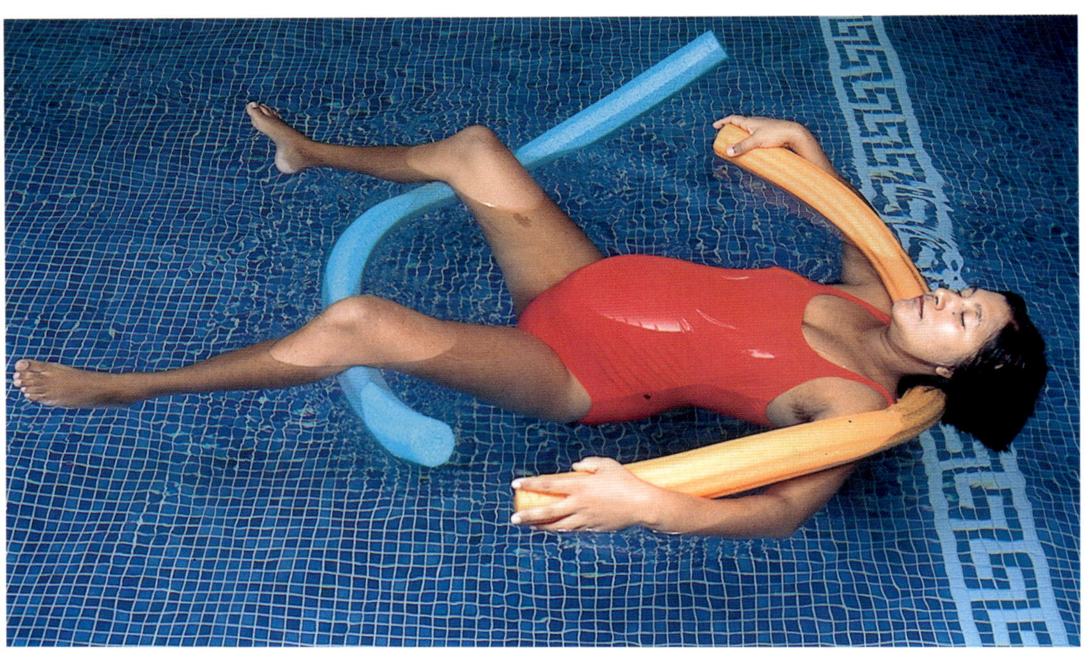

## 119 With one woggle under the knees and another under your neck

**This is perhaps the position in which women can relax the most deeply. Be careful that there is someone watching you in case you completely lose track of time.**

◁ Stand in the water with two woggles in front of you. Place the first under your knees as before, then place the other behind your neck. Bring your hands over it loosely on each side to keep it in place. This allows you to stretch yet relax fully.

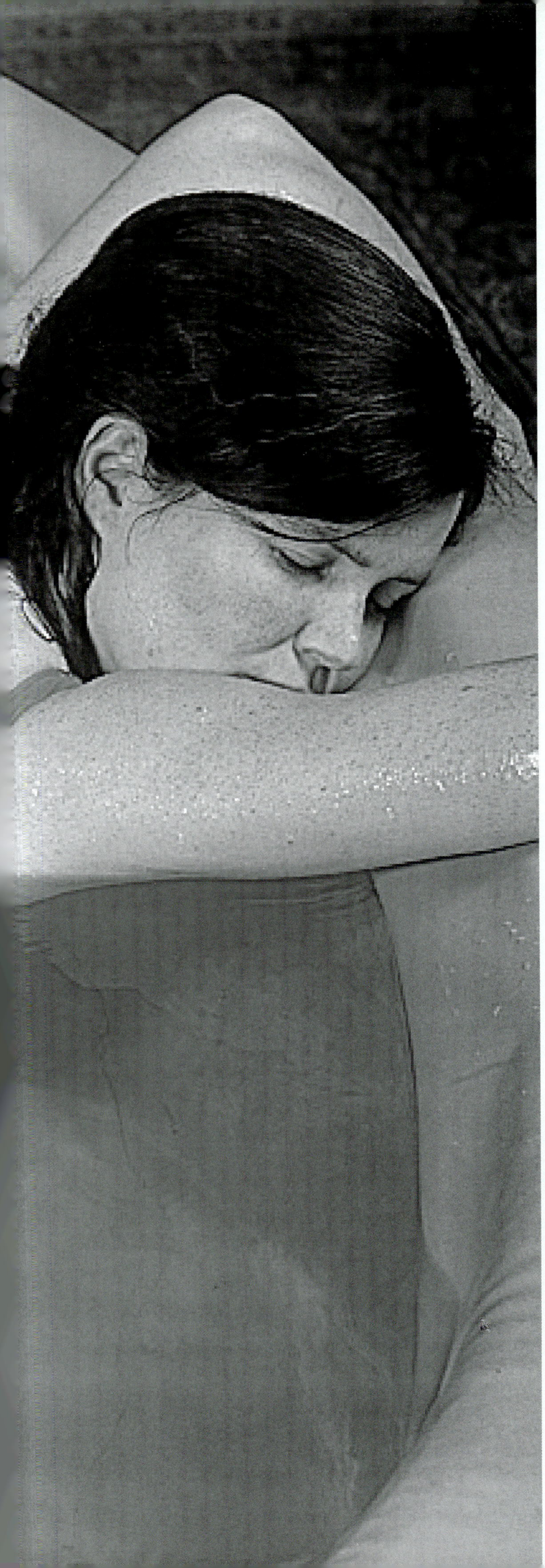

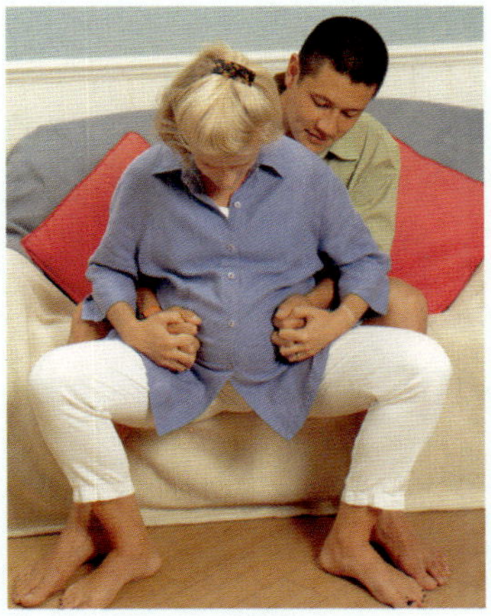

# preparing for the birth

Your baby's birth is a time of great excitement and some uncertainty, of exhilaration and suspense. All your stretching and breathing practices will come into play during labour and the birth itself. Waterbirth is the renewed discovery of our ancestral affinity with water applied to birth. Water is gentle on the mother's body and the baby's entry into the world. Your aqua yoga practice during pregnancy will have prepared you for a fuller use of the power of water to alleviate pain during labour and to ease birth.

# Preparing for labour with kneeling poses





Sitting on your heels, with a cushion between your buttocks and your heels for comfort, is one of the best positions you can adopt at this stage of pregnancy. Your spine is erect, with the coccyx hanging freely, and the trunk's weight is flowing down naturally through your legs and into the floor. This open position means that your baby's head has the maximum amount of space in your pelvis. With the padding from the cushions, you can comfortably maintain this position while you are doing other things, such as chatting to a friend. Kneeling poses also prepare you for a birthing position on all fours – a comfortable and popular choice.

## 120 Chest openers

**Clasping the hands behind the back can be difficult for some people, yet it is well worth persevering because it is a good way to open the shoulders and chest, straighten the upper spine and make more space – especially to ensure a better position on all fours.**

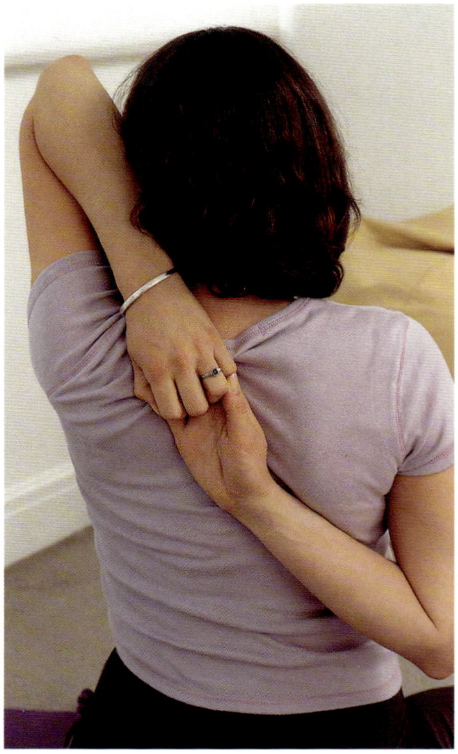

◁ **1** This is the classical position. One elbow is brought up to ear level and then bent to bring your palm against your upper back, while the other elbow is brought down by your side and bent to bring the back of your hand against your upper back. The two hands find each other (sometimes with help from a friend) and are clasped. They pull on each other to create the stretch at the front of the body.

△ **2** Take a few deep breaths in the position, then relax.

▷ Here is another chest opener with variations for different levels of suppleness in the shoulder joints. Take both arms behind you. For an easy version, hold each elbow with the opposite hands. For a stronger stretch, press your palms together behind your shoulder blades in the Namaste (prayer) position. Lean forward to stretch the spine at the back, making room between your knees for your baby. If leaning far forward is uncomfortable, then just lean a little way, or lean on to a low bed – whatever you are happy with.

## 121 Tiger stretch and relax (2)

**Do you remember Tiger Stretch and Relax (1) (67)? It is important to carry on with this stretch in the final few weeks of your pregnancy, as it is an excellent way to revive the circulation in your legs as your growing baby presses upon the major arteries, veins and nerves in the lower back and groin. Alternate this exercise with the Active Kneeling Stretch (122) shown below.**

▷ Begin in the Cat Pose (64). Stretch your right leg out behind you, parallel to the floor. Let it drop and trail out behind you, dropping your right hip. Shake it to relieve stiffness after kneeling or sitting. Readjust your position and do the same with the left leg.

## 122 Active kneeling stretch

**Another good kneeling stretch for the final weeks of pregnancy. Alternate with the Tiger Stretch and Relax (2) (121).**

△ **1** From a kneeling position, put your weight on both hands, lifting your upper body, and slide your right leg over to place your right foot firmly on the floor. Now raise your buttocks on an in breath and stretch your lower back as much as possible as you flex your bent right knee and open your right hip joint. Keep your weight equally distributed on your left knee, your right foot and your hands, using a gentle rocking movement. Repeat on the other side.

△ **2** This is a gentler version of the active kneeling stretch, using a bed, as you may not feel strong or supple enough to kneel on the floor comfortably as birth approaches or during labour. Kneel on a low bed, resting on your forearms, and let one leg drop toward the floor at the side of the bed. Breathe deeply, focusing awareness on your lower back. Repeat on the other side of the bed.

# Massage, breathing and relaxation

These last few weeks are the time to take full advantage of all the help and support that family and friends can give you. You need to build up your reserves of physical and emotional strength in preparation for the birth, and the changes in your life once your baby is born. So rest and rest again, at odd moments and in whatever position you find comfortable. While relaxing, breathe deeply in order to nourish both your baby and yourself, and to let go of aches and tensions. Massage can be a great help, and the person doing it does not need to be an expert, as long as they are happy to do what you ask.

▷ **Cuddles and closeness are especially soothing and sustaining during this final period of waiting. Let the whole family join in.**

## 123 Back massage for deep breathing

**This is one of the most soothing things that one friend or partner can do for another. It can be heaven for the recipient and also very soothing and relaxing for the person doing the massage. The recipient kneels with her knees wide and toes touching, and stretches over a beanbag in a relaxed and comfortable position. The beanbag will yield to fit the baby comfortably. The helper can kneel comfortably to one side, leaning forward slightly to massage her friend's back in soothing, circular movements. Both of you should make sure you are relaxed and comfortable before starting the massage. If pregnant herself, the helper should not lean forward too far, as this could cause backache.**

◁ The helper lays both hands gently on the recipient's back and leaves them there for a moment. This establishes a gentle contact while she co-ordinates her breathing with that of the recipient. "Two breathing as one" is a key feature in massage. The helper then moves her hands as the recipient is breathing out (and therefore relaxing), lifting them slightly to allow the recipient room to breathe in deeply into her back lungs beneath the helper's hands. See exercise 68 for back massage guidelines.

## 124 Ankle massage in supported Warrior Pose

**The purpose of this exercise is to relax the thigh and calf muscles passively while a friend supports your stance and massages your lower leg. Leaning against a wall with your head on your hands lifts your upper torso and creates more space for you to breathe deeply into your abdominal, pelvic floor and buttock muscles. You will find that this brings blissful relief generally, and relieves tight calves and lower backache in particular. Cramping in the calf muscles is common in late pregnancy as your legs cope with the extra weight and your blood circulation slows down.**

▷ **1** Stand tall and lean your head against a wall with your forearms at head height. Take one foot forward. Bend the front knee and stretch through the back leg, as you take your weight into your back heel. Your helper should now get into a stable position where it is easy and comfortable for them to massage your leg.

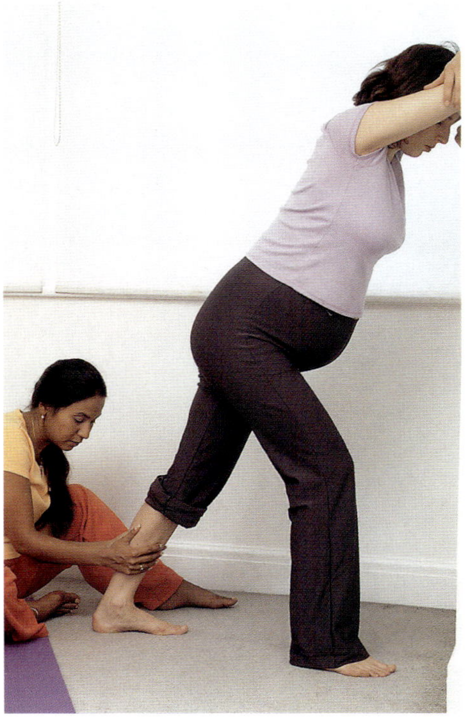

▷ **2** The helper should hold the ankle of your back leg to ensure that it doesn't lift from the floor as you lean forward. This increases the stretch in the calf. Lean into the stretch as you breathe deeply.

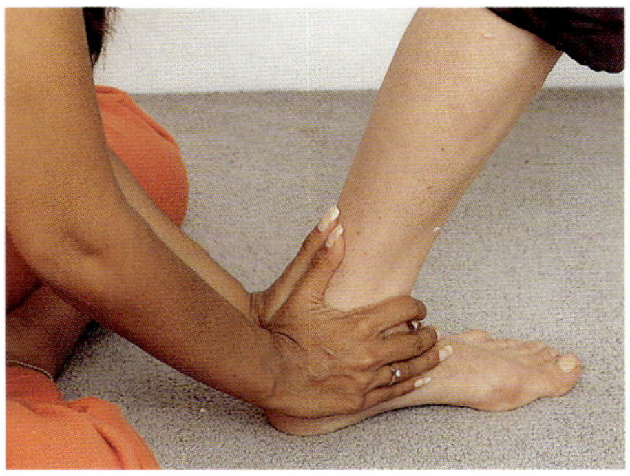

▷ **3** The helper can now slowly massage your lower leg, breathing in time with your own breathing, to release stiffness and tension and improve blood circulation.

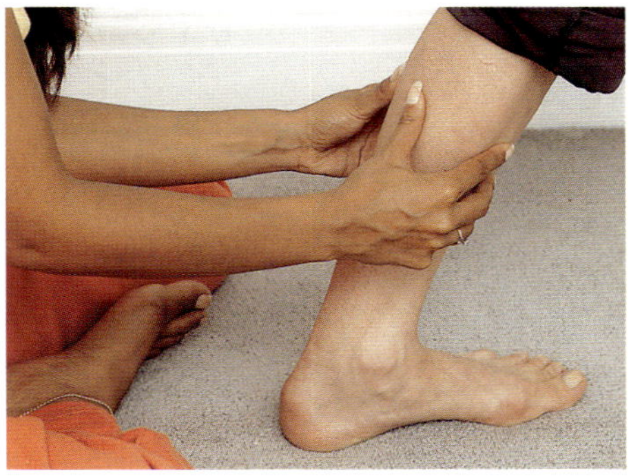





## 125 Supported reclining

**Lying on your back after about 31 weeks is neither comfortable nor recommended, as the weight of your baby can put pressure on the vena cava, which carries blood from the uterus to your heart. Instead, recline at a comfortable angle on a nest of cushions, on your bed, a sofa or the floor. Have your "nest" ready and waiting for you, so that whenever you get the chance you can crawl in, lie back, close your eyes and relax.**

▷ **1** Lean back against a beanbag or a pile of cushions. Make sure that your trunk is raised and your head is at a comfortable angle. Add cushions under your bent knees to lessen the pressure in your lumbar area.

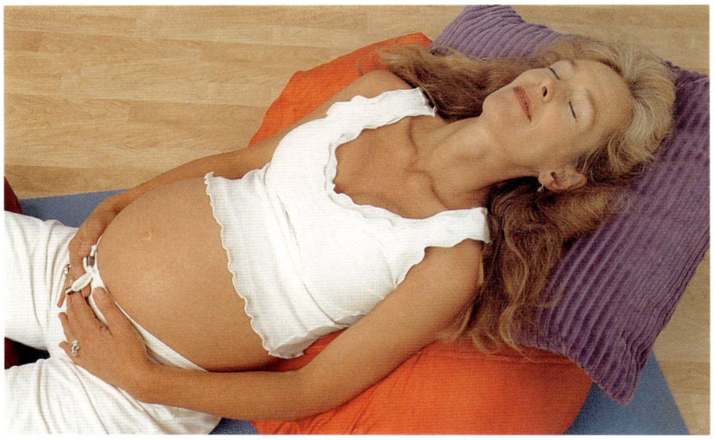

△ **2** You can place your hands over your baby to increase your loving connection to him or her – or them.

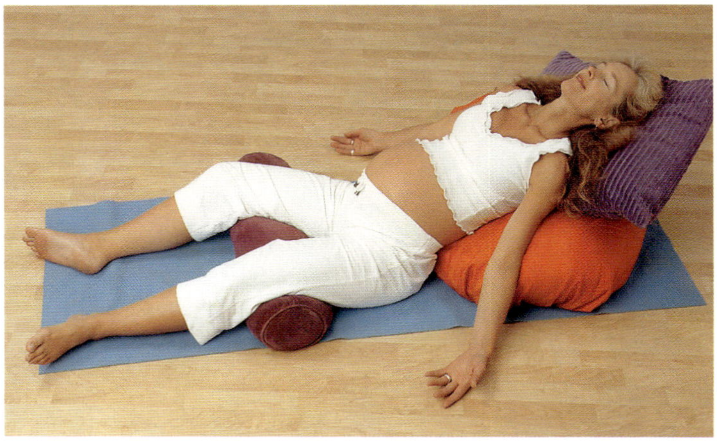

△ **3** If you prefer, let your hands simply flop to the sides. Breathe deeply and feel yourself letting go of any strains or tension.

# Preparing for birth through self-massage



Self-massage is a technique that pays great dividends in terms of ease during the birth and after it, as breastfeeding is being established. It is easy and relaxing to do, and well worth spending some time on. You do not need to use any oil for your massage, but if you wish to, then use pure plain oils as some oils are not recommended during pregnancy – check with an expert aromatherapist first. There are five main areas to focus on.

1 The base of the body, the perineum, has to be strong to support the contents of the abdomen, especially as your baby grows much heavier in later pregnancy. At the same time, however, it will also have to yield and stretch in order to let your baby pass down the birth canal. Nature provides for this change in texture by releasing "loosening" hormones that soften the ligaments. You can also help to improve elasticity in this area by self-massage. Massaging the yogic way can greatly increase the comfort and ease with which you give birth, and possibly prevent a tear or the need for a surgical cut (episiotomy).

2 Up to 36 weeks into your pregnancy, your breasts can be prepared for breastfeeding by regular massage. In Western societies, women's breasts are always covered up and so become unnaturally soft. Massage helps to tone and strengthen the breasts and make the surrounding areola more elastic.

3 The abdomen has to stretch a great deal during pregnancy and can be made much more elastic by regular massage. This also helps to prevent stretch marks.

4 Your feet and ankles may be swollen by fluid retention. Massage can often help to relieve this congestion, thus easing pressure and swelling and the resultant aches and pains.

5 While you have the massage oil on your hands, don't forget your face. Gentle circular movements over the face relieve tiredness and tension and feel soothing and relaxing.

## how to massage yourself

You may like to take a relaxing bath first or just apply a hot, wet flannel to the area to be massaged. The hot flannel brings the blood closer to the surface, which is soothing in itself. Settle yourself with the oil, if using, beside you. Find a comfortable, supported position. Reclining is probably best, either against a beanbag or on your bed.

Apply a little oil, if used, to your hands. Your touch should be exploratory but relaxed and gentle, indeed almost passive and reflective. Use your breathing actively as part of the massage. The stretching of tight skin and tissues is not caused by your fingers but by the relaxation of the tissues against your fingers when you breathe out. So, whatever part you are massaging, work with awareness of your breathing, moving your fingers on the out breath.

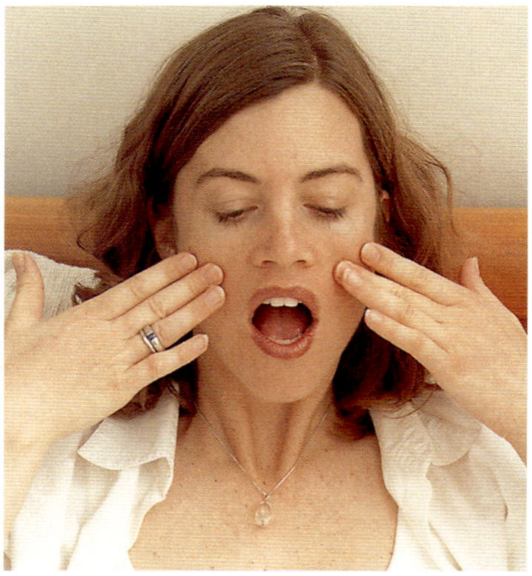

△ **Massaging the muscles around your mouth is helpful for keeping your lower jaw dropped and your face generally relaxed during labour.**

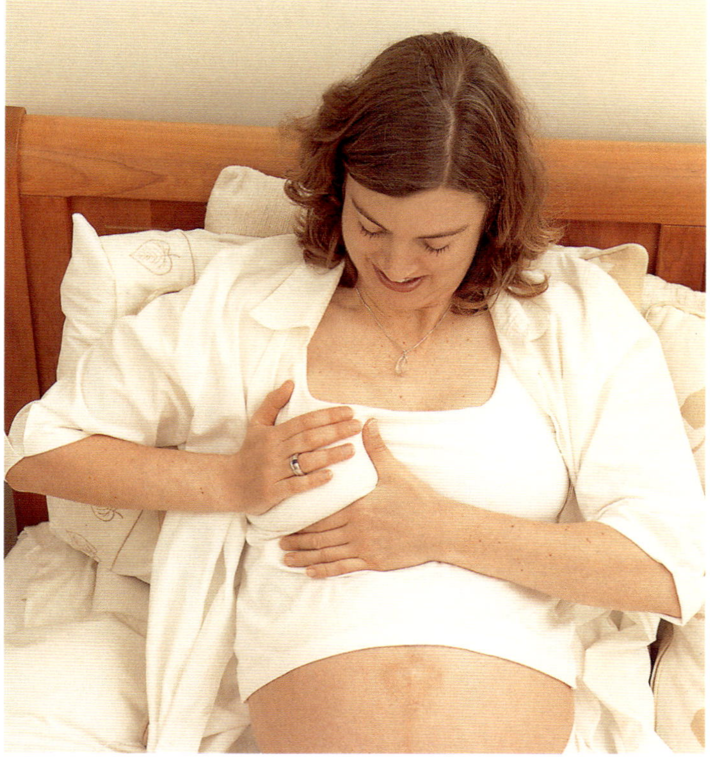

▷ **Massage your breasts with gentle strokes, going toward the areolas. Do not massage the nipple area itself (see the Caution box) and avoid any breast massage after about 36 weeks.**

**CAUTION**

**Nipple massage**: Do not massage the nipples themselves. However, if you have reached your due date, then tweaking your nipples gently between thumbs and index fingers can be an effective way of stimulating producton of the hormone oxytocin and so helping to bring on labour.

**Perineal and vaginal massage**: Never pull or attempt to stretch these tissues manually.

"From early days,

Beginning not long after that first time

In which, a Babe, by intercourse of touch

I held mute dialogues with my Mother's heart..."

*William Wordsworth*



◁ **Very gentle abdominal massage helps to prevent stretch marks.**

## perineal massage

It is truly amazing just how quickly the normally tight tissues in the perineum, vagina and abdomen will stretch with regular massage. The more that you are able to pre-stretch these tissues before the birth the better you will return to your original shape after it. Start around 36 weeks and practise once a day.

Use a light touch to explore the layers of tissues along the back wall of your vagina and the skin that separates your vagina and anus. It is this area that will be most stretched during the birth of your baby and is most prone to tearing.

Insert two fingers into the vagina up to the first knuckle, progressing to the second knuckle with practice. Press against the back wall of the vagina, against the spine, while breathing deeply. Feel the muscles under your fingers as they engage on the breath out. As space is created, move in further and exert a little more pressure. Using your breath in this way is like blowing up a balloon. Nothing much seems to happen at first, but soon your perineal tissue starts to give and then begins to stretch. You will be amazed how much you can stretch it, simply by breathing out into the areas under your fingers.

▷ **Massaging swollen ankles and feet relaxes the tissues here, which allows your blood and lymphatic fluids to circulate more freely, bringing nutrients to the area and removing waste products and excess fluid.**

▽ **Most women find that the most comfortable and convenient position for massaging the perineum and vaginal areas is reclining on their side against a beanbag or bed.**

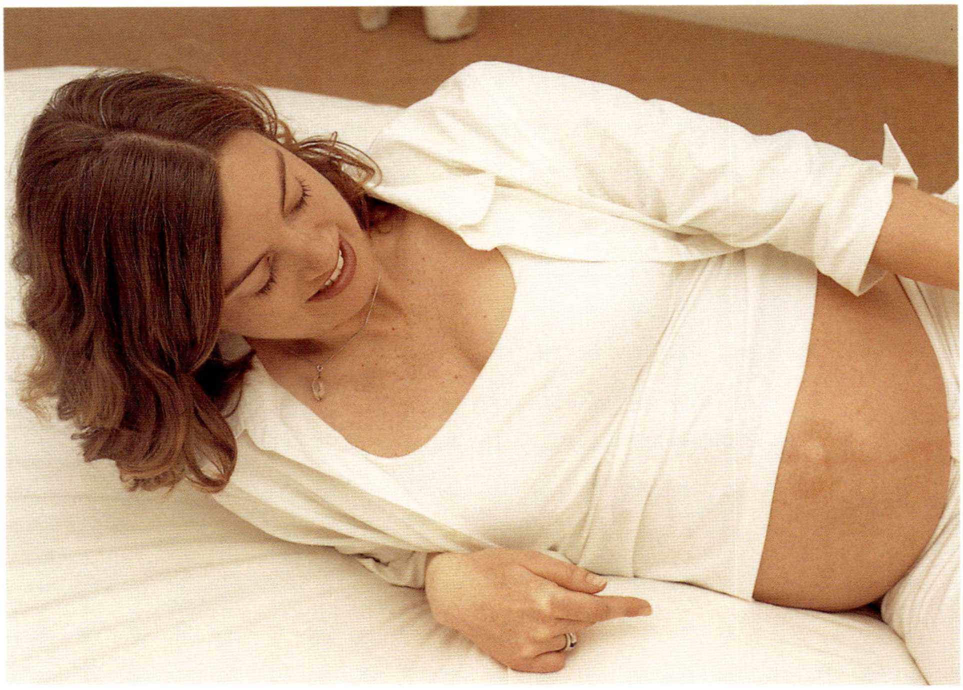

# Yoga for labour and birthing

Day by day, your baby is getting ready to be born. As the time of birth approaches, your body responds to your baby's signals with practice contractions of your womb and the release of birth hormones. You need yoga more than ever during this time, to create and maintain feelings of peace and surrender in preparation for your baby's journey into the world.

## the labour circuit

Each birth is unique and each labour starts differently. As you approach your due date, it can be helpful to choose and practise several positions to use during early labour. These should keep you comfortable and help you to breathe through your contractions, making them as effective as possible. These positions can be put together in a sequence, to make up your "labour circuit". The labour circuit allows you to stay in your own unique rhythm and to ease the descent of your baby by making full use of gravity. If all goes well, it may help you right up to the point where you are fully dilated.

Every 15–20 minutes, move from one position to another position around your circuit. You will find that one or two of the positions you try will begin to feel the most comfortable and secure and you will tend to stick with those.

From time to time during labour, you can also use movements 109 (Pink Panther Strides) and 110 (Hip Drops). These will loosen up your hips and back and release tension. Alternating positions is particularly helpful if labour is slow to get established, as the movement will help the baby's head to press down on to the cervix. What follows are some suggested positions for inclusion in your own labour circuit.

**CAUTION**
Make sure the surfaces you lean against during your labour circuit can support your weight.

## 126 Supported squat against the wall

**These positions help engage the muscles of the abdomen and the lower back to assist uterine contractions during labour. They also make full use of gravity to open the cervix effectively as well as to alleviate pain, particularly in the lower back. To conserve your energy, lean against the wall with your elbows resting on a windowsill, and a stool in position in case you need to sit down.**

▷ **1** Stand with your legs a comfortable width apart. Now adjust your position until your back is supported by the wall as you bend your knees in a semi-squat position.

◁ **2** If this position puts too much strain on your thighs and legs, or you already need to sit down to breathe through regular contractions, lower yourself down the wall until you are sitting on the stool, still with your legs apart. Make sure that your back is upright against the wall.

## 127 Standing poses during labour

**After squatting for a while, stand up and practise the Pink Panther Strides (109) and Hip Drops (110). When you feel a contraction starting, try these supported standing poses as they are an effective way of facilitating the descent of your baby's head. You may prefer to press down on a chest of drawers or counter with your hands rather than against the wall, but in the same standing position. Circling your hips rhythmically can feel very soothing.**

◁ **1** Face a wall and lean against it. Bend your knees and press against the wall with your forearms, resting your head on top of your joined hands.

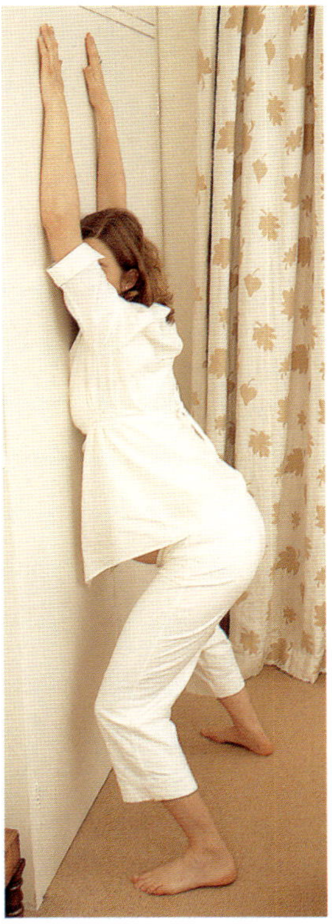

◁ **2** Then, keeping your forearms in the same place, bend your knees and let your hips drop down on an out breath. "Hang" in this position and breathe deeply, focusing on the out breaths.

## 128 Supported kneeling

**Supported kneeling is a favourite labour position for many women and can provide you with periods of active rest during your labour. It can also be a good birthing position. It is important to adjust the position of your knees so that they are not too wide apart for comfort. Take time to install yourself in such a way that your spine is extended as much as possible while the shoulders remain relaxed. Cushions or pillows can be placed under your knees and feet for greater comfort if you need them. This position is especially soothing if you experience backache during labour, particularly if your baby is lying in a posterior position – that is, with his or her back to your back. Change position again after 15–20 minutes.**

▷ **1** Use a beanbag or exercise ball to really stretch your back during labour. A ball is excellent as you can move back and forth very slightly, which is highly soothing. Hug the ball and rest your head on your arms to keep your neck comfortable.

◁ **2** Use a windowsill or high bed if you prefer a more upright position. Support yourself with your forearms and make sure your neck and shoulders are relaxed.

△ **3** Kneeling over a low bed with your arms above your head gives your shoulders a particularly good stretch.

# Yoga breathing for labour





Many of the complications of labour arise from physical exhaustion, often made worse by lack of sleep, so you need plenty of deep rest as the birth approaches. Conserving your energy is also a priority from the moment you discover that labour is starting, and the best way to achieve this is through deep breathing that follows the rhythm of your contractions. Taking a sip of water after each contraction is helpful too. When you are fully dilated, the breath takes on another role by helping you to give birth with minimal strain.

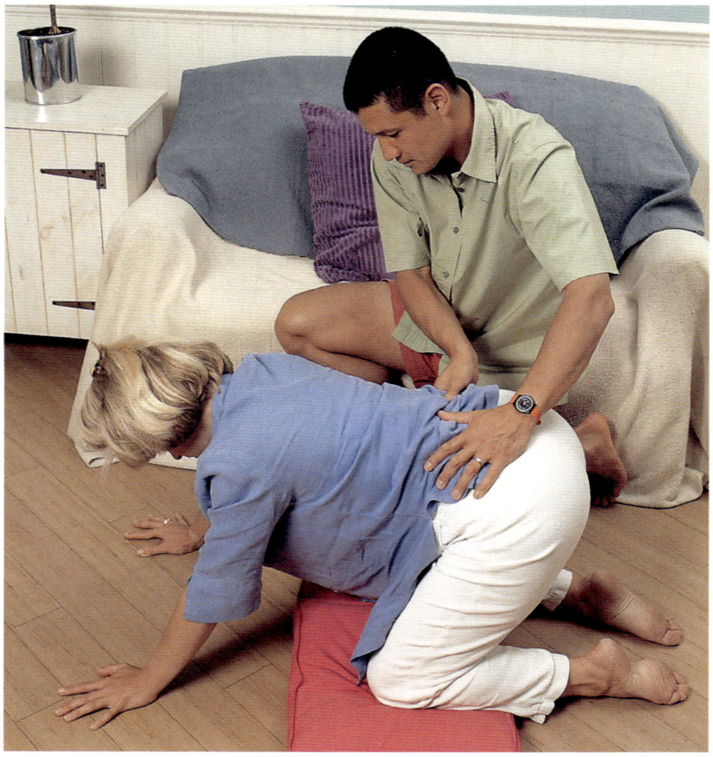

◁ **Kneeling on all fours, keeping your head relaxed, can be a very effective position for grounding you and helping you to cope with backache during labour.**

## breathe out to welcome the contractions, then let them go

In the first stage of labour, most women have contractions at intervals that gradually become shorter as the labour progresses. From the very beginning, your most important task is to relax as much as possible between the contractions and to avoid dissipating your energy, particularly by talking. Your breath out needs to be used for getting rid of tension as the contractions come and go. During each contraction, focus on breathing as deeply as you can, depending on its strength. Then start to relax again, even if only for a minute.

## centring with breath during labour

Your labour circuit positions may involve your partner, who can be holding you or massaging you, or you may prefer to labour on your own, drawing deeply upon your inner resources. Whichever way is best for you, the ebb and flow of your breath can help you to remain centred through awareness of the flow of breath – both during and between your contractions. You will find that breathing is your most powerful tool for surfing the contractions rather than attempting to resist them. After any conversations or medical procedures, use your breath to re-centre yourself.

◁ **Each time you feel a contraction on its way, breathe out deeply. This allows you to welcome it with relaxed muscles, and this, in turn, helps the contraction to work more effectively to open your cervix. Breathe throughout the contraction in whatever way feels best for you. When the contraction peaks, it is time to breathe out again deeply, to send it on its way and to dispel as quickly as possible the inevitable tension that results from pain.**

▷ **Sitting astride a gym ball allows you to use gentle pelvic rocking, in time with your breath, to relax between contractions and to centre yourself once more.**

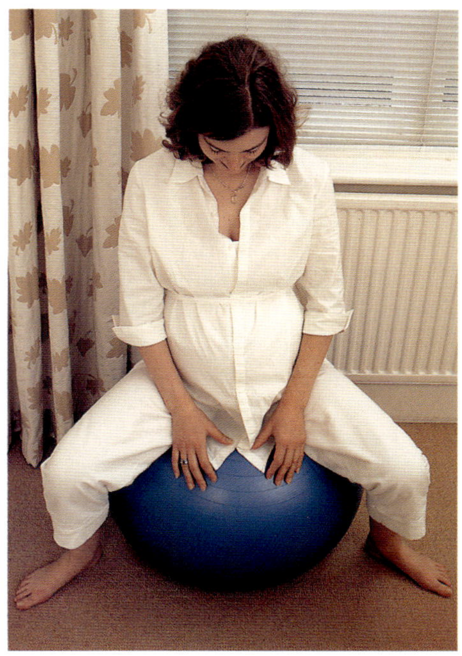

## breathing for birthing

The second stage of labour begins when your midwife confirms that the birth passage is fully open and ready for your baby to pass through. You may already be feeling a strong urge to push your baby out, or you may feel nothing at all. Every woman is different. The two priorities in all cases, however, are to relax as deeply as possible to make space for the baby, and to relax all the muscles of the pelvis, particularly those in the buttocks, for birthing.

When it comes to breathing, voicing your breath out, on any note that feels good to you at the time, helps the abdominal muscles to work together with the powerful bearing down contractions. The longer that you can extend the breath out, the farther your baby is able to move down the birth passage during one contraction. Engage your inner pelvic muscles on your out breath, pushing from within. Try to keep your facial muscles, and the rest of your body, as relaxed as possible as you do this, to lessen the strain.

Your midwife will guide you as to when, or if, you should breathe lightly – as if you were blowing on hot soup. This need arises if you have to hold back and wait for your perineum to stretch as the baby's head crowns. By blowing lightly, you are disengaging your abdominal muscles from your breathing and so weakening the impact of the uterine contractions.

◁ Voice your breath out with a "Haaah" sound deep into your lower abdomen. Extend it for as long as you can to increase the pressure of your contracting uterus on your baby's body as he or she moves down the birth canal.





Gravity, centring and a voiced breath out can be combined in a powerful yet light action to push your baby out. Let awareness of your baby guide your breathing. Breathing your baby out into the world is a loving action that is open to most women and brings many possible long-term benefits to both mothers and babies.

Even if medical intervention is necessary during your labour, breathing and relaxing with yoga will facilitate any birth process.

## breathing to deliver the placenta

To deliver the placenta after the baby is born, use the same breathing that you employed for the birthing.

## Zoë's story

**Mine was a highly positive birthing experience – due to my husband's very vocal encouragement and essential breathing advice from Françoise. Having attended a yoga class throughout my pregnancy, I felt well-prepared, but when contractions suddenly started on my due date, I was taken by surprise by the strong back discomfort. I stayed at home for as long as possible with my husband and friend, timing contractions and pushing on my back to relieve the pain.**

**When I arrived at the hospital, my friend and husband arranged my pillows, sat me on my birthing ball and set up my specially chosen music. I started to meditate, breathing through the contractions. After a long labour, where the contractions hit me hard, and I became rather frustrated by watching the head bob back and forth for a couple of hours, I heard the word "episiotomy" from my midwife and with one contraction focused on my breathing and pushed five times to deliver my wonderful daughter, Kira.**

# Yoga and birth positions with a partner





For many thousands of years, women in all cultures have given birth in positions that make use of gravity, although for much of the last century, Western hospitals tended to encourage women to give birth on their backs. The advantages of not lying flat on your back for giving birth have now been recognized and currently women are encouraged to sit up, or to lie on their side, for delivery on hospital beds. This is a step forward, although here we present further birthing positions that allow you to be more active still. If you have practised yoga regularly during your pregnancy, these positions should feel both familiar and comfortable. Supported standing in a semi-squat, supported squatting and variations on kneeling are all options that you can try out beforehand to discover which one feels best for you. Some women consistently favour a leaning-forward position while others prefer to lean back. Supported birth positions also mean that partners can be actively helpful and closely associated with the birth of their baby. In this book we refer to a male partner, but of course you can enlist the help of a female friend.

## 129 Birthing: supported standing positions with partner

**The supporting partner must be confident that his back is strong. He leans against a wall with his feet a little away from the base of the wall and his knees slightly bent to ensure a strong bracing position. Stand as close as possible to your partner. You must feel able to let go completely, trusting that your partner's back is pressing against the wall and that he can take your weight safely during contractions. Both of you should relax between contractions.**

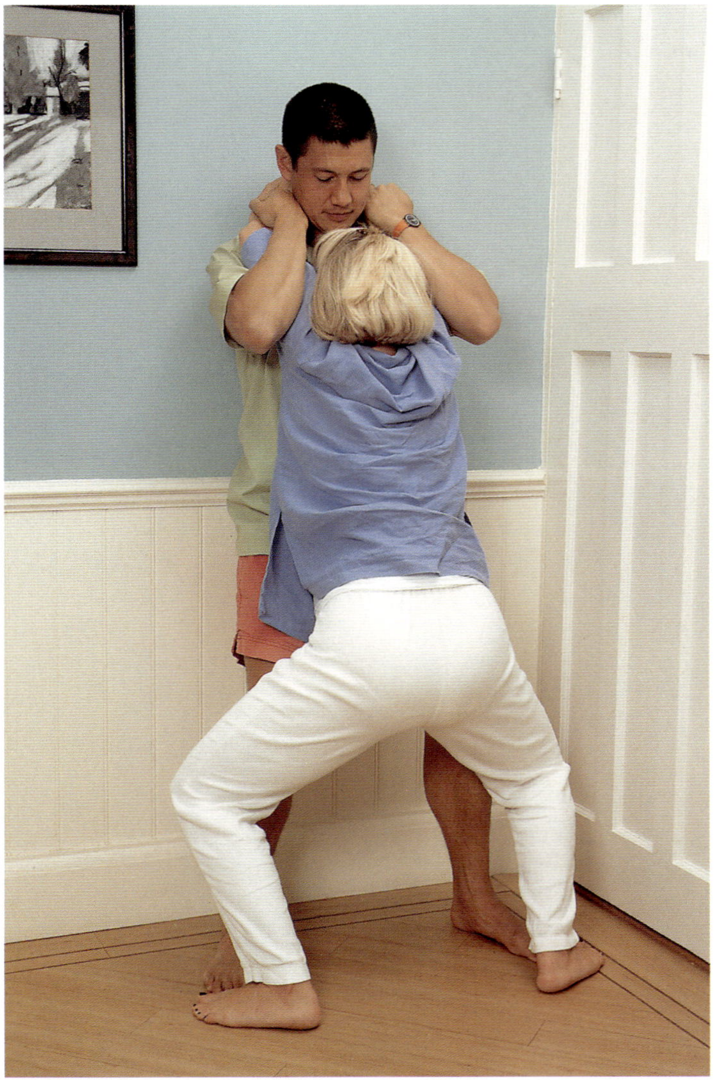

△ **First position** Face your partner and link your arms around his neck. Bend your knees and let yourself hang down.

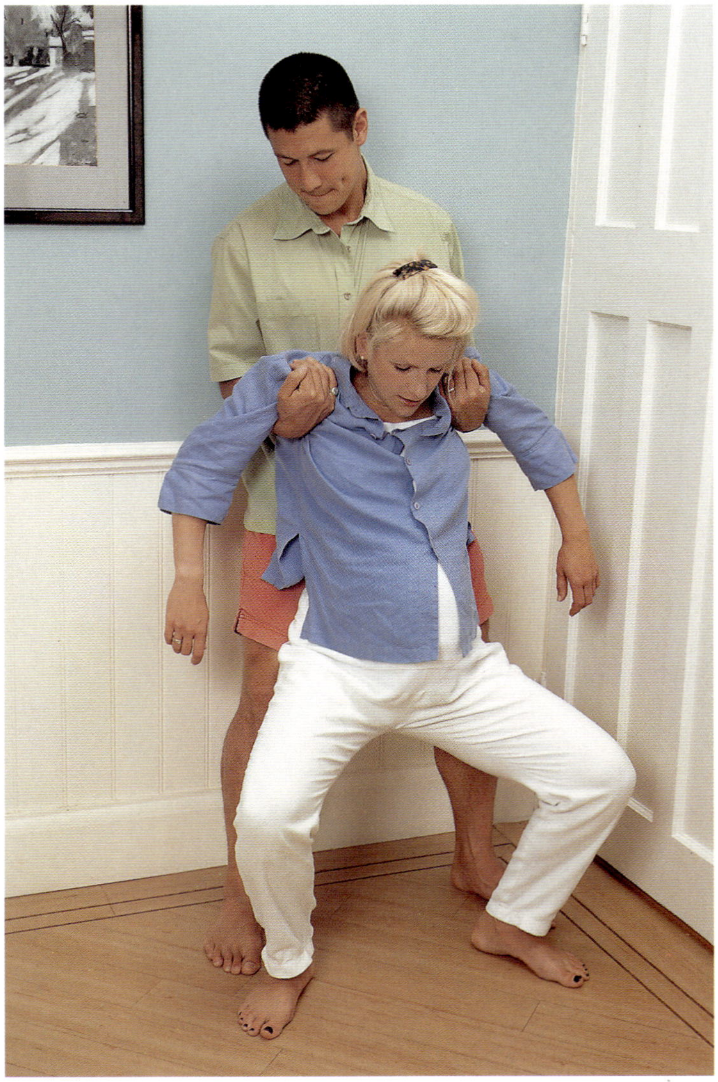

△ **Second position** Stand with your back to your partner. Let him support you with his forearms under your arms while you bend your knees in a semi-squat.

## 130 Birthing: supported squatting positions with partner

**Women who feel that they can create more space in their pelvis when they are leaning back can experiment with this position in one of its variations. The first variation is an extension of the standing semi-squat, which can also be used with a birthing stool.**

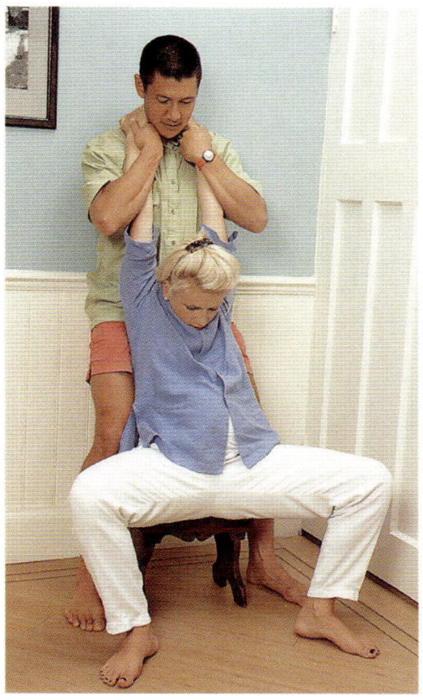

△ **First variation** 1 Use the support of a low stool so that you can squat easily while hanging from your partner's shoulders.

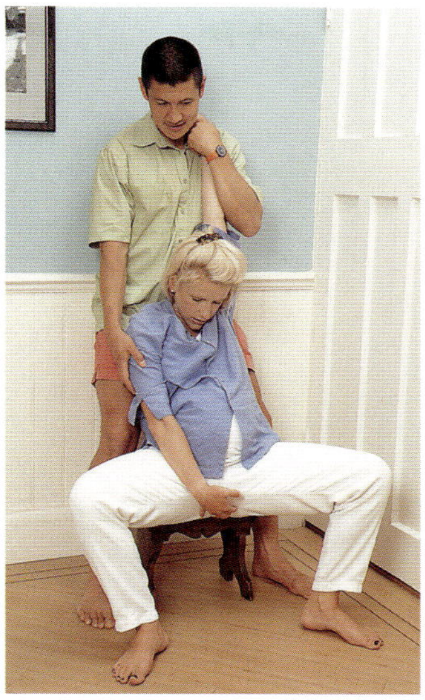

△ 2 During the final birthing contractions, touching your baby's crown can help you to pace and centre your breathing.

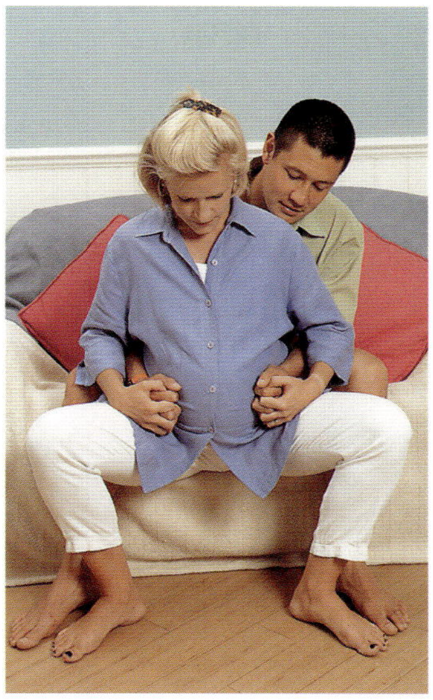

△ **Second variation** Your partner sits behind you on a sofa or wide chair while you sit on the edge, between his knees. Holding hands helps you both to centre your breathing in close harmony with each other.

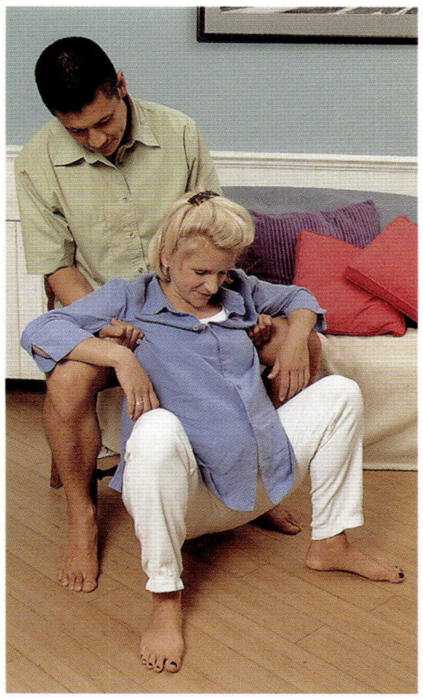

△ **Third variation** Your partner sits on a chair with his legs apart and his back straight, supporting you under your arms as you drop into a wide squat. Adjust the position of your feet so you are as straight and relaxed as possible.



## 131 Birthing: supported kneeling positions with partner

**If you choose to spend a major part of your labour on all fours, then a supported kneeling position may be the best birthing option. There are many variations, depending on how you choose to kneel, the angle of your back and the height at which your partner sits to support you. Be guided by your experience as you focus awareness on your pelvic floor. Put cushions under the knees for comfort.**

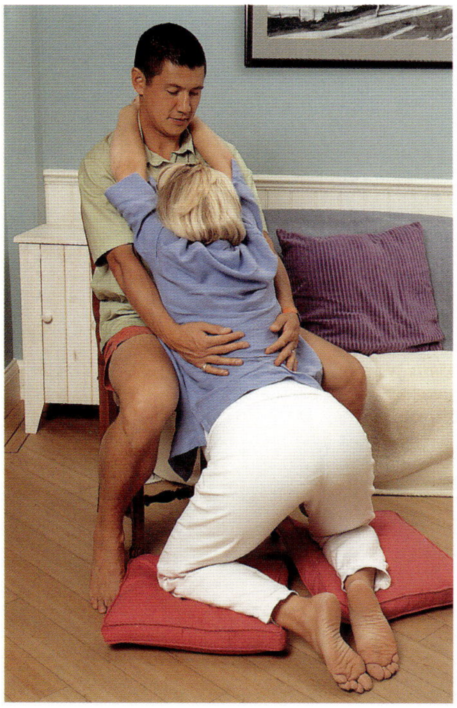

△ **1** Kneel in front of your partner, putting your arms around his neck for support. This position makes good use of gravity and relieves pain if the baby is pressing against your lower back.

△ **2** Kneel as before, but this time spread the knees wider and sit further down. The tilt of your pelvis can be modified to widen the birth passage. Let your body guide you into the best position.

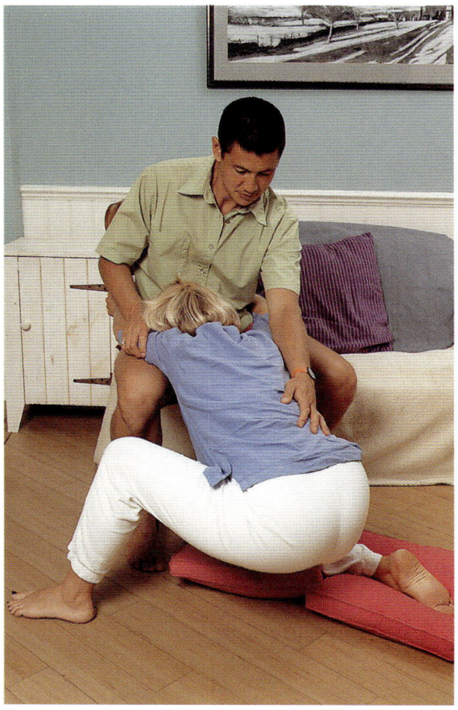

△ **3** Kneel as before, but then bring one foot forward outside the knee. This position allows the widest opening in a position that may combine the advantages of both squatting and kneeling.

# opening for birth in water





Although research has not confirmed that labouring in water makes it easier for the perineum of unprepared women to stretch without tearing, yogic pelvic-floor breathing, to prepare both physically and mentally for this stretching, is equally effective in dry births or waterbirths. Practise it every day during the last six weeks of pregnancy, in the pool, in a birthing pool or simply at home in the bath.

Opening the body for birth is accompanied by a state of being open to what can happen and surrendering to it. You may have prepared well and feel strong, relaxed and confident in yourself, but the journey of your baby's birth can take unexpected courses. Open your mind, letting go of all expectations and plans. Let this birth take its course and be ready to flow with it fully.

If you stay in touch with your baby throughout your labour, it becomes a shared journey and is likely to be a satisfying experience, whatever happens. If the need for intervention arises at any time, remember that breathing and relaxation are invaluable tools. Fear of the unknown is a primary source of muscular tension: so, with each out breath, let go of your fear.

## 132 Open stands, drops and hip swings

**Right up to the day of the birth, open stands and drops help to stretch the lower spine and ease the back. They also facilitate the descent of the baby's head in the pelvis and, after it has become "engaged", promote optimal presentation in an anterior position. This maximizes the space between the coccyx and the pelvic symphysis at the front, so that the baby's head has as much room as possible to rotate forward into the birth passage once the cervix has dilated during labour. Many women feel a need to hang from a support and move their hips before and during labour to achieve this effect. The more these movements are practised during the last six weeks of pregnancy, the greater the chances of an easier and less painful labour.**

◁ **1** Standing facing the pool wall, inhale. Flex your knees open and let yourself drop – with a straight back – holding on to the bar or the edge of the pool as you exhale slowly. Breathe deeply a couple of times before standing up and letting yourself drop again.

◁ **2** If holding the bar or edge constrains you or is uncomfortable, use a woggle under your arms. Support from the back allows you to drop in a very open semi-squat, while resting your arms on a woggle at the front helps you drop, leaning slightly forward.

◁ **3** Your partner may hold you while you swing your hips in a semi-squat position, holding on to the bar, the edge of the pool or a woggle in front of you. This helps you to drop the base of your spine lower in the water and open your hips more. You can swing your hips from left to right or complete a circling movement. Keep your neck soft, relaxing your lower jaw.

△ **4** The same movements can be done in a more supported way with your partner behind you, holding you with his arms under your arms.

## 133 Float-drop

**While the drops can be done both on dry land and in water, you can uniquely open your pelvis freely in the water, forgetting gravity and without any pressure on your legs. This is a useful exercise if you would like to have a birth in which you can be absorbed in the process of labour rather than trying to control it. It is also helpful if you wish to have a vaginal delivery after a previous Caesarian section and you need to avoid putting any strain on your scar tissue. Women who wish to have a gentle birth in water can use this exercise to make the most of water as a supportive environment.**

▷ **1** Holding on to a woggle in front of you, inhale and let yourself drop gently in the water as you exhale with your legs open and completely relaxed. Continue breathing in this position, half floating, half sinking, feeling every muscle of your pelvis relaxed around your uterus.

▷ **2** You can also let yourself "float-drop" while being supported by your partner under the arms. He can then swing you from side to side without your legs touching the pool floor. Breathe deeply and enjoy the freedom from gravity in this supported movement, opening your hips as much as possible.

## 134 Breathe yourself open

**The first and most important tool that you will have at your disposal during labour, which can be made even more effective by water, is your breath. As your due date approaches, you may find the following exercise helpful. Breathe in as you start any of the above positions. Lengthen your out breath slowly as you lower your body in the water, opening your pelvis wide. You may vocalize the breath, if it helps you, as a long "Haaaaah" or "Hooooh" sound. As you do this, release any fear that you may have about how your baby is going to be born, the changes that motherhood will bring in your life, the unknown. With your vocal out breath, calmly empower yourself and feel your energy centre strong and yielding deep inside your abdomen.**

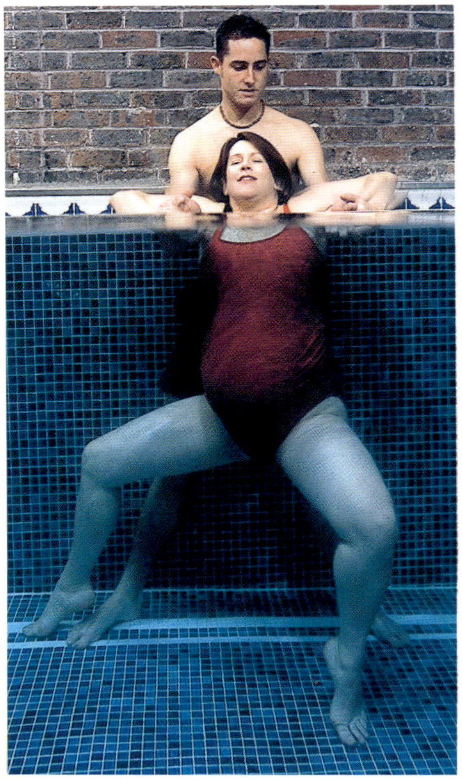

◁ You can practise this breathing on your own or supported by your partner with his arms under your arms while he stands against the pool wall, which is also a possible birth position whether in or out of water.

## 135 Floating relaxation before birth

**As you reach the end of your pregnancy you may wish to practise floating relaxation with your baby's father or your labour partner in anticipation of the birth. Joint floating relaxation can be a powerful way of preparing for birth, which many women recall during labour as a way of centring themselves and keeping a close contact with their baby.**

◁ **1** Your partner should place one hand under your lower back and the other at the base of your neck.

◁ **2** The additional support of a woggle under the knees is often desirable. This takes the strain off the supporter and it also enables both partners to relax together while focusing on the baby between them.

# The benefits of water in labour and birth

In the last two decades, the use of water to facilitate birth has shifted from the esoteric and the legendary into everyday practice. In the 1980s, experiences of waterbirth fired the enthusiasm of midwives and obstetricians so that women from all walks of life and many nationalities now choose to labour and give birth in water.

Waterbirth is an option that is increasingly available to women in hospitals, homes and birthing centres around the world. Labouring women with low-risk pregnancies, which accounts for the majority of mothers-to-be, can labour in a bath or birthing pool and, in many cases, give birth to their babies in water. The use of water in labour and birth has now been studied and documented sufficiently to allow emotional views for or against it to be replaced by known facts. Few people still fear that babies may drown when born in water, but it is now better known that babies need to be lifted to the surface fairly soon to initiate their first breath, as the blood that continues

## A story of a waterbirth: Hester and Bathsheba

**Although not many births are as romantic and laid back as the birth of Bathsheba greeted by siblings and the family dogs, Hester's story captures well an experience shared by many women labouring in water. Hester practised yoga to prepare for her three previous births and found aqua yoga exercises most helpful in making full use of movement and breathing in this birth.**

My fourth baby, Bathsheba, was born early in the morning by candlelight into a pool by the fire. Near the beginning the children were still asleep upstairs, my husband was filling the pool and our two midwives arrived and settled calmly on the sofa with the dogs and a pot of tea, not interfering at all.

During early labour I used the pool as a calm, dark space in which to float. It contained me, helped me to focus energy on my mission and connect with the baby. An hour later I was consciously appreciative of the deep heat and massaging effect of the water. The force of contractions felt much less harsh, less frightening in the water. I found this out when I got out for a while to have a walk about and a little dance to speed things up – the strength of the contractions really hit me hard and I got back in quickly.

As the intensity increased, the pool allowed me to move with freedom and vigour. I no longer felt heavy and the water relieved my sciatic pain and stiffness. For the last hour I was moving all the time, keeping the water swooshing around me in a low squat, using a sweeping, arcing movement of the pelvis from side to side, stretching the left leg out far to the side when swinging round to the right and vice versa, hanging on to the side of the pool with both hands. Sometimes I changed the movement to whole circles with the pelvis, a bit like belly-dancing, or I used a swinging backwards and forwards motion. I continually repeated the words, "Open, open" to myself and concentrated all my energy down, breathing long controlled out breaths through my mouth, sipping water, and really trying to help the baby move down. I was totally driven to keep moving; the more strongly and rhythmically I moved the greater the relief.

I did then completely lose it during transition, and sloshed about wildly like a maniac for a couple of minutes, until Fred caught me from behind and supported me under the arms for the birth.

I bore down for maybe half a minute and the baby's head slipped out quite easily. I shrieked a bit then and the dogs took the cue and started howling and woke all the neighbours. The baby's body stalled so the midwife reached into the pool and unhooked the cord from behind the baby's neck and brought her gently up into my arms. She lay clean and glowing in the firelight. Her two sisters and brother reached in to stroke her little body, and for the fourth time Fred and I felt humbled before the power of birth, exhausted and thrilled.

Later, the children from next door who had woken to the howling of the dogs came in on their way to school to see the new baby. They saw Bathsheba feeding by the fire, two hours old.

The midwives had already gone.

Hester with Bathsheba

flowing through the cord has less oxygen once they have been born. The monitoring of babies born in water has been improved by the use of submersible dopplers. A sound code of practice has been developed for waterbirth both in hospital and at home.

Research has confirmed what midwives have known for generations: water has a relaxing effect on both the mother and her baby. Mothers experience less pain when they labour in water and therefore have less need for pain relief. Water also offers some protection to the perineum in giving birth, although it does not totally eliminate the risk of tearing as early enthusiasts claimed.

## the birth experience

For many women who give birth in water, the difference is in the quality of the birth experience. Their statements are difficult to quantify but they share a lyrical, euphoric feeling. Besides comfort and freedom of movement during labour, water gives women the privacy that they need to be able to let go of their fear and enter the mental space in which their labour can progress unhindered. Although it does not eliminate pain, water allows more control over the rhythms of labour.

Many women who want a "natural birth" find that once they are in a hospital environment much of what they have read or learnt is superseded by the protocols and routine practices of the labour ward. Being in water makes it easier to feel centred and in charge. They are then in the best possible state of mind, and body, to meet their new-born babies, perhaps lifting them from the water themselves.

Not all women who plan to have a waterbirth have their babies in water. There are many reasons why a planned waterbirth can become an unplanned dry birth, a practical example being that some babies arrive before the tub is filled up. Babies whose heartbeat slows down during labour may be at risk of oxygen deprivation and may have to enter into the air for greater safety. Equally, many women who have never thought of a waterbirth feel so comfortable labouring in a birthing pool that they just find themselves giving birth in it.

△ **When a new baby is about to enter the family, water is also a medium to renew the bonds with your other children.**

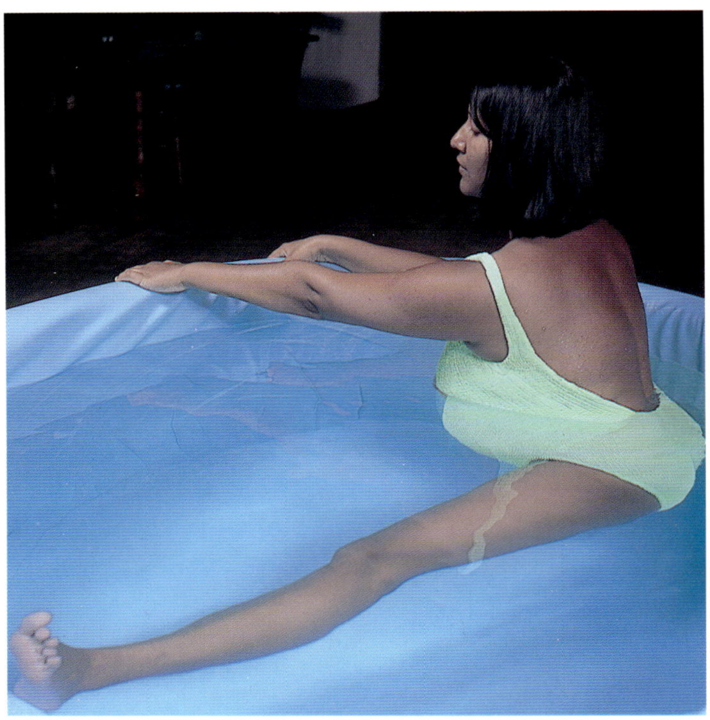

▷ **During labour, aqua yoga helps you move around to find the most comfortable positions in the birthing pool.**

## good for your baby too

While the element of water can help mothers to have comfortable pregnancies and easier, less painful births, birthing in water also has advantages from the baby's point of view. The transition from the womb to water, rather than cold air, is the gentlest possible. Babies are born in a warm environment without the pressures of gravity. Uncurling from the confined space of the womb into the unboundedness of water may create a different quality of birth experience for the baby, and this may have distant repercussions in the make-up of his or her personality. Some people claim that "water babies" have special qualities, being both lively and calm.

Should you not be able to use a pool or even a bathtub during your labour, remember that you can still derive great benefit from water, particularly if you have practised aqua yoga during pregnancy. Even running water from a tap, or a wet sponge on your face, can conjure up the deep relax-ation that you have enjoyed in water.

# Aqua yoga for labour



When you labour in water, you escape to a peaceful protected world where you can be at one with the rhythm of the contractions and your breathing. The water massages, supports and envelops you in a way that is far removed from being watched in a labour ward. It gives you total privacy and comfort, in your own world with your baby.

Experience gathered from thousands of women by midwives and doctors who attended the first International Waterbirth Conference at Wembley, London, in 1995 showed that the more the body of a labouring woman is immersed in water, the more effective is the pain relief. Most women did not go underwater during labour, but it helped some to concentrate during painful uterine contractions.

Labouring while in warm water has the advantage of maximizing the supply of rich oxygenated blood to the hard-working uterus in several ways: the muscles that maintain your posture against gravity are supported; major veins and arteries are not obstructed in any position; temperature is even and less blood is diverted to the periphery of the body.

Exercises in the swimming pool or the birthing pool in early labour can help greatly to open the cervix. Short active periods can be alternated with quieter restful ones, during which you can practise visualization techniques or just relax and breathe through your contractions as they come and go.

## 136 Pelvic rolls and swings in the birthing pool

**Rolls and swings increase the pressure of the baby's head in a rhythmical way and involve you actively in the process of making space for your baby to come down into the birth passage.**

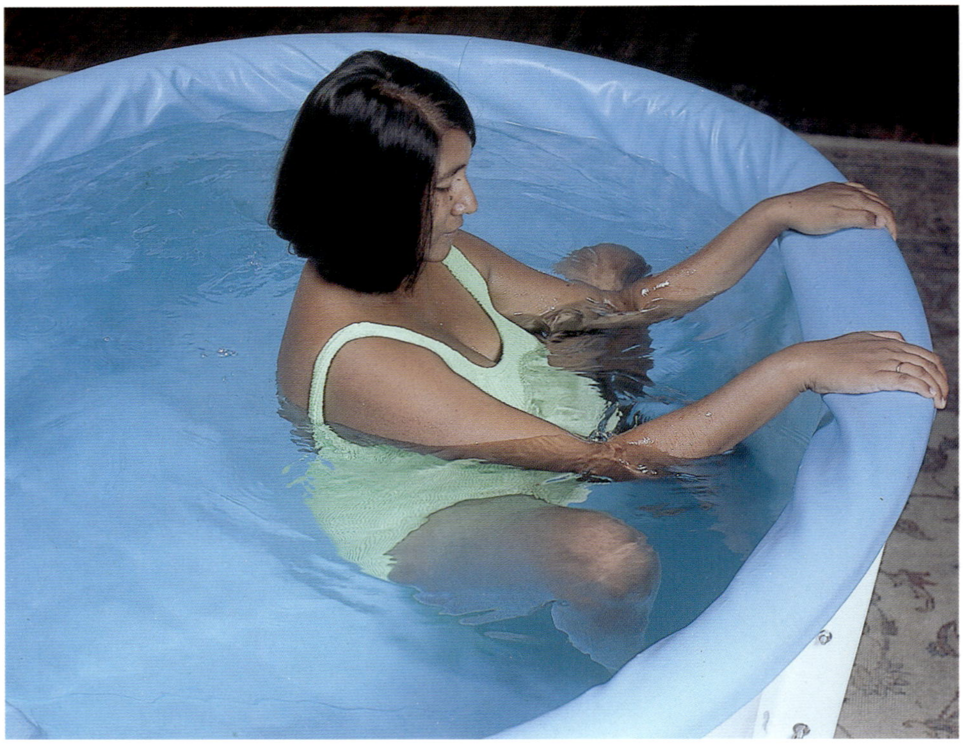

△ **1** Get into a low squatting position, holding on to the edge of the birthing pool.

▷ **2** Swing your pelvis forward and back: this will make you bend and stretch your legs in a broad movement. Breathe in as you stretch back, out as you bend forward.

## 137 Knee-bent variations

**These are useful movements which can get a baby "unstuck" from an awkward presentation and help promote stronger labour when contractions become weak during the first stage, as this is usually because the head of the baby is not pressing on the cervix at the best angle.**

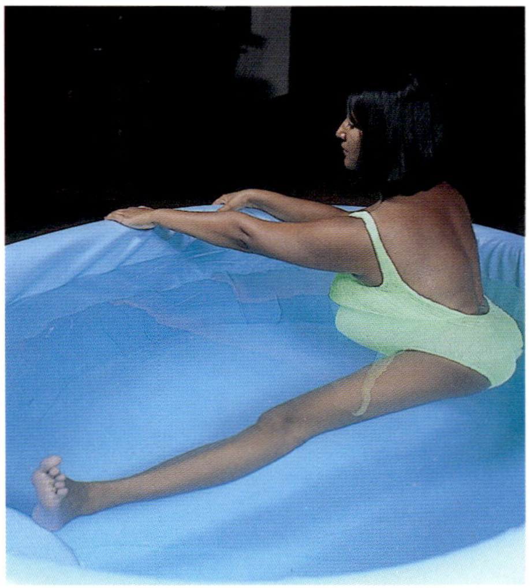

◁ **1** Kneel in the birthing pool, holding the edge in front of you, and straighten one knee and then the other, extending the leg sideways at the bottom of the pool. Breathe deeply, exhaling as you extend either leg to the side, and take your time to feel intuitively which position "opens" you the most.

◁ **2** The same leg movement can be practised facing the pool in a squat, with the back against the side of the pool, or in a sitting position. Breathe in the same way.

▷ **3** In an all-fours position, with the hands resting on the bottom of the pool, the same movement can be done as a wide swing of the hips to one side and then to the other, soothing the whole back and giving you a feeling of space.

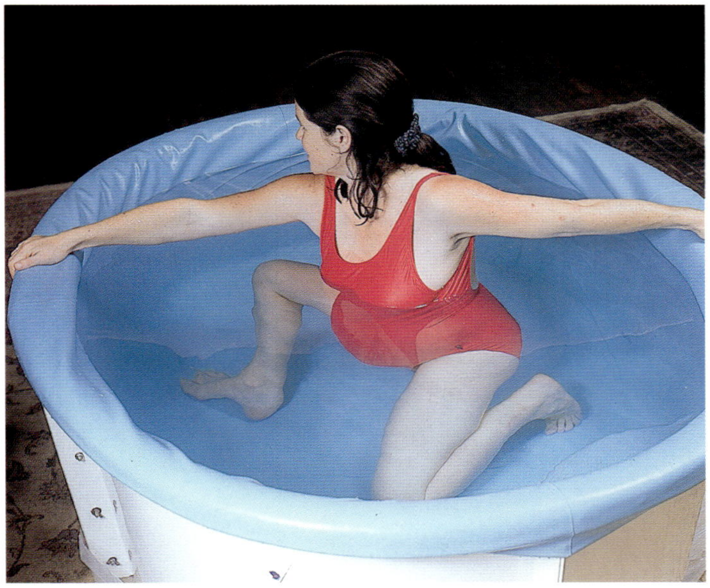

△ **4** With the arms stretching sideways holding on to the opposite edges of the pool, the same alternating leg movement becomes more active and has all the advantages of a deep squat without putting undue pressure on the pubic bones or the perineum. A simultaneous opening of one knee and closing of the other is a very effective way of changing sides. Turn the head in the direction of the raised knee, as in a low-lying Archer Pose in classical yoga.

▷ **5** Between these movements, take rests in a kneeling position, in which you can also do comforting pelvic rolls now and again. In the early phase of labour, when your contractions are just getting established, you may not mind being visited by your older children if you are having a home birth. Seeing you in the birthing pool involves them in the journey that their little brother or sister has initiated to join their family.

# Aqua breathing for waterbirthing



Make it a priority to find a rhythm that will help you move at regular intervals and change position. This will enable you to remain centred and feel the progression of your labour in a positive way. Whether you continue using pelvic rolls and knee-bent movements in the birthing pool or not, try alternating between a forward kneeling position, a lying float and sitting down or, if you are very confident with yoga and breathing into your pelvic floor muscles, squatting. Try different angles, as some may suit you better than others, and then use your favourite positions throughout the first stage of your labour. You may need reminding to move as your labour gets stronger and you become more absorbed in the rhythm of contractions.

## relaxation between contractions

The ability to relax between contractions during labour saves a great deal of energy, which is better used to keep you alert to welcome your baby into the world. It also reduces negative stress, and with it a great part of the discomfort of labour. The only part of your body that needs to contract in labour is the uterus, and active relaxation makes this possible. Sometimes the pain of contractions causes other muscles to tighten up, but a deep exhalation, giving your body, mind and emotions the message to relax, can dissolve all the tension again and again just after it has reached a peak.

During labour the primitive parts of the brain are involved. The safer and more relaxed you feel, the less likely you are to produce "run away from danger" hormones, such as adrenalin, which counteract the "peace and harmony" hormones, such as prolactin, that are sproduced when relaxing. Floating relaxation promotes the production of endorphins, the body's own painkillers, to help you tolerate the physical pain of birth, and also help you to forget about it as soon as it is over.

## using the birthing pool

There is no strict rule about when to get into the water or how long to stay in it during labour. Make sure you keep drinking little sips of water so you do not become dehydrated and that the water temperature remains constant (33–40°C/91.4–104°F in the first stage of labour and 37–37.5°C/98.6–99.5°F during delivery).

When you stand up to get out of the pool in pre-labour or during labour, you may feel dizzy while your circulation adjusts to the effects of gravity. Take it slowly, accepting help to sit on the edge of the pool and swivel your legs over it one at a time. Stand up carefully and take small steps, bending your knees slightly to ease your lower back.

### A story of a waterbirth: Alison and Luke

**Alison's story illustrates the greater effectiveness of yoga breathing and water in combination during labour. While being accomplished in yoga since her first pregnancy, deep breathing in water proved invaluable to Alison in alleviating a challenging backache in her third birth.**

Luke is my third child to have been born in water. Just as the children bring with them their own personalities, each labour has brought new challenges and experiences.

Water has played a significant part throughout all three pregnancies and labours. The stretches and movement that can be achieved in water are quite different from those on land and it has been so reassuring for me to enter a labour knowing that, through yoga, my body has been prepared for the event.

The pool has always given me my own private space – somewhere to let go in and to feel a sense of freedom. In my previous labours I found it much easier to be active and to move around, but this time the contractions came so fast and furiously that I didn't feel like moving at all. However, the simple support that the water offered enabled me to focus on expanding my breathing and channelling the breath in a direction that I had often rehearsed in yoga practice. The pain was intense but for me breathing was the only way of staying grounded and of being able to work with the contractions as they rippled the water around me. Having benefited from Françoise's generous support and wisdom over the last five years, it was particularly special that she was with us to witness Luke's arrival.

## 138 Breathing through your contractions in water

**In any of these positions, each time you feel a wave of contraction starting to tighten the wall of your uterus, exhale to relax and welcome this process, which is squeezing your baby further down to put pressure on your cervix and "open" you further. The more relaxed you are, the more effective each contraction is bound to be. As soon as you feel the completion of the contracting force, often around your navel, exhale again to dispatch this wave and let it follow its course, without engaging in it any longer by feeling pain after it has accomplished its task. This gives you a little extra time to relax and restore your energy before the next contraction comes along, which can be invaluable when they come fast and strong.**

◁ **1** Alternate between positions that suit you throughout your labour. For example, you may find it helpful to kneel upright during a contraction.

△ **2** As the contraction passes, rest forward on the edge of the pool to start relaxing again.

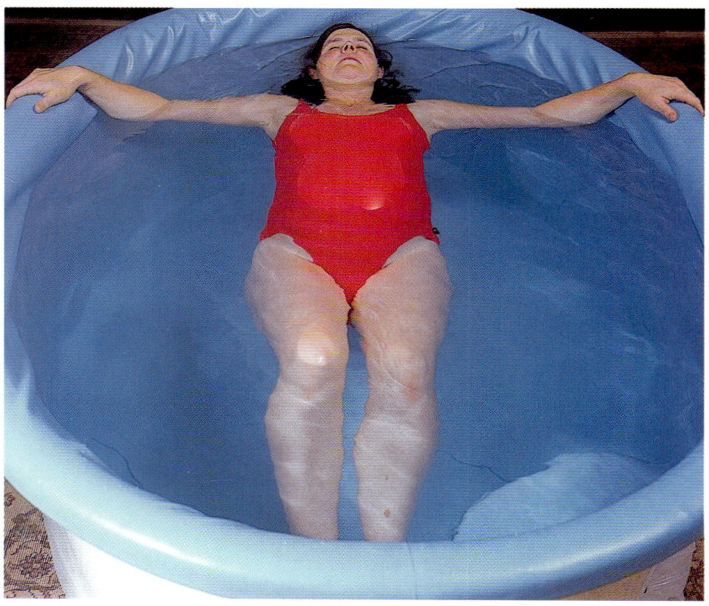

△ **3** You can also rest, breathing quietly and deeply, between contractions by stretching on your back in the water, resting your feet against the opposite wall of the pool while your arms stretch on each side to hold the edges and keep you afloat.

# Positions for waterbirthing



Mothers who have moved freely in their late pregnancy and labour tend to move spontaneously into the best possible position for childbirth. While some women feel more open in an upright or slightly backward-leaning position, in a semi-squat or standing, an equal number prefer to lean forward, usually kneeling. Water allows a unique, gravity-free way of giving birth. You can be supported by your birth partner in the tub or support yourself on the edges of the tub and "float" with your bearing-down contractions without having your feet on the bottom of the tub.

If your contractions slow down or seem to peter out when you are fully dilated, recall that traditional midwives call this the "rest and be thankful" stage before bearing down. Standing up in the pool or even getting out for a short walk, interspersed with semi-squats, can do wonders to get you back on track. Keep calm, saving energy.

The time when you are ready for your baby to be born is called the "second stage" of labour, during which more powerful yet not necessarily more painful contractions push your baby through the birth canal (your vagina) and into the outside world. At this time, both the position you are in and your breathing can make a great difference to how you will experience the birth and how your baby will be born. The unfamiliar sensations of second-stage contractions can make you hold back, contracting your buttock muscles involuntarily. Water helps you to let go of fear and open your whole self – body, mind and spirit – to make space for your baby's journey through you.

Without hurrying, allow your body to settle into the most comfortable position to give birth, even if it is not one that you had prepared for.

## 139 Squat or semi-squat

**Pace yourself and concentrate on the sensations around your perineum as it stretches to allow for the passage of the baby's head. To avoid tearing, stay as relaxed as possible and if necessary voice your exhalation to slow down the force of the contractions until you feel that the head can make its way through the elastic, expanding tissues of your vagina and perineum. You can have the extraordinary experience of accompanying the descent of your baby's head with your breathing, perhaps touching it with one hand just before it appears. You may be able to raise your baby out of the water yourself. This can certainly be a peak moment in your life, but something that you can wish for rather than anticipate in expectation.**

◁ **1** In squatting or semi-squatting positions, make sure that you have a broad, comfortable base with your feet flat on the bottom of the pool. What matters is to create as wide an angle as possible between the base of your spine and your pubic bone so that your baby has plenty of room to move out of your pelvis. Once you start feeling the head in your vagina, focus on lengthening your exhalation at the same time as you feel the strong bearing contractions overwhelming you.

## 140 Kneeling or half kneeling

**This position is helpful to relieve back pain caused by the baby's head pressing against your sacroiliac joint. If your baby started labour in a posterior presentation – that is, with his or her back to yours – you may experience less backache with your contractions in this position.**

◁ **1** This position is about the best you can adopt to relieve back pain and make yourself comfortable, and in water it is particularly effective.

# Yoga and medical intervention during labour

## Medical intervention: questions and answers

**• How will yoga affect whether or not I have medical intervention?**
Practising yoga while pregnant gives you the best possible chance of a happy, intervention-free outcome, although complications can still occur. Hope for the best possible scenario and then calmly revise your expectations should difficulties arise. If they do, yoga will still help: deep breathing and relaxation reduce stress; body-awareness helps you adjust your position effectively even when movement is restricted; and yoga helps you remain connected with your baby throughout any interventions, and in harmony with your care team.

△ Try to remember this position just in case you are attached to a monitor at some point during the birthing. It is also recommended if you have had epidural analgesia.

**• Do yogic techniques work when attached to a monitor?**
You can adopt several active birth positions when attached to a monitor. Adjust the bed head to the most comfortable sitting position, usually around a 25° angle. When you are comfortable, bend your legs alternately for about 10 minutes, placing the sole of the foot of the bent leg against the inner thigh of the straight leg. Breathe calmly for as long as possible through contractions. Alternatively, kneel on the bed and lean against the bed head (still at a 25° angle), using pillows for support. Lastly, try resting on your side in the relaxation position, with one bent leg above the other and a pillow between your knees. Alternate between these positions every half hour or so. This creates a sense of rhythm that may provide relief from contraction pain.

◁ Good breathing practices help greatly throughout pregnancy and labour. Deep down-breaths can also be used to encourage the contractions needed to deliver the placenta.

**• How would I cope with instrumental delivery?**
Ventouse or forceps deliveries can be stressful for you and your baby. Try to relax as deeply as possible to eliminate all resistance. Even if you have an epidural analgesic, mental surrender can make a big difference and facilitate delivery. Try to remain connected to your baby during this procedure and take extra time for bonding as soon as your baby is born.

**• Can yoga help in the case of an emergency section?**
During this operation, you will be anaesthetized but remain conscious. Remember that your baby will be with you very soon. Use deep breathing, focusing on the breath out, to centre yourself and to minimize the overall impact of this operation on your nervous system. Relax with each breath out and surrender yourself to the process. Visualize yourself holding your baby's hand from inside as you are prepared for theatre. The deeper that you are able to relax, the less morphine you may need after the operation, and therefore, the more alert you will be to welcome your new baby into the world.

**• What happens if the placenta's delivery is delayed?**
You can help to trigger the uterine contractions needed for the expulsion of the placenta, so resume your labour circuit. The yoga exercises will help here, as they did for the birth.

# postnatal yoga and aqua yoga just after birth

Now you have done it. You are a mother and here is your amazing baby. Take time to look back at what happened during your labour and birth. Whatever happened, allow feelings of acceptance to surface and be grateful for the presence of this child who has come to share your life.

# birthing lightly with yoga





So here you are, with your new baby. Congratulations!

Nothing can quite prepare you for the flood of emotions that can overwhelm you when your baby is finally in your arms and here to look at, feed and marvel at as he or she also discovers you. The moment of making contact and welcoming your baby is a precious one indeed, unique to each parent and each birth. Make the most of this initial closeness. (If you have chosen a water-birth, you can hold your baby in the water to allow him or her to adjust gently to being born. After you have rested and your baby has discovered the joy of feeding, it will soon be time to be in the water again. Perhaps a bath with dad too?)

△ **Breathing deeply can relax and revitalize you. Each inhalation tones and strengthens your back muscles. Pressing your hands together directs the energy produced by your breath.**

## the transformation of birth

Giving birth transforms women's lives in profound, and often unexpected, ways. The experience of each mother is different, and yet all births call for a new integration of physical and spiritual well-being. The flow of breath in yoga opens a steady calm path in the midst of all the emotions and changes that new mothers inevitably go through. Having a baby can be a very demanding physical event. It can also give rise to strong emotional and spiritual experiences. Who can gaze at a tiny baby without being stirred by feelings of joy and awe at the miracle of new life? When the baby is your own newborn, such joy may be accompanied by feelings of apprehension. The well-being of this helpless child depends upon your ability to nurture him or her, to satisfy his or her needs.

Yoga can give you much-needed support at this time of radically changing responsibilities. Continuing regular yoga practice after you have given birth will quickly increase your overall feelings of health and fitness. You will grow stronger, more confident, calmer, and better able to nurture your baby, as well as the other members of your family. You will experience and be able to spread real happiness as you nurture yourself and those close to you.

◁ **Keep your baby near you during yoga practice. He or she will enjoy watching you, and will be safe and comfortable lying close by you on the floor, propped up on cushions or a beanbag. This is also an ideal place for your baby to fall asleep while you are doing your yoga practice.**

## yoga and aqua yoga after birth

The following pages will lead you gradually through exercises designed to help you acquire increased pelvic strength and long-term pelvic health.

The postnatal programme starts with the underlying core elements of yoga: awareness, breathing, relaxation, positive attitude and physical stretching. To this core are added, as the weeks and months after the birth flow by, progressively more vigorous and demanding postures and

△ **Sitting upright strengthens your lower back. You may need to sit against a wall at first, but as your back muscles strenghten you can sit without support as you play with your baby.**

asanas (classical poses). You can refer back to the earlier stages of each exercise as you develop and strengthen the posture over time. This progression will encourage you to keep the suppleness that comes with pregnancy and to add to it increasing strength and stamina. Aqua yoga exercises help to realign your spine, using deep breathing in relaxed stretches.

The yoga relaxation you practised before the birth will refresh and restore you during busy days and disturbed nights. As your practice continues, you will be able to slip into the space of relaxation quickly and completely, whenever you need to.

▷ **Sitting cross-legged is a comfortable position to do your yoga breathing while playing with your baby. Try to keep your spine straight and you will feel the benefits of this stretch.**

# Yoga after giving birth

After your baby is born, regular yoga practice will help you ease gracefully into your new life as a mother. Your aim is to use the core aspects of yoga to bring you to a state of full health and vigour, starting from where you are now, soon after giving birth. You can expect to:

- Regain strength in the pelvic and abdominal regions.
- Relax and enjoy deep rest, to compensate for lack of sleep.
- Tone the body back into perfect alignment of hips and spine.
- Learn and practise self-nurture, so that you can nurture and enjoy your baby.

## start at the beginning

Right now you may be feeling very well, or you may have all sorts of problems resulting from hormonal imbalances, poor muscle tone or lack of sleep. However you are feeling, please start at the beginning of this section of the book. The stages are carefully worked out to take you safely from your present postnatal state to your personal maximum level of well-being. Many of the problems that women face in later life – such as uterine prolapse or incontinence – can be traced back to lack of care after childbirth. They are usually avoidable, through an awareness of posture and the right kind of progressive exercise after childbirth. Don't worry about your figure at this stage. It will be regained, perhaps improved, by inside toning.

"Each birth, each baby, each mother, is unique."

## posture

Regaining good posture is especially important after the birth. The abdominal muscles become very stretched during pregnancy. They may have been cut. Until

△ Standing in Tadasana (198), tilt your pelvis forward and backward slightly. Feel the link between your pelvic floor muscles and both your abdominal and lower back muscles.

◁ Use a futon or a firm bed, with cushions for extra support, for breathing and relaxation practice. It is comfortable for your baby, too.

▷ **As your baby grows and you regain strength, it is best to use an upright chair for breathing practice. Always make sure that your knees are level with your hips, using support to raise your feet if needed.**

they are healed and strengthened they cannot hold the spine firmly in place.

As a new mother, you therefore need to take special care of your lower back. This section of the book teaches you how to move with greater awareness, using your legs and upper back to sit and stand, to lift and carry. You can gradually progress safely into gentle movements that build up into flowing sequences to strengthen the weakened and overstretched muscles. Too much vigorous exercise, too soon, would simply strain them further. Full classical yoga postures should not be taken up until the after-effects of the pregnancy and birth have disappeared. It usually takes about six months to reach this stage.

It is best to take advice from your doctor about when you can start going to the pool again to continue with aqua yoga exercises, particularly if you have had a Caesarean section. You will benefit from this gentle yet very effective form of exercise earlier than from land-based exercises (these are not advisable until four or five months after a Caesarean section).

## making time for yoga

You do not always have to find the time to install yourself in your "yoga space", or on a special mat or chair, in order to practice yoga. There is no special time to practise deep breathing, stretching, relaxation, meditation or quietly observing your body, your feelings and your thoughts. All these are yoga practices that you can do as you look after your baby and go about your daily activities, or fit into those moments when you create a brief pause between one activity and the next. A few minutes of yogic awareness, frequently repeated, becomes a habit that gradually builds up into a state good health, positive feelings and a clear and focused mind.

If you cannot manage a practice during a particular day, then just a few minutes of yoga can still help you. No effort, no matter how small, is wasted in yoga. The aim of this book is to help you to integrate yoga practice into your daily life as a new mother, both in your home and outside it.

◁ **Postnatal aqua yoga exercises focus on closing the body. They include this Wide Twist (157), which keeps your hips supple and helps to recover your waistline.**

# Basic breathing techniques





Before you start any postnatal exercise, the first thing to focus on is your breathing. This is called "Yoga Breath Awareness". Watch yourself breathing. Become aware of your breath just as it is. Then, without forcing your inhalation, very gently extend your exhalation, allowing your natural breath to become gradually slower and deeper. This can have a profoundly calming and settling effect at any time. The breath is closely linked to the nervous system. Shallow breathing will make you physically tense, mentally distracted and emotionally anxious. Deep breathing has the opposite effect, making you centred and steady.

A deep breath in will quite naturally charge body and mind with new energy, and a deep breath out will release muscular tension, chemical waste products and feelings of tiredness and strain. For this reason, you should breathe deeply and slowly at all times during yoga practice, and the descriptions of the poses give you guidance on when to breathe in or out. This joining of mind and body through breath and movement is yoga. After a few days' practice, you will be able to use your breath in new ways.

You can use Alternate Nostril Breathing (4) to energize and/or calm yourself, and Reverse Breathing (141) to tone the deep muscle layers of your abdomen and spine. Take every opportunity to practise and perfect these breathing techniques. A good time to do this is while you are feeding your baby, as long as you can remain relaxed while you are practising.

## 141 Reverse breathing (1)

**During pregnancy you used breathing exercises to open the body, make more room for the growing baby and facilitate the birthing process. Now the situation is reversed: your aim is to close the lower part of your body, pull the stretched muscles inward and upward, and strengthen them so that they hold the spine, pelvis and abdominal organs in correct alignment. This is the purpose of Reverse Breathing. Practise it for a few rounds, or until you feel tired or lose your rhythm. Stop and rest, and repeat whenever you feel ready. With practice, you will feel very toned and strengthened after breathing in this way.**

△ **1** Sit or lie comfortably, with your spine supported. Place your hands on your lower abdomen, to become aware of what is happening. Breathe in deeply, imagining the energy of the breath being drawn up through the base of your body into the abdomen.

△ **2** As you breathe out, pull in your waist, drawing your navel up and closer to your spine at the back. Feel this out breath continue to flow up into your chest, toning you powerfully from inside. Release at the end of your exhalation. The out breath is longer than the in breath, but this should never be forced. You can either take a "resting breath" in and out before inhaling and drawing up again, or repeat the Reverse Breathing without a pause.

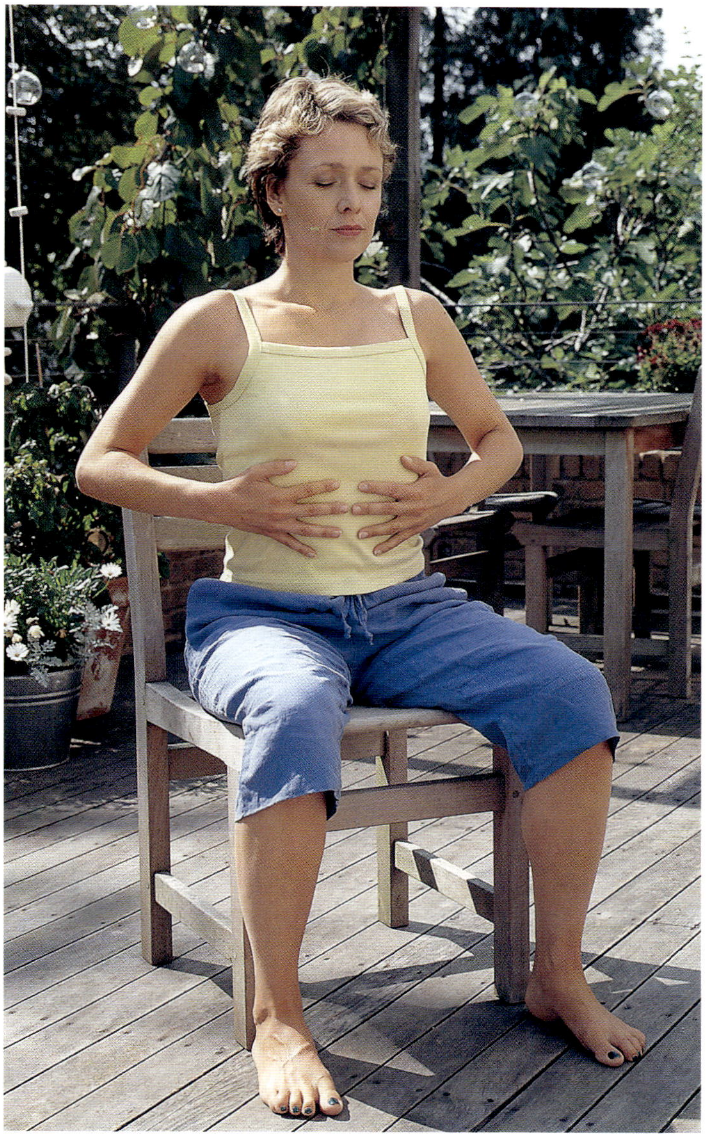

◁ Feel your breathing muscles working by placing your hands in turn on your ribs, your lower chest and your abdomen.

△ Alternate Nostril Breathing (4) works on the nervous system, quickly soothing the emotions and calming the mind. Use it whenever you feel stressed during the day, as well as making it part of your regular yoga practice. Your breathing will deepen naturally after a few rounds; you should never force it.

◁ Whenever you feel the need for energizing, perhaps just after your baby has gone to sleep, Alternate Nostril Breathing (4) will refresh you in two to three minutes. You can invite other children to do it with you before you play with them too.

"The moment I first touched my new born, a love I had never felt before swept my heart."

# Feeding and energy

You will enjoy your new baby most if you are feeling good in yourself. This good feeling largely depends upon two things: regaining your fitness and vitality, and being able to rest and relax despite the inevitable lack of sleep. Fitness and relaxation are the two keys to happy mothering and a happy baby, so these are the two "arms" of yoga that we will be focusing on. Everyone in your family will enjoy the benefits of your yoga practice.

No sooner have you welcomed your baby into the world than feeding becomes an all-absorbing task. However well prepared you have been for this, it takes a great deal of adjustment for both your baby and yourself. Relaxing in a comfortable position can make a significant difference to your early experience of breastfeeding and make it more enjoyable from the start. If you are bottle-feeding, practising breath awareness can contribute towards creating a closer physical bond with your baby.

△ While sitting up or reclined, make sure your lower back is well supported. Use a cushion to raise the baby's body if needed.

## feeding positions

In the first weeks following birth, it is important that your back should always be well supported when you breastfeed. You may prefer a reclining position at first, in bed or on a sofa, but favour an upright position as soon as this is comfortable. If you have had a Caesarian section or a traumatic birth experience, lying down with your baby at your side may continue to be your most

◁ If you had a Caesarean section you will need, at first, to find positions where the weight of your baby does not rest on your abdomen.

◁ As you grow stronger you will be able to feed your baby in a variety of positions. The important aspect is relaxed comfort.

▷ If you were in the middle of doing something else when the baby wakes for a feed, take a few deep breaths before you pick up your baby. This allows you to transmit a message of loving nurture to your baby, rather than one of irritation at being interrupted.

comfortable feeding position for longer. If you need to, raise your baby on a cushion so that your back can remain straight while you feed. If you are sitting on a chair, you may need to place a cushion or use a support to raise your feet so that your knees and hips are level.

Check your feeding position again and again, week by week, anywhere you happen to be with your baby, to make sure your back has adequate support while you feed. You spend so much time in feeding that forming good habits with regard to feeding positions is a fundamental step in regaining, or creating, a sound posture after birth. Always relax your shoulders.

## breathing and relaxing while feeding

Feeding your baby is a precious time to practise breath awareness and save, if not generate, energy. Once you are settled in a comfortable position, use a deep exhalation to release any tension you hold in your body at the time. If you are breastfeeding, you can do this while the baby is "latching on" and while hormonal changes are occurring in your body. Slow down your breath, and feel that you are beginning to rest. If your baby does not feed easily and gets frustrated, start again calmly. Early obstacles can be overcome more easily and rapidly if you can break for relaxation while feeding your baby. Then feeding becomes a positive rest time in which you can practise some other breathing techniques, such as Reverse Breathing (141), and also relax deeply while remaining close with your baby. Making the best use of feeding times to renew and save your energy as a new mother is one of the main aspects of regaining fitness and vitality the yoga way.

## bottle-feeding

It is even more important when bottle-feeding to breathe yourself into a welcoming, nurturing attitude before you pick up your baby. Relax while the baby is awake and alert at the beginning of the feed.

▷ Hold the bottle at a comfortable angle for your baby to suck on it. Relax and enjoy this moment of physical closeness and rest with your baby.

# The art of relaxation





Yoga relaxation involves four elements: slow, calm breathing, comfortable posture, physical and mental relaxation. Slowing your breathing right down and breathing out slowly will calm the nervous system. You may already know how rapidly and well this works through your practice of expanded breathing. Relaxation is both a tool and a completion.

## basic relaxation

In relaxation you do more than rest. You enter another state of being in which you are neither sleeping, nor engaged in activity. Think of it as putting your gearbox in the neutral position, disengaging from all your voluntary thinking and acting.

The more you stretch all the muscles of your body with yoga, the easier it becomes to relax them. The more you breathe in your stretches, the deeper your breathing becomes and the more you can make use of your breathing to either energize or quieten yourself. Life with a baby changes from day to day, nearly from moment to moment. Before you learn the classic yoga relaxation in Shavasana (197), or Corpse Pose, it helps to practise this basic relaxation whenever you can, through the day and night.

Although you will relax more deeply if you can lie down, any position in which you can settle comfortably for a minute or two is

△ **Lie on your back with your head, neck and spine in a straight line. Avoid letting your chin poke upward by lengthening the back of your neck. Let your arms lie stretched out loosely, a little away from your body, with the palms up and fingers gently curled. The shoulders and upper back are spread wide and soft. Stretch out your legs, with your feet apart and rolling slightly outwards.**

△ **If you intend to relax deeply for 10 minutes or more you may wish to cover yourself with a shawl (and socks in winter), as your body temperature will drop. Include your baby and relax deeply together.**

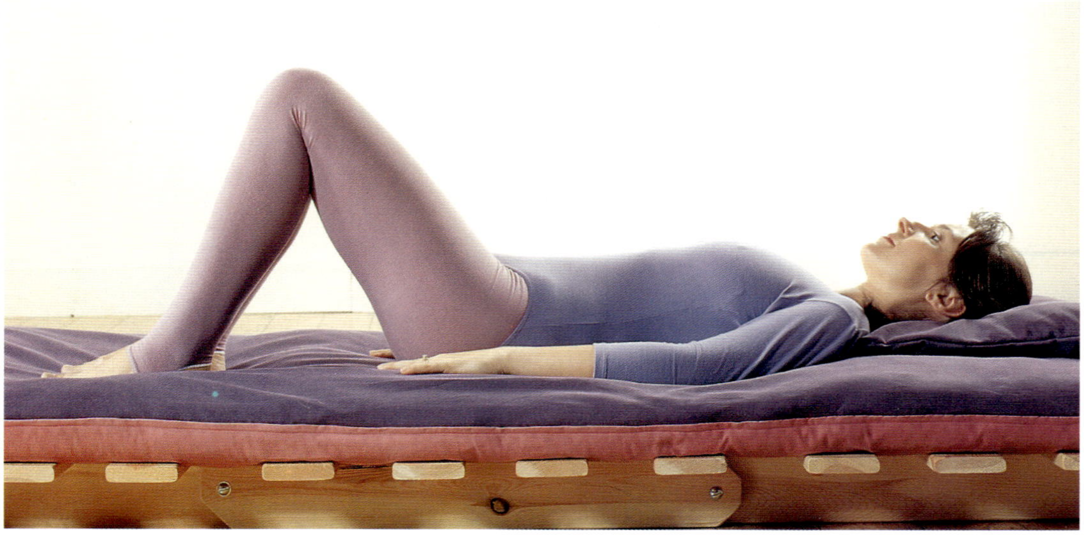

◁ **If your pelvis tilts in this position, making a hollow under your waist, you may be more comfortable bending your knees and placing the soles of your feet flat on the floor to begin with, until in time your back remains flat with your legs outstretched. Meanwhile, press your back gently towards the floor as you breathe out.**

▷ **Once you have learnt how to make your body "let go" on demand, you can practise relaxation in many positions and situations. This is the Child Pose (237) which we look at later in the book.**

fine. Inhale, then extend the exhalation as much as you can. If you feel that you need to, then voice it, as a "Haaah", or yawn it, a few times. Then close your eyes and be aware of your breathing. If you learnt to breathe in your abdomen while pregnant, feel yourself breathing deeply. Then let go of your conscious breathing and feel yourself resting. Experience the quality of rest that results from relaxing in stillness and quietening your breathing. At this stage you are entering the open space of relaxation, where your whole physiology can be refreshed and restored.

▷ **Once you have learnt the art of non-doing you can slip into this mode of being anywhere, any time you wish.**

## mental relaxation: use the power of visualization

This aspect of yoga practice helps you to let go even more, releasing tensions within your body and also within your mind. Imagine yourself in a happy scene, such as lying in a beautiful garden. Build up this scene and make it very real for you. Bring your baby into your visualization. Feel close and bonded, with both of you basking in the sunshine of universal love, both of you being nurtured together. Include others who are close to you in this happy scene. Feel loving and loved... After a while, let the vision fade away, knowing that it is always there for you to recapture. Focus on your breathing and start to come out of your relaxation.

▽ **Learning to relax and let go creates space for quality time with those we love.**

## emotional relaxation: the attitude of surrender

This is the true purpose of your relaxation: to let go, to surrender to the flow of life, to be rather than to do. Learning to "go with the flow" makes a mother's life happier and her relationships more rewarding.

You can relax deeply while you are feeding your baby – to the great benefit of both of you. Use relaxation to help you to go back to sleep during disturbed nights, or to soothe your baby to sleep.

# Breath, relaxation – and now movement

By increasing your awareness of your everyday movements, you can eliminate a great deal of postnatal tiredness and strain. Consciously allow your legs and upper back to carry your weight – and often that of your baby as well – rather than relying on your lower back and abdominal muscles. If you had a Caesarean section or episiotomy you will need to be especially vigilant while the scar tissue is healing. Practise the following exercises regularly, to restore muscle tone in the perineal and abdominal muscles. When these muscles are weak, the spine and pelvis move out of alignment, causing both poor posture and lower backache.

## 142 Reverse breathing (2): for the pelvic floor

**Practise the first stage of Reverse Breathing (141) for a while, until you feel absolutely comfortable with it. Then add the following: as you breathe in, tighten and pull up the perineal muscles at the base of your body, drawing them up into the abdomen. Tighten the muscles at the centre of your "seat" (the vaginal muscles), drawing also on the anal muscles and the front area (the muscles that support your bladder). This exercise, when practised regularly, can save years of discomfort and problems – including stress incontinence and prolapse – caused by perineal muscles that have been overstretched during childbirth.**

**Continue to tighten these muscles even more as you breathe, releasing them at the end of your out breath. Practise using these sets of muscles in a smooth, wavelike flow of the breath. This exercise can be done almost anywhere and at any time. Rest for a few seconds between breaths, or between sets of six breaths. To alleviate any problems due to the weakness of your perineal muscles, do two sets of six breaths three times a day for two or three weeks.**

## 143 Getting down to the floor and up off the floor

**Getting down to the floor and up off the floor is something new mothers soon find themselves doing many times a day. If you have done yoga during pregnancy, you will already be familiar with the Cat Pose (64). You can enjoy the benefits of this pose right away to soothe your back and avoid straining it as you go down to floor level and up again. This first basic sequence introduces yoga movement in your life as a new mother in a simple but effective manner. In yoga, body symmetry, suppleness and stretching are constantly practised so as to eventually become effortless during everyday activities.**

▷**1** Once on the floor, position yourself on your hands and knees in a firm, symmetrical and well-balanced position on all fours.

▷ **2** To get up off the floor, lean forward first so that you can easily turn your toes under. Then, in one flowing movement, walk your hands on the floor towards you while rolling your back to find yourself sitting on your heels, as shown. Remember to keep your neck relaxed.

△ **3** By stretching your legs and pushing on your hands you find yourself getting up off the floor in one easy movement. With your legs bent at first, then extended, you can now stretch your spine to a full upright posture. Your lower back has been protected at all times during this sequence.

△ **4** Practise going down to the floor again on all fours by bending your knees and extending your arms towards the floor, palms stretched out. Your heels will probably lift from the floor as your knees reach down. Stretch on all fours and get up off the floor again, making this a rolling motion up and down.

# closing the body in water

After giving birth, aqua yoga exercises that are the counterpart of antenatal aqua yoga will help you realign and "close" your body, as well as toning and strengthening the muscles of your pelvis and lower back. Water is uniquely healing for the perineum and a good medium in which to tone the pelvic floor muscles. Breathing remains an essential aspect of postnatal aqua yoga.

Rather than aiming simply to "get back to normal", your goal is to create a new strength and stamina which are no less than those of your body before pregnancy but are also enriched by the transformation of birth and – if not yet, before too long – by the fulfilment that being a mother can bring.

## toning with breathing

In the same way that you used your out breath to "open" your body for birth, relaxing all the muscles of the lower abdomen and pelvic floor, you can now use it in reverse to tone the same muscles. Within a few days, your uterus will have returned to its pre-pregnancy size (an average-size pear). The fitter you are, particularly if you have used deep abdominal breathing in pregnancy, the more elastic the four layers of muscles in your abdomen will be and so more able to tighten, forming a strong and firm abdominal wall. Involving your pelvic floor muscles in aqua breathing will help you achieve thorough and long-lasting results in a relatively short time.

## 144 Reverse breathing (3): in water

**The first place to try Reverse Breathing in water is in the birthing pool or a bath tub, at home or in the hospital. Either a sitting or a kneeling position, which will allow you to keep your back straight, is suitable.**

**For a few days after giving birth, take a breath drawing in your abdominal muscles only, without involving your pelvic floor muscles. As you breathe out, draw in these muscles even more. Relax them at the end of your exhalation. It is often a shock to women to discover how soft their abdominal muscles are after having a baby. Do not get discouraged as you can be assured that a steady practice of Reverse Breathing in water will help you tone your abdomen from inside out, from the deepest layer of transverse muscle to the top layers under the skin.**

◁ In the pool, it is best to stand with your feet straight under your hips, knees slightly bent, for this breathing to be most effective. Feel the flow of breath having a powerful action on your muscles, to the point that the lower back muscles are also drawn in with your exhalation. Now is time to start lifting the pelvic floor muscles as you inhale and continue lifting them even more as you exhale. Relax them at the end of your exhalation.

## 145 Cross-kneeling to warrior pose

**This exercise can be demanding on new mothers. It tones the oblique abdominal muscles early and effectively after birth, in a way that would not be advisable with land-based exercises until after three months. There is a natural progression from the cross-walks to the classic Warrior Pose (251), which you can use now in its aquatic version to stengthen and energize you.**

△ **1** Kneel or stand in the pool, depending on the depth of the water, and advance by moving one leg across the other, extending your arms on the surface of the water. If you find it difficult to stride forward, move your crossed front leg back to the centre before moving your other leg forward and across.

△ **2** Extending your step straight in front of you, bend your front knee so that it is above your foot. Stretch from your back foot, bringing your arms together on the surface of the water in front of you. Breathe in and out in this pose, bringing your back foot forward on the next out breath. Repeat with the other leg.

## Closing the body after birth

**After birth, the uterus contracts down to its pre-preganancy size and position within three to six weeks. This process is known as involution. Yoga breathing can ease any discomfort until you have stopped bleeding and feel ready to return to the pool.**

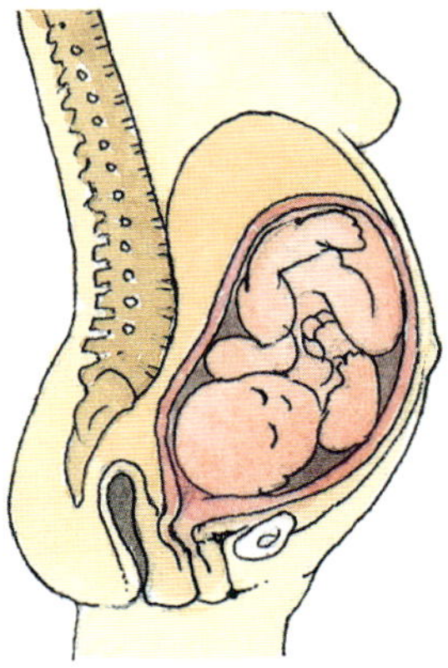

At the end of pregnancy

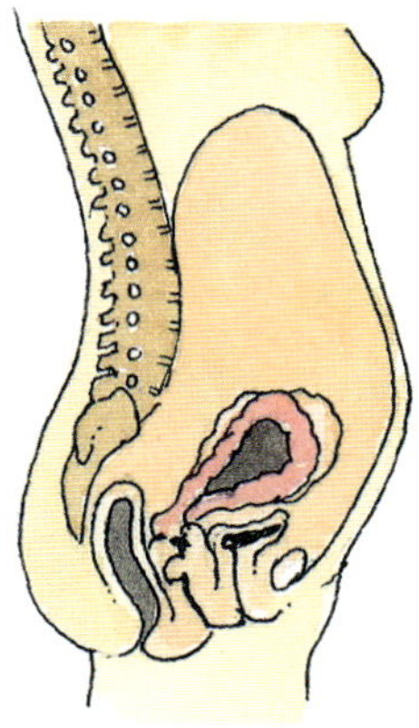

Immediately after the birth

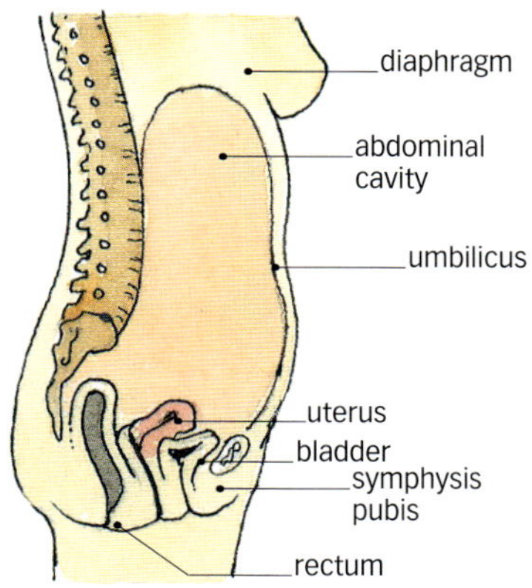


6 weeks after the birth

## 146 Cross-arms

**The resistance of the water increases the toning of your arms, upper back and chest muscles in this exercise.**

◁ **1** Standing in the water, bring your arms horizontally across your chest with one above the other.

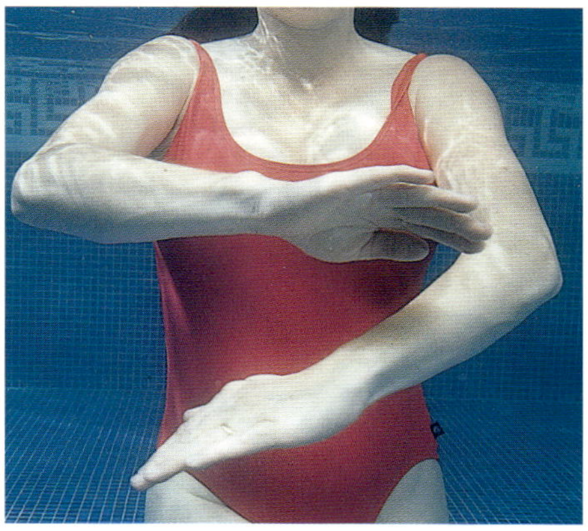

◁ **2** Open them out slightly then bring them back across your chest again, changing the arm that was on the top so that you alternate the crossing of your arms in a vigorous rhythm under water. Breathe in as you extend your arms, out as you cross them.

## 147 Kneeling close and lift

**After months of exercises that helped you to open your pelvis in preparation for birth, kneeling with your knees together is now needed to knit back all the muscles of your abdomen. Reverse Breathing (144) is particularly effective in stretches in which the legs are parallel to each other. The front thigh muscles lengthen and breathing involves both abdominal and back muscles in a tightening effect during the exhalation. In all these exercises make sure that your neck and shoulders are free of tension.**

△ **1** Standing against the pool wall, align your back against the wall as you bend your knees, keeping your legs and feet together. You can use a woggle – a half woggle is very comfortable – under the backs of your thighs to help you keep your trunk upright in the water with your knees bent.

△ **2** Your feet can now take off from the pool floor; unexpectedly, you are perfectly stable in this supported upright position which allows you to draw in your abdominal muscles as you practise your Reverse Breathing. The focus is on your hips and legs. You can extend your arms sideways or forward on the surface of the water for additional balance, or hold the edge of the pool behind you.

△ **3** Bring your knees up, holding on to the edge of the pool behind you. Inhale as you lift your knees, keeping them close together, and exhale as slowly as possible with your knees up. Your lower spine will be extended. Doing Reverse Breathing in this pose makes it quite intense for your innermost muscles deep in the pelvis.

# water relief before and after birth





Aqua yoga exercises can be used to relieve backache in pregnancy. They also prove invaluable in soothing and treating the pelvic floor or your abdominal muscles after a Caesarean section.

At some point during pregnancy you are likely to experience a form of backache. It is due mainly to the relaxation of your ligaments and joints in the pelvis that stretch you open, or to the destabilization of your sacroil-iac joints (where your pelvis meets the lower spine) due to the increased weight of your growing baby when you walk or stand. Sometimes the pressure of your enlarged uterus may affect your sciatic nerves and cause acute pain. If your discomfort is constant and impairing, consult a doctor. Most common backache in pregnancy, however, responds well to yoga and even better to aqua yoga. In the buoyant environment of water, you can soothe your sore back and tone the muscles that will enable you to keep your spine aligned as you grow to full term. Regular aqua yoga will prevent any re-occurence.

The most soothing exercises are those in which you kneel or bend your knees and, if you are a swimmer, the leg movement of backstroke. All the hip rolls and loops will help you keep backache at bay once the pain has receded. After birth, aqua breathing will help you to heal and tone your perineum and pelvic floor, as well as the muscles of the lower abdomen. If you have had a Caesarean section, some postnatal aqua yoga twists and stretches will be most beneficial, while deep breathing can help to heal the scar tissue.

## 148 Backache

**A great deal of backache in pregnancy is due to posture. Aligning your body in stretches with your knees bent and your back straight often helps to improve your posture and allows you to breathe more deeply, oxygenating the back muscles. Do the postures slowly, lowering your body in the water as much as you can and extending both your inhalations and your exhalations with each practice. If aqua yoga relieves your backache in two or three sessions at the pool, do not stop practising the postures that have helped you, as they continue to be effective in a preventive way. When you go to the pool with backache, be careful with draughts when you get out of the pool and make sure you have a large towel to wrap yourself in. If you have lower backache at any stage of pregnancy, here is a suggested sequence.**

△ **1** From hip circle to full stretch: stand holding on to a bar or a woggle and practise all the different circular movements you can make with your pelvis until you find one that particularly stretches and soothes your back. Then practise this one focusing on your breathing for a few minutes. You may find that the next time you go to the pool, you may need a slightly different movement.

△ **2** To do a kneeling bend-stretch, place a woggle under your arms and lean forward as you lower your bent knees in the water. If the pool is shallow enough, kneel on the pool floor.

△ **3** Inhale, and as you exhale, allow your relaxed legs to extend back on the bottom of the pool, letting yourself drop as you hold on to the woggle. Then bend your knees again to return to your starting position and repeat this movement with the flow of the breath a few times, aiming at being more relaxed in it each time. The gentle contrast between the bending and stretching of your legs is particularly helpful with sciatic pain.

## 149 Healing the pelvic floor

**Water is healing after giving birth and you have probably used baths at home to soothe your perineum if you had a tear or an episiotomy. It has been found, through controlled experiments, that a drop of lavender essential oil in the bath makes it even more effective. The first and main aqua yoga practice to rely on for better and speedier healing of the perineum is deep breathing sitting in water. Simply breathe at first and then lift your pelvic floor muscles using Reverse Breathing (144). This increases the blood circulation in the area and involves all the muscles together in their connection with the lower back and the lower abdominal muscles.**

**When you go to the pool there are two additional exercises that have proved to be helpful if you continue to be aware of your tear or cut, or if you have lost your vaginal tone or feel that your pelvic floor muscles remain weak.**

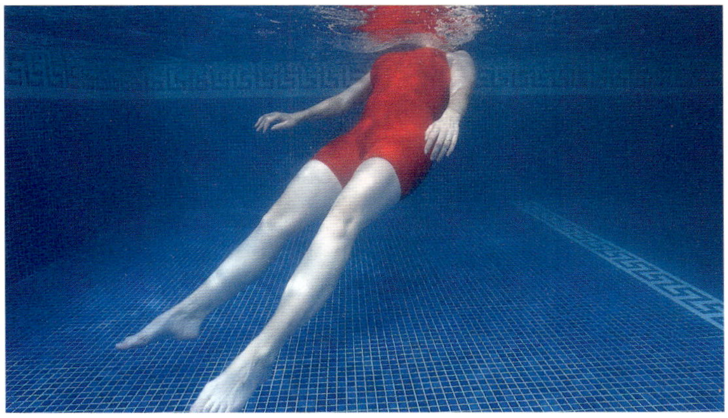

△ **1** Lie on your back in the water and stretch, trailing your extended legs. Use a woggle or board for support if you need to. Inhale and stretch more.

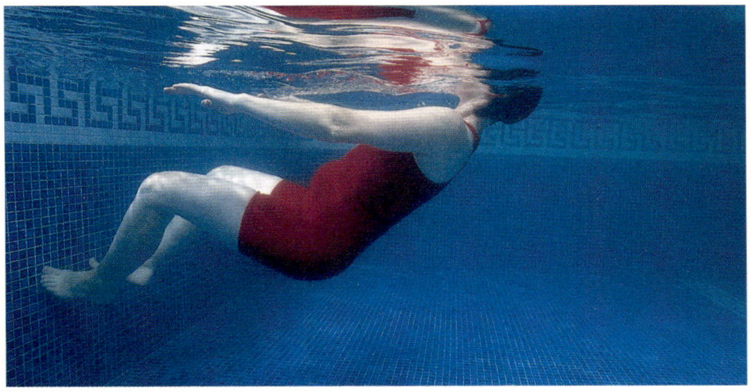

△ **2** As you exhale, bend your knees and bring them towards your body. Stretch again and let your legs drop, bend again, stretch again and so on. If your legs drop to the bottom of the pool, relax and stop, or start again from the beginning. If you get confident, you can combine this exercise with one of the aqua twists.

△ **3** Backstroke with wide leg movements, focusing on the stretching phase rather than on the opening of the knees, is also very effective.

## 150 After a Caesarean section

**While all the postnatal aqua yoga stretches and adapted swimming are suitable if you practise them without exerting yourself after a Caesarean section, once you have healed your scar tissue with deep abdominal breathing and included Reverse Breathing (144), you can use aqua twists to breathe more deeply and tone your transverse abdominal muscles. Three of these twists can be practised together as a short sequence. Include them particularly in your postnatal routine.**

△ Wide twist, standing against the pool wall (157).

△ Twist-roll-bend (158).

△ Eagle pose, legs only at first, then with the arms (159).

# Standing aqua stretches

After pregnancy, it is necessary to realign your spine. Standing in the water allows you the maximum stretch between your hip bones and your ribs as you lift your arms above your head. Aqua yoga makes use of deep breathing in relaxed stretches that are easier and safer in water than on land. Your ligaments are still soft and should not be overstretched for at least four months after giving birth.

## 151 Realigning the spine

**Practise these simple standing stretches to lengthen your spinal muscles and breathe deep under your diaphragm where your baby was lying just a few weeks ago.**

◁ **1** Consciously, with a deep, long breath, close and lengthen your whole body.

◁ **2** As you stretch your arms above your head, extend to the maximum as you inhale and exhale as deeply as you can. At the end of your exhalation, relax completely and "flop" your arms before you start stretching again on the next in breath. The fullness of the relaxation is as important as the extension.

## 152 Overarm stretch

**After expanding your breathing capacity during pregnancy, breathing for two, you need to continue using the same muscles, which are no longer stretched by your fully grown baby.**

▷ **1** You can make the previous stretch more extreme by extending one arm over your head and breathing more intensely in your intercostal muscles: the little muscles between your ribs. Repeat on the other side.

▷ **2** After extending your arm to the maximum above your head, lower it towards your other arm, keeping your chest wide open. Breathe as deeply as possible.

## 153 Side-stretch

**Even more stretch can be achieved by adding a sideways extension to the previous exercise.**

△ With your straight legs together, stretch your whole body in an oblique line, holding on to the bar or pool edge to stabilize yourself with one hand. Stretch first to one side, then to the other, and breathe fully on each side, being aware of creating one long stretch from your feet to your extended hand.

## 154 Knee-bent stretch

**This creates an intense stretch in which you breathe deeply for two or three full cycles before you change legs.**

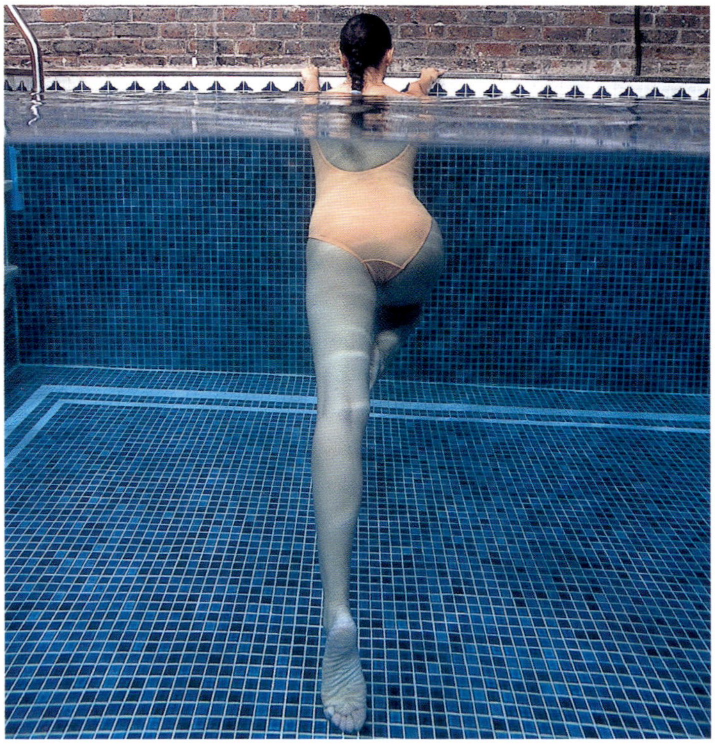

△ Facing the pool wall, take a wide step so that your front foot can rest at the base of the wall. Bend your front knee and lift your foot to bring it on to the knee of your extended back leg.

## 155 Leg stretch

**As you become stronger and fitter, you can practise this classic yoga leg stretch in different ways. At first you may want to rest your leg on the bar, if there is one (the pool edge may be too high). If there is no bar, it may be sufficient to start with to bring your extended leg up, at any height comfortable to you on the wall, while keeping your standing leg bent. Being in water allows a greater stretch than most people can achieve rapidly when doing dry land yoga and strengthens the muscles at the base of the spine that contribute not only to physical fitness but to vital energy in the body.**

◁ **1** You can use a short woggle to support your leg. Hold both ends and rest your foot in the centre.

◁ **2** Straighten the leg, bringing your foot up to shoulder height at the surface. Eventually, you will be able to extend both legs, using your stretched legs to pull your back even straighter as you breathe in the pose.

# aqua twists and rolls





These standing twists are a great help in recovery of your waistline, and you will get it back sooner by doing them in the water than you would on dry land. Do the twists facing the wall and holding on to the bar or the pool edge, or facing the pool and holding on to a woggle, or standing freely.

As in all the yoga postures, it is deep breathing that makes the twists effective. The combination of twisting and rolling movements helps to keep your hips supple after pregnancy and prevents postnatal lower backache. If your pool is shallow, you can use kneeling versions of the standing postures. Keep your neck soft and relaxed as you twist.

## 156 Narrow twists

**Both these postures are very helpful if you have split your abdominal muscles in late pregnancy or during birth, and they are recommended if you have had a Caesarean section. Stand with your back straight and your feet together, bending your knees slightly if necessary to get a better alignment.**

△ **1** For the straight twist, bring your right leg in front of your left leg and place your right foot firmly on the pool floor about 30cm/12in to the far side of your left foot. Keep your hips facing forward. Breathe deeply in the twist a few times, then change legs.

△ **2** The sideways version gives a more extreme stretch which does not involve opening your hips. Turn both feet to the same side while keeping your trunk facing forward.

## 157 Wide twist

**For this twist, hold on to the bar or edge if you face the wall; hold a woggle or stand freely if you face the pool. Start from a standing position with your feet wide apart.**

▷ Scissor your legs one in front of the other. Extend your front foot sideways as far as you comfortably can in order to increase the twisting stretch and breathe deeply in this posture a few times. Gradually, both shoulders will become aligned as you face the wall. Let your head follow the extension of your spine naturally. Don't force it. Change legs and repeat. If you wish to make the posture more dynamic, you can jump and scissor your legs one way and then the other, inhaling as you change sides and exhaling as you stretch down.

## 158 Twist-roll-bend

**This is a soothing movement for the lower back which also tones the abdominal muscles as you breathe rhythmically with the roll. It can be done facing the wall or the pool, supporting your arms on the bar or on a woggle. If you are in a shallow pool, you can "twist-roll-bend" in a sitting position with your back straight, supporting your arms on a woggle and moving your knees to one side.**

▷ **1** Start from a standing position with your feet together. Keeping your back straight, bend your knees slightly and turn them to one side, creating a gentle twist. Then roll your knees in small circles on that side, bending more as you come to the centre. Make it a fairly energetic movement, breathing in a rhythm that helps you twist further. Repeat on the other side.

## 159 Eagle pose

**This is one of the most "closing" classic postures in hatha yoga. It is also beneficial for centring and helps you focus your attention. It is an excellent pose to practise after giving birth. Even if you are already familiar with yoga, you may find this pose easier in the water than on land after opening your body in childbirth. You can get into the posture progressively, starting with the legs and arms separately before binding both at the same time, and you can use the pool wall as a support behind you to help you balance. You may find that this pose, which perhaps differs most from all the yoga you have practised during pregnancy, will help you "close" your body and gradually encourage you to turn your attention outward again as your baby is growing.**

△ **1** Start with your back straight and your knees slightly bent. Lift one leg and bring it over your other leg, binding your foot behind it as high s you find comfortable between the ankle and the knee. Feel the closing twist of your hips and breathe as deeply as possible for a minute or two. Then unfold your legs, returning to a standing position, and change sides.

△ **2** Open your arms wide and bring your right arm over your left arm, crossing them at the elbows if possible. Pull your right forearm to the right and bring your right hand forward to meet your open left hand. Breathe deeply for a minute or two before unfolding your arms. Change sides and repeat. This is a powerful toner for the muscles of the upper arms.

# Swimmers' bends and stretches





If you are a swimmer, after stretching with standing poses in the water to elongate your spine and close your pelvis, you can now stretch while swimming to realign your body and remodel your figure after giving birth. Swimming helps you achieve further stretching with twists, bends and rolls in fluid movements which are all the more effective if you do them very slowly and thoroughly.

## 160 Front and back stretch

**Enjoy a plain stretch of your arms and legs together, extending your whole body on your front and then on your back. It is your breathing that makes this stretch tone you, so make sure that you extend more each time you exhale, three to four times on each side. If you are familiar with the start of backstroke swimming from the wall, with your knees bent high, or if you practised the back arch in yoga before your pregnancy, you can also use this movement in water as a safe and gentle postnatal stretch.**

◁ **1** If you are not a confident swimmer, you may wish to use woggles to stretch.

△ **2** If you are a swimmer, extend your arms and legs freely as close to the surface as you can.

◁ **3** Stretch one side and then the other, keeping your arms and legs parallel and, if possible, together, and breathing deeply in your waist area.

△ **4** You can extend your back stretch further into a back arch. Start by facing the wall with your knees bent, push yourself off the wall and open your front ribs, letting your head and arms follow the movement of your spine.

## 161 Screw stretch

**You can do this movement supporting yourself on a bar at the side of the pool, but it can also be done with a woggle or freely if you are a confident swimmer. Find a rhythm of breathing that suits you in this movement and make sure you roll equally in both directions. The combined rolling and stretching may give you a feeling of physical freedom.**

△ **1** In a continuous movement, roll over in the water, extending your right arm and right leg over your left arm and left leg. This combines an extreme stretch with a twisting movement of your whole body.

△ **2** Inevitably, you will have your face in the water some of the time, so you may avoid this movement if you would rather not be under water.

◁ **3** As you become familiar with this rolling twist, you can intensify its "screwing" action by bending the leg that you twist over, while the other leg continues to extend in a relaxed way as you roll.

## 162 Bend-stretch

**This is an expanded, combined version of standing aqua stretches. It elongates the spine and tones the lower back and abdominal muscles together, while stretching the upper back and arms as well. While in pregnancy your aim was to open your knees and hips wide in this movement, now in its postnatal version the emphasis is on the closing of the hips and the stretch.**

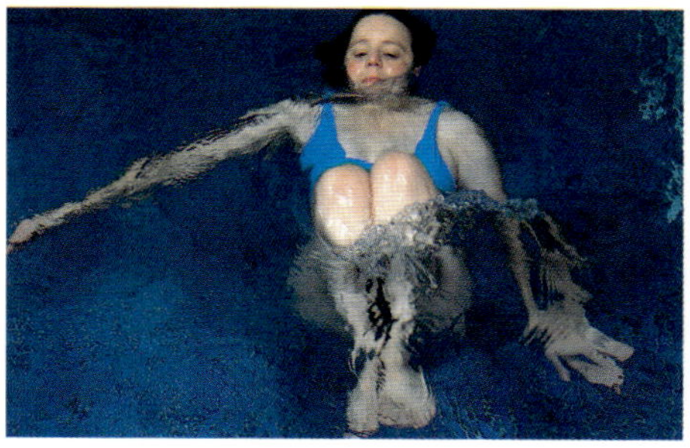

△ **1** Lie on your back in the water with your arms outstretched. Hold on to a bar or a woggle if necessary. Inhale, then, with your legs together, bring your knees as close as you can to your abdomen as you exhale. Stretch again as you inhale and continue alternate stretches and bends for four or five cycles of breathing.

△ **2** In the same starting position, inhale, bring your knees close together then stretch your legs and your whole body as you exhale. Find a steady rhythm that allows you to stretch fully with the flow of the breath. The sculling movement of your arms in and out is an intense exercise in itself.

△ **3** Bend your knees and allow your thighs and trunk to stretch as your knees drop in the water. If you are in a shallow pool, you may find yourself kneeling on the pool floor. Swing your legs back towards your arms and then forwards, raising them to the surface as much as you can. Do not force this bending and stretching movement but let it be fluent even if you find that it is very small to start with.

# Swimmers' twists and bends





These twists and bends build on the Bend-stretches (162), including further twisting movements of the whole body in the water. They are quite strenuous and you may not feel ready to start doing them until your baby is five or six months old. Never force yourself. Although you are unlikely to strain your muscles in the water, you can deplete your energy if your practice exceeds your current level of fitness. Every woman is unique and experiences the postnatal period in a different way that she cannot always predict from her degree of fitness before or during pregnancy. Reassure yourself that you can take the time you need to tone your body in depth and always practise under your limit rather than to your limit. Take your time and enjoy each pose fully.

## 163 Extended twist

**As you extend your legs in this position, your arms stretch too so that you get an intense stretch of your whole body in a vigorous rhythmical movement. The higher you bring your knees up before rolling them to the side, the more extended the twist as you then stretch your legs. To start, lie on your back in the water, holding on to a bar or woggle if necessary, with your arms extended.**

△ **1** At first you can warm up by bending your knees to one side, stretching your legs and then bending your knees to the other side, bringing them as far up as possible each time. Inhale as you stretch, exhale as you bend your knees up.

△ **2** Then continue with an expanded version of the standing Twist-roll-bend (158), alternately bending and circling your knees to one side, then extending your legs on the surface of the water before bending and circling your knees on the other side, breathing deeply throughout the movement, keeping your neck soft.

▷ **3** A more advanced version of this exercise is to roll over as your knees drop to the side, bringing your arm over to reach the bar or woggle so that you are now facing down and stretching on your front. Then bring your bent knees together under your body and turn them to the opposite side, opening your arm and lifting it to reach the bar or woggle so that you find yourself on your back once again. Roll three or four times in this way with a steady flow of your breath, enjoying a complete movement that involves all your spinal and abdominal muscles at once.

## 164 Snake bend

**The gentle bend of your back in this pose is soothing after stretches and twists, and you can use it as a counterpose and a rest. You can also, however, make it into a vigorous pose in its own right, using the movement of your shoulders and hips to propel yourself. You can practise the pose either with your head in water or above the surface. Whether you are a confident swimmer or not, you may wish to use a woggle at first to achieve a very relaxed stretch.**

**Deep breathing in this exercise makes it a powerful waist trimmer as you involve both your intercostal and dorsal muscles in the stretch. With each exhalation, you can tone the area between your ribs and your hip bones, with visible results after a few sessions at the pool.**

▽ **1** Start from a standing position and align your body on the surface of the water, floating face down. If you like, you can use a woggle to support your arms and keep your head above water and another to support your legs and help keep your back straight. Extend one side of your trunk at a time, elongating all the muscles.

▽ **2** Turn your head to the other side and stretch more, breathing as deeply as you can and keeping your bending side relaxed.

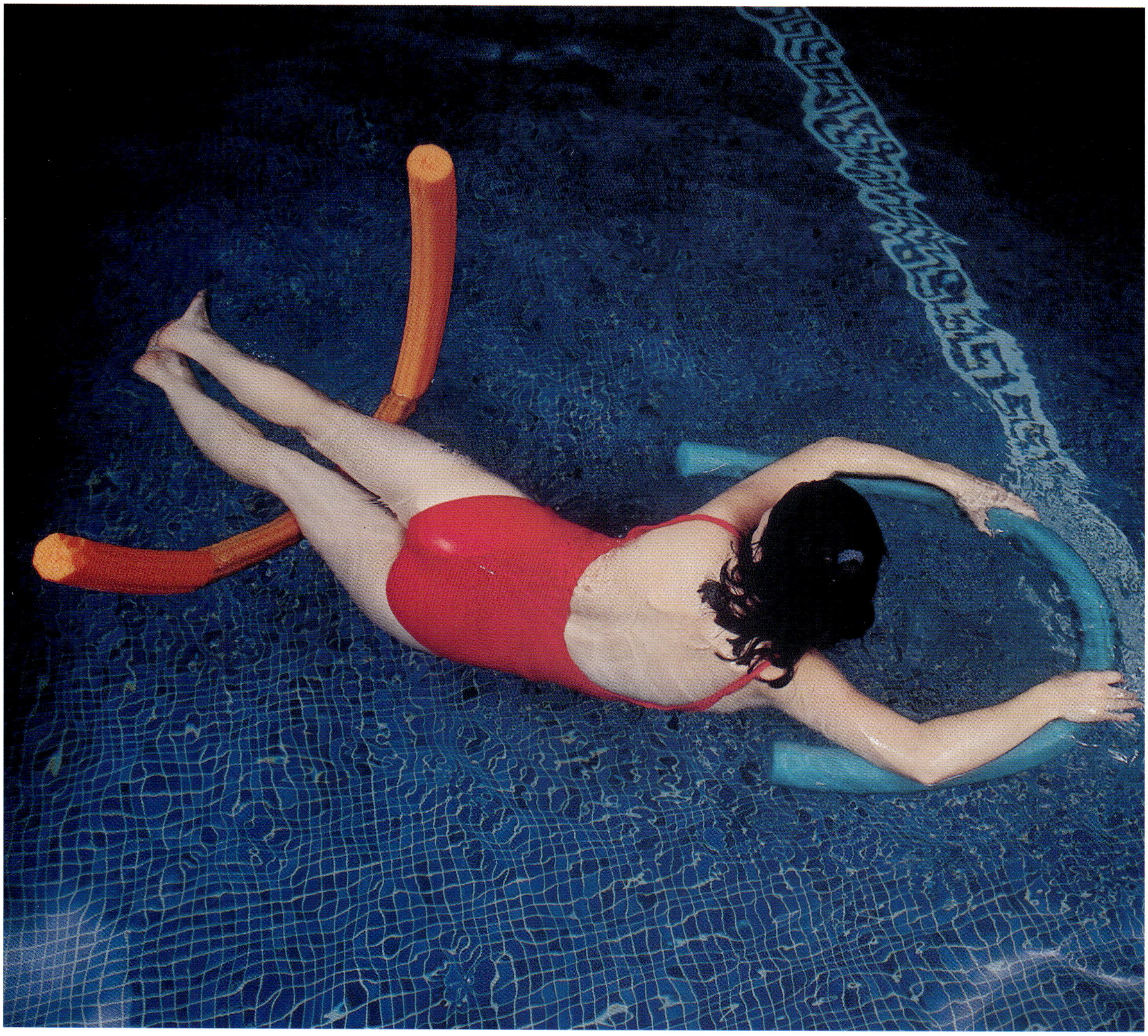

# Postnatal front crawl

If breaststroke and its leg movements were ideal to open the hips in pregnancy, front crawl is best to elongate the spine and tone the abdominal muscles of new mothers, whatever their birth experience has been. Front crawl is suitable for those who have had a Caesarean section if it is practised as aqua yoga, using the flow of breath combined with slow motion. This stroke helps new mothers to maintain the expanded breathing they have gained if they have done aqua yoga in pregnancy, and use it now to create new strength and stamina. For those starting aqua yoga postnatally, the goal is to use the full flow of the breath with the swimming movement and gain as much extension as possible with each stroke, rather than aiming at a speedy movement. This is a good stroke for reshaping your buttocks and legs after pregnancy and for elongating your whole body.

## 165 Leg movement only

**The leg movement of front crawl is most effective to tone the abdominal muscles postnatally if it is done in an aqua yoga way: that is, with the legs extended yet relaxed, and the alternate "kicking" motion of the feet coming from the ankles, with the feet remaining soft and relaxed like flippers throughout the movement. In this way the stretch extends via the legs to the abdominal muscles and the deeper muscles of the lower back that control leg movements. Combined with deep breathing, this movement involves and tones the whole body including the legs, trunk and arms.**

**It can be practised holding on to a bar or to the pool edge, which makes the kicking action more energetic, but it is best done holding on to a float or a woggle as it is less likely to be mechanical and stretches the whole body in movement. Make sure that your arms are fully stretched ahead of you, whatever you are holding on to.**

△ **1** Practise relaxing your legs more and more in the kicking action until you feel the movement extending your leg from the hip to your toes, keeping your ankles floppy. Experiment with various amplitudes of movement, from very small kicks just under the surface to a wider movement of your legs under water before your feet splash slightly on the surface.

## 166 Arm movement only

**To practise the arm movement, support your legs so that they remain motionless, with your feet under a bar, or on top of a woggle. You may also place a woggle under your thighs for more support. The movement is very vigorous if you have your feet under a bar but you will almost inevitably have your face in the water. With your feet on a woggle, you can keep your face above the surface, although your body is better aligned if the water comes to your forehead. Turn your face towards your arm to inhale, then exhale in the water as you complete your arm movement.**

**You make this practice "aqua yoga" by focusing on the extension of each arm, which should be as slow and complete as possible, accompanied by a long exhalation. Inhale on one side each time you extend your arm back on this side, but change sides regularly to avoid getting used to breathing always on the same side.**

◁ **1** Extend one arm behind you in a sweeping movement and bring it forward as far as you can alongside your ear, turning your hand outwards as it reaches the water. At the same time, start extending the other arm back with the same movement, so that you pull the water vigorously with each arm alternately to the side before extending it ahead.

◁ **2** If you are a confident crawl swimmer, keep your feet together and let them trail in a relaxed way close to the surface while you practise this arm movement as slowly as possible, extending your whole body with the stretch and concentrating on the flow of the breath.

## 167 Front crawl stretch

**After practising the leg and arm movements of front crawl separately, this stroke is easier to do in an aqua yoga way, with a slow and thorough extension of each side of the body in turn. There are several possible breathing rhythms you can adopt with this stroke. You can continue to expand your breathing capacity by inhaling on each second, third or fourth arm movement, extending your exhalation more and more.**

▷ **1** Stretch each arm to the fingertips and use a very relaxed propelling motion of the legs and feet.

# Postnatal back crawl

Back crawl is probably the best postnatal stroke. It suits most women as it does not involve having your face in the water as front crawl does. It has a direct and effective action on the abdominal muscles, thighs and buttocks. It can be practised effectively with supports even if you are not a confident swimmer, and you may get great satisfaction improving your performance rapidly by practising the leg and arm movements separately, making it aqua yoga rather than simply a swimming stroke.

A good alignment of the whole body, particularly of your head, neck and back, is essential to achieve both a relaxed stretch and optimum balance when the leg kick and the alternating arm pull are combined. The more relaxed you are in the movement then, the easier it is to gain a steady balance and a fluent arm movement. Give priority to breathing in both separate leg and arm movements. In the actual stroke, explore rhythms that give you the greatest free-flowing mobility.

## 168 Leg movement only

**If you start doing this leg movement less than four months after the birth, you may find it difficult to bring your feet to the surface. Persevere and try to keep your movement small, which is a challenge after your hips have become used to wide movements in late pregnancy. It is also important to keep your knees straight so that the legs are stretched yet relaxed at the same time. If you find that you cannot do this leg movement without bending your knees a little, keep practising and concentrate on the motions of your ankles and feet. Gradually, you will find that you become able to keep your legs extended while your feet make a small splash on the surface of the water.**

**Practise the movement holding on to a bar or a woggle or, if you need more support, use one or two woggles under your arms. You can also hold a float under your head as if it were a pillow. Alternatively, you can hold one or two floats on your abdomen with your hands crossed on top.**

△ Lie on your back in the water with your arms stretched out behind your head. Scissor your legs alternately in the water with a relaxed kicking motion of your feet, legs and ankles, remaining relaxed throughout. Breathe deeply in the movement, extending your exhalations as long as possible. Be aware of the effect of your leg kick on your abdominal muscles and modify it as the muscles that surround your uterus tone again month by month.

## 169 Arm movement only

**In this exercise priority is given to the opening of the chest and the use of the muscles under your ribcage in order to achieve a maximum stretch. Whether you are an accomplished swimmer or not, practising the arm movement of back crawl in this way will stretch each side of your whole body as you swim on your back.**

**If you are an experienced swimmer, you can do the arm movement in the aqua yoga way, keeping your feet together close to the surface. There is no need to tie your feet together and you may get a better stretch without using a foam block between your feet.**

**You can also practise with your feet under a bar or with the backs of your legs resting on a short woggle. A bar allows more stability and vigorous movement, while the woggle enables you to stretch more slowly and lightly. It is important that you extend your arms and hands in a line, all the way to the fingertips. Stretch to the tip of your middle finger. Find a rhythm of breathing that suits you, every two to four movements according to your capacity.**

△ Raise one arm with the palm of your hand facing toward your body and in the course of the upward movement, turn your hand so that it faces outward. Do this with a deep inhalation that opens your chest and make sure that your arm is as close to your ear as you can have it before you extend it behind you as far back as you can. By the time your hand approaches the water behind you, your arm is beginning its oblique pulling that propels you in the stroke. At the same time the other arm comes up with the same circular movement. Keep your chin tucked in so that you are able to see the opposite side of the pool, if not your own feet.

## 170 Back crawl stretch

**You can now combine the leg and arm movements in the stroke, but if you find that you remain relaxed and aligned in the separate movements but tense up when combining them in the stroke, it is preferable to continue practising the leg and arm movements separately. The more you stretch, the better you will eventually swim, besides gaining stamina and developing strong yet graceful muscles. Swimming in the slow lane, you will soon discover that you cover greater distances with a remarkable economy of movement, making full use of both the relaxed stretch in your arms and legs and your deep breathing.**

△ Give priority to your alignment and the alternate full stretching of your arms along your ears and back. Keep swimming very slowly, breathing as fully as possible and lengthening your exhalation gradually.

## 171 Rolling back crawl/front crawl

**If you enjoy performing the Screw Stretch (161) you may wish to roll and stretch from front crawl to back crawl. If you do it very slowly and breathe deeply as you stretch to your maximum, you are unlikely to get dizzy and you will probably enjoy the rolling motion of this twin stroke.**

△ Turn your shoulders over in each movement as you extend your arms alternately, one forward as in front crawl and then the other backward as in back crawl.

# Postnatal dolphin dives

During pregnancy, Dolphin Dives (49) are a way of feeling weightless with a broad undulating movement in the water. Indeed, close to the birth, it is even difficult sometimes to go under, and the most pleasant part of the dive is the middle part, before floating back up. After birth, the situation changes and you can enjoy streamlining your body again in the dives, stretching fully in a more vigorous movement that alternates bending and arching your middle spine. Practising these dives helps your back to gradually regain or acquire the flipping motion of the dolphin stroke, which is a perfect toner for back, abdominal and thigh muscles.

## 172 Dolphin dives (2)

**The alternate bending and arching of your back in succession enables you to take these dives with an even, flowing movement as you practise. Enjoy coming back towards the surface with a greater stretch which may remind you of the stretch-breathing you practised in late pregnancy, although now the feeling you have is quite different.**

**As you run out of your out breath, with your arms fully extended in front of you, keep stretching into your waist area. The emphasis is now on "stretch-relaxing" to get further stretch, rather than merely on relaxing as it was before birth. If you swim butterfly stroke, you may wish to first recover the movement of your lower back with dolphin dives before practising the leg movement of the butterfly stroke, holding on to a board with your extended arms.**

**Diving from the edge of the pool or from diving boards can be uncomfortable for some time after giving birth unless you are an experienced diver. Dolphin dives allow you to get ready for diving again in a gentle way. Once your baby is over four or five months, you can combine them with a Back Stretch (160), arching your back as you dive with your arms extended back.**

△ **1** Start standing free in the pool. Bend your knees and raise your arms over your head very straight as you inhale. Bend over toward the water and, as you get near, spring on your legs to take a small dive.

△ **2** As soon as you go under, stretch your lower back and open your chest.

△ **3** Let yourself come back up to the surface, keeping your arms extended right to the end of your exhalation. Then spring again on to your feet, inhale as you stretch and take another dive forward.

△ **4** You can choose to dive and "stretch-relax" quite close to the surface or go deeper, right to the bottom of the pool, wherever it feels best for you. You can also practise dolphin flips holding on to a board.

# Involving your baby

You can involve your baby in your postnatal aqua yoga practice practically from birth at home in your family bath. Many parents prefer to wait until their babies have been immunized before taking them to a public pool. Your baby is protected from polio with the first vaccine, but always follow your doctor's advice about full protection and be aware of your responsibility when you take a young baby to a pool. You are the best person to decide when to take your baby to the pool for the first time. If you have access to a warm, clean pool, the earlier the better.

It is enjoyable to swim with your baby, both as a continuation of your antenatal aqua yoga and because it is also the best introduction to swimming for your child. These pages offer suggestions for mothers who are confident in the water. The main challenge is to stay relaxed: if your baby falls off your body into the water, gently pick him or her up and continue. Your baby is likely to be more affected by your agitation than by being immersed. Many babies do not cry at all when they "go under". It is, however, a good idea to have someone with you when you take your baby to a pool, at least for the first few visits until you gain confidence. If your baby's first introduction to the pool is not a happy experience, do not be discouraged. Try again a week later.

Keep up your aqua yoga practice as your baby grows, whenever you go swimming in the months and years to come. It is one of the simplest and best forms of exercise, contributing to the prevention of sickness and a feeling of total well-being as well as the promotion of good health for your family as a whole.

## 173 Water stretches with your baby

**Postnatal stretches in water can be practised with your baby. You can hold your baby safely with both hands under the arms at first and then with one arm only. It is relatively easy to hold your baby against your body, facing out, with one of your arms across her chest extending to hold her arm between your thumb and index finger. Make sure you hold your baby in the most relaxed way you can and, whenever possible, allow her to find her own buoyancy in the water as well as relying on the support you give her.**

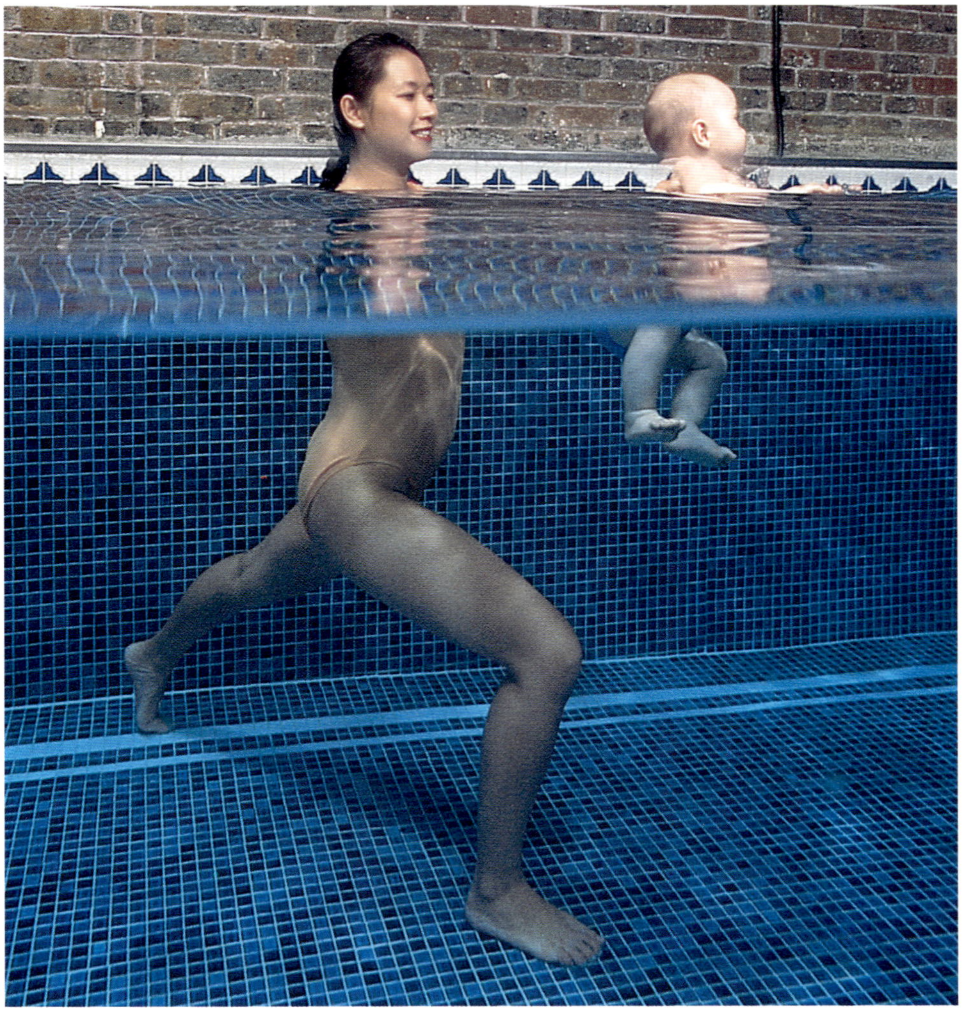

◁ Many classic yoga poses can be done in water with your baby as part of your postnatal routine. Having your legs in the water gives you a stable and supple base from which to stretch and tone your body in the posture. Practising the Warrior Pose with your baby gives you strength and stamina that are communicated to her too. Extend your back leg and breathe as deeply as you can in your abdominal muscles on a strong base.

## 174 Relaxed floating with baby on board

**Floating with your baby on your body is a marvellous feeling that completes all your practice of aqua yoga during pregnancy. When you are able to stretch back in the water and relax, if your baby is happy, let her lie freely on you, ready to hold her if needed only. You can also splash water gently on her body, which most babies find pleasurable. The more relaxed you are as you float, the better the experience for both of you.**

**You may ask your partner or a friend to give you support as you lower yourself in the water holding your baby, in the same way that you learnt to get into the position for Floating Relaxation (115). If you are on your own in a pool with a bar, you can use your feet under the bar as a departure point while you settle your baby on your body before taking your feet off to float. You can also have your baby resting on a float on top of you as you float on your back in the water, holding on to the sides of the board or to your baby's body on the board. In this case, your baby can be on her back, as described previously, or on her front, facing you. This may give you more confidence and some babies like it too. The body of a baby on a float will, however, be less immersed in the water than when resting on your body as you float, and you must make sure that the ambient temperature is high enough for comfort.**

△ Most young babies enjoy lying on their backs on their mothers' bodies and you may experience sensations of rest similar to those felt during your pregnancy relaxation in water, except that now your baby is outside rather than inside. The freer you are in water, the more enjoyable the relaxation is for you both.

△ At first, even if you can float, the idea of your baby falling off may cause you to tense up. It may therefore be best to start with a long woggle or even two woggles under your arms, which allow you to have your two hands free to support your baby gently on the sides of her body.

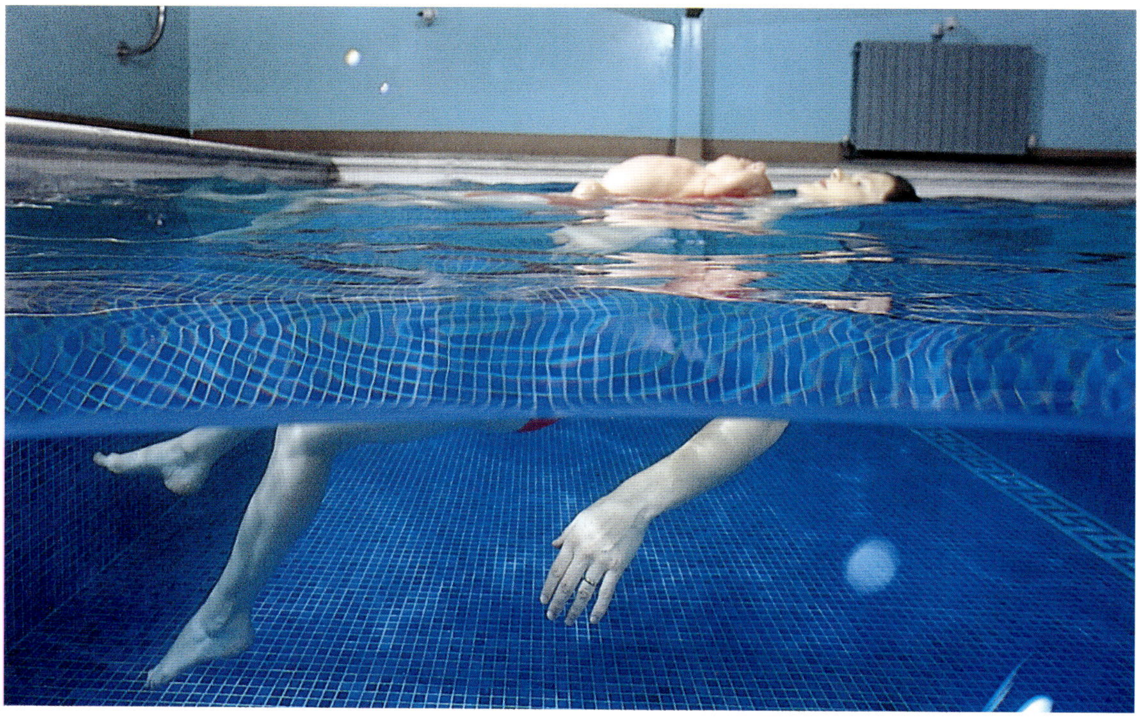

◁ At first you may prefer one foot to remain close to the pool floor to give you a feeling of security. However, if you can relax without any support with your baby on your body, then do so, as your baby is sensitive to the movement of your body and will be happy to enjoy the freedom water gives, yet be in close contact with you.

# postnatal yoga routines

After the joy of welcoming your baby into the world, you may remember the firmer, slimmer body of early pregnancy and wonder if, when and how you will wear those clothes again. Trust the power of the breath to tone the deepest muscles in your body. They are your best allies to developing not only a fine figure but also your future strength.

# Your first yoga routine





Every woman progresses at her individual rate, depending upon many factors: how well she is after the birth, how dedicated she is to her yoga practice, how busy her life is, and how well the baby is settling down. Some days flow smoothly while others seem to snarl up. The most important thing is to do what you can – today. Yoga is totally non-judgmental, so to compare yesterday with today is pointless. Every day is an opportunity to progress towards greater pelvic strength, better alignment of the spine, deeper relaxation, more serenity and inner balance. The weeks after giving birth bring huge changes, physically, emotionally and mentally. Your aim is to relax and heal, to energize and tone your body, your emotions and your mind. Regular deep breathing will keep you on course even when your emotions are all over the place. Above all, make time for rest.

If you have just a few minutes to spare, remember that relaxation comes before stretching. Alternate Nostril Breathing (4) is instantly relaxing – you will stretch all the better afterwards. If you are interrupted, take a few deep slow breaths to give your practice a completion.

## yoga in the first six weeks

The routines here include postures on the floor (lying down, sitting and kneeling) and a few standing postures. Exercises can be practised on their own, or one page or more at a time.

Make sure that you do not do too much, too soon. The exercises included in this section are designed for the first six weeks after giving birth. You can continue, with great benefit, to do them for the rest of your life. But please do not go beyond them, to the next stage, until six weeks have passed. Even then, please wait if you do not feel ready for new challenges. It is far better to practise simple routines regularly, and to grow stronger and more relaxed, than to push yourself too fast and become stressed.

## 175 Legs up the wall

**Even if the birth was relatively easy and you feel fit and well, take time to practise your Reverse Breathing (141) with your legs raised. If your birth was difficult, or you had a Caesarian section, it is important to tone your inner muscles with deep breathing. In the position below, the floor and wall will give you a solid support to help you to expand your abdominal breathing.**

△ **1** Sit sideways against the wall. The aim is to place your legs parallel against the wall.

△ **2** Bend the knee nearest to the wall, leaning back on your hands.

△ **3** Swivel round on your bottom, leaning back now on your forearms. Straighten your legs and move your upper body round.

▷ **4** You should be lying in a straight line with your legs together, hands on your abdomen. Flex your toes, lifting your heels, to strengthen your legs.

△ **5** You can strengthen your abdominal muscles by bending one knee and placing the sole of your foot on the wall, then repeating with the other leg. Remember that, after giving birth, you are working to close your body, so keep your legs together to tone your inner thigh muscles more effectively.

△ **6** Once settled in this position, you can include your baby. He or she will enjoy closeness with you, lying peacefully against your heart. Without even moving, you are using the calm power of your deep breathing to tone the lower back and abdominal muscles.

# abdominal and lower back muscles

After your baby is born, lying flat on your back again is a new feeling. It is also the first, the safest and the best way to re-align your spine and tone the pelvic muscles in depth after giving birth. Feel your lower back settle into the floor and open up. One or both knees stay bent at all times to protect your lower back and ensure that you remain relaxed while you stretch. As your uterus returns to its normal size, yoga breathing allows toning through all the layers of abdominal muscles.

## 176 Knees to chest

**In this exercise, Reverse Breathing (141) is used to tone the muscles of the lower back, together with the pelvic floor. Vaginal tone is also improved. If you have had a Caesarian section, do the first part – no. 1, below – only, for several weeks.**

△ **1** Lie on your back with your knees bent and your feet flat on the floor. Stay comfortable and relaxed. Breathe freely in your abdomen.

△ **2** Clasp your hands below your knees and, using Reverse Breathing, breathe in, drawing your pelvic floor muscles up, then further up as you exhale. Release.

◁ **3** Inhale again and pull your thighs closer towards the chest as you breathe out, bringing your waist down toward the floor and widening your upper back. Repeat a few times.

## 177 Leg over

**This exercise introduces a gentle twist which helps tone your transverse abdominal muscles as you practise your yoga breathing.**

▷ Straighten one leg along the floor and place your other foot outside it, bending your knee. Place both hands on your abdomen. Breathe deeply, drawing your abdominal muscles in toward your spine as you exhale, and pressing your feet on the floor.

# upper back and shoulder muscles



The exercises on this page aim to tone the dorsal muscles that were supporting your baby inside you, in your "bump". It may seem both enjoyable and strange to feel and regain ownership of this space with your yoga breathing. If your baby is awake you can welcome him or her into your practice. Yes, baby, here you are, out in the world, but still close to your mother.

## 178 Hug yourself

**This exercise helps to open your upper back and at the same time to recover the sense of your body as your own after giving birth.**

◁ Fold your arms across your chest, with fingertips on opposite shoulders. Hug yourself and breathe deeply, feeling the expansion in the back. As you exhale, press the base of your spine on the floor and let your whole back spread out.

## 179 Side stretch

**This stretch elongates your spinal muscles. As you breathe more and more deeply between your hips and your ribcage, feel your waistline again.**

▷ Straighten one leg along the floor. Bring the arm on the same side over your head and stretch it along the floor behind you. The whole of this side of your body should feel stretched and open. As you breathe in, flex your foot and stretch your arm, extending from heel to fingertips. Stretch more as you breathe out. Release and relax. Repeat several times, then change sides and repeat with the other leg and arm. You can also stretch diagonally, extending the opposite arm and leg first one way and then the other, and breathing in the same way.

## 180 Namaste

**The pressure of the hands held together in this Indian greeting allows you to breathe more deeply in your upper and middle back. At the same time, you build up inner strength in your open heart area.**

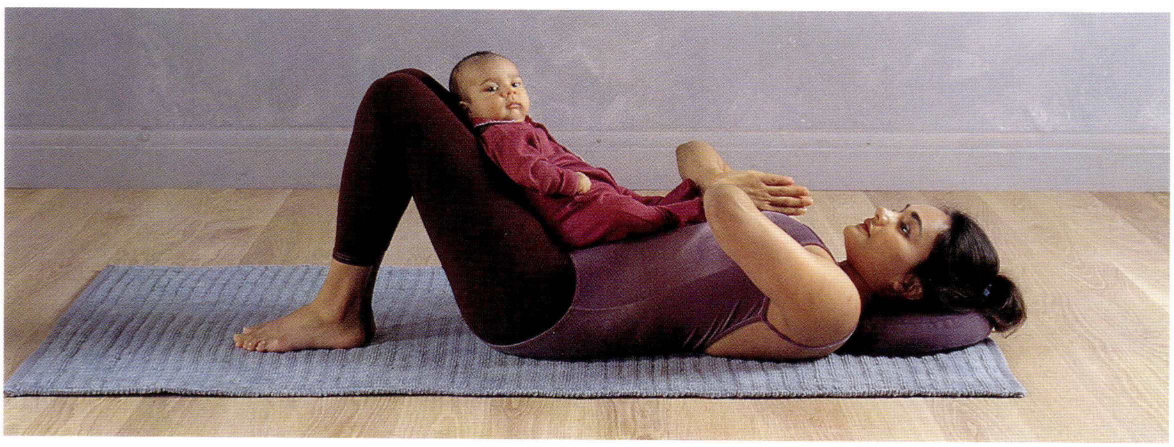

◁ Lying down with your knees bent, join your palms together in front of your heart, in the prayer position. Inhale and press on your palms as you breathe out slowly. Feel the upper back and shoulder muscles strengthening and the front of the chest lifting. At the end of the practice, relax and greet the moment as it is.

# Regaining strength and stamina





As you practise the stretches that follow, use Reverse Breathing (141), which will help you stay relaxed and to stretch further. If any area feels tight or tense, breathe out into it to relax it before continuing. Start your stretch from the lower back or pelvis – that is where strength enters, with the breath in. Keep your body relaxed so that you experience the flow of breath while you are stretching.

## 181 For leg and abdominal muscles

**Lie on the floor, reclining against a beanbag or other support. Make sure that your lower back is well supported and your shoulders and neck can stay relaxed. This is a flowing movement in which your legs alternately extend and bend with a relaxed stretch, toning the whole abdomen. If you are able to stretch your legs completely without tensing your abdominal muscles at this stage, you can do so.**

◁ **1** Inhale as you extend your relaxed leg up.

△ **2** Then bend your knee.

△ **3** Exhale slowly as you extend your leg towards the floor. Extend your leg up again as you inhale and enjoy a smooth circle of movement and breath.

## 182 For abdominal and pelvic floor muscles, lying down

**Practise this exercise as often as you can. Lie on the floor with your legs propped up on a beanbag or other support.**

▷ Bend one knee towards your chest and clasp both hands around your shin. As you breathe out, press your knee to your chest while you also pull your navel up and back toward your spine. This makes your chest widen at the back and lift at the front. Release the pull on your leg before you breathe in again. Repeat a few times, then change legs.

## 183 For abdominal and pelvic floor muscles, sitting

**Sit on a cushion on a firm chair. If you have a Caesarean scar, place a large, soft cushion on your lap to protect your abdomen. Keep your back very straight and your waist against the chair back.**

△ Pull your knee to your chest, pressing your foot on the chair. Use Reverse Breathing (141) pulling your knee towards the chest on the breath out. Repeat several times on each side. Keep your face soft and your neck relaxed.

## 184 For upper back muscles, lying down

**Lie on the floor with your legs on a beanbag or a pile of cushions for similar support. Make sure your lower back is comfortable on the floor; if it is not, raise it with a pillow. Relax both your lower back and your legs.**

◁ **1** Raise one arm as you breathe in. Stretch it up and then behind your head as you breathe out slowly. Flop the arm back to your side at the end of your out breath.

◁ **2** Repeat with your other arm. After a few rounds, work with both arms together. Make sure you keep the back of your waist in contact with the floor throughout, even if you cannot reach the floor behind you with your arms.

## 185 Wall stretch

**Many new mothers find that the weight of their enlarged breasts makes their upper back droop and ache. If you feel like this, this stretch will help you extend your spine and use deep abdominal breathing to tone and open your back muscles. It also helps prevent mastitis as the overall circulation in the breasts is improved.**

△ **1** With your knees hip-width apart, kneel on a cushion in front of a wall so that when your hands are flat on the wall, your spine is straight.

△ **2** Keeping your coccyx tucked in, let your hands slide down the wall very slowly while you breathe as deeply as possible.

△ **3** Feel your whole spine stretch as you sit on your heels. Continue to elongate your spine for a few breaths. Repeat for a few rounds, or rest.

# Spinal stretch





After extending your spine on the floor in the lying down exercises, sitting postures practised on a chair enable you to stretch further and strengthen your lower back from the base of the spine. Sitting upright will also help you to practise Reverse Breathing (141) and pelvic floor lifts more intensely against gravity, as you are working.

## 186 Sunwheel stretch

**Sit on an upright chair with your spine erect and feet planted firmly on the floor. Pull your spine upwards from its base to the crown of your head. Keep your neck long and your shoulders down and relaxed.**

▷ **1** Breathe in. With your out breath, push your palms down toward the floor, fingers facing out to the sides and wrists bent back in line with your spine. Your shoulder blades draw closer together and your chest expands. Push as if you were moving air currents away from you on the out breath.

△ **2** Bend your elbows and raise your hands higher as you breathe in, then repeat the downward movement, pushing more on the out breath.

△ **3** Next time you breathe out, push your palms out to your sides at chest level. Keep a flowing movement, breathing in and out.

△ **4** As you breathe in your hands are now above your shoulders, opening your upper back and stretching your chest and arm muscles.

△ **5** Turn your hands out and lift higher and further on your out breath, opening the rib cage. Enjoy your full span, stretching to your fingertips.

△ **6** On the next round, lift your arms straight up above your head, stretching more as you breathe in. Start your downward wheel by reversing the steps, breathing in your own rhythm with a slow movement.

△ **7** When you have completed your sunwheel, bring your hands together into a seated Namaste (180) position. Press the palms together and breathe quietly, enjoying the effects of this sequence on your whole back.

# Gentle twists and bends sitting on a chair

Twisting movements are central to yoga. They are powerful toners, firming the body from inside out in the abdomen and around the waist. Practised gently to begin with after giving birth, twists and their counterparts, forward bends, are very effective means to help new mothers "close" their body again after opening it to grow their babies and give birth.

Yoga twists start from the base of the spine, involving the lumbar area and then progressively the whole back. They stimulate the functioning of all the organs, as the leverage helps you breathe more intensely in the abdomen and chest together. It is usual to twist to the right first, then to the left, as this sequence follows the line of flow in the large intestine. In sitting twists, make sure you keep the spine stretched up as you twist, from the lower back to the shoulders. The head follows rather than leads this upward slow movement, which you expand with your breathing. Twisting is always done on the out breath, and with each out breath, you twist a little further. Today's limit will seem easy after only a week's practice, but never force, just let the extension come.

## 187 Simple twist on chair

**The first twist can be practised soon after giving birth to regain your awareness of your waist. It also opens the chest, which helps when you start feeding.**

△ **1** Allow your right arm to hang down loosely by your side. Place the back of your left hand against the outside of your right thigh. This hand is your lever: press it against your thigh to help you to twist to the right. As you breathe out, start the twist at the base of the spine and continue it all the way up, so that your neck and face turn last, and you are looking over your right shoulder. Release the twist a little as you breathe in, then increase it as you breathe out again. You can make this simple twist stronger by holding the back of your chair with your right hand. You now have two levers to help you, pushing away from your left hand and pulling toward your right hand. Come back slowly, to face front, as you breathe in.

△ **2** When you have finished, bend your right knee and pull your shin toward your chest as you breathe out. Then twist and bend to the left side. Repeat all these twisting movements to the left.

## 188 Circling one arm

**This is a gentle stretching twist that counters the tension of feeding and stretches the spine. Do it often.**

△ **1** Sit upright on your chair, with the back of your left hand outside your right thigh. Stretch out your right arm behind you.

△ **2** Breathing deeply, make a slow circling movement with the extended arm. Repeat on the other side. Then, use your right hand as the lever as you twist to the left and circle your left arm.

## 189 Crossing your legs

**This twist allows a long diagonal stretch that is invigorating.**

△ Cross your left leg over your right knee and – if you can – tuck your toes behind your right calf. Use your left hand as the lever, pressing it against the outside of your right thigh. Twist to the right, circling your right arm in a wide sweep up in front and down behind you, breathing deeply. Repeat on the other side.

## 190 Forward bend (1)

**Bending forward after giving birth may feel slightly uncomfortable at first. You have not been able to bend for a long time, and now bending may remind you that your body has changed. Trust that yoga will help you tone your body in depth day by day. If you have had a Caesarian section, place a pillow on your lap before bending forward.**

▷ When you have finished the twisting movements, relax completely. Extend your right foot along the floor and ease your lower back by flopping forward, breathing out. Extend your arms to your shins, ankles or, if you can, to your toes. Repeat with the left foot, and then extend both feet, breathing deeply with long, slow, relaxing breaths out.

# Standing twists with a chair





The arm movements for this sequence are the same as for the twists sitting on a chair, but this time you should stand in front of the chair with your right foot placed firmly upon the seat. Make sure that the chair is the correct height for your knee to be bent at a right angle with your standing leg straight. There are two twists: "open" and "closed".

Only practise the "closed" twist when you are comfortable with the full extension of the "open" twist. In standing twists, the whole torso turns and extends following the circling of the arm. The leverage of the arms helps you to draw in your pelvic floor muscles as you twist.

## 191 Open twist

**In this twist, one arm is used as a lever on the inside of the same leg to allow the trunk to open and rotate.**

◁ Place one foot on the chair with the back of your hand acting as a lever on the inside of your thigh. Twist away from the raised leg and circle your other arm. Repeat on the other side. Breathe deeply as you circle your arms, always using the out breath to twist further with the stretch.

## 192 Closed twist (1)

**In this twist, one arm is used as a lever on the outside of the opposite leg to bring about a more intense rotation at the base of the spine. As the trunk turns, the kidneys and abdominal organs are activated and exercised.**

△ Place one foot on the chair with your opposite hand as a lever on the outside of your thigh, then twist towards the raised leg and circle your free arm. Repeat on the other side. Keep your chest very open.

△ After doing standing twists it is a good idea to lie down with one or both knees bent for a short rest. It will soon be playtime!

# Relieving tension in the back





The floor twist can be practised either as a gentler completion of a sequence of sitting and standing twists, or just on its own to relieve tension in the back whenever you need it. Sometimes this may be several times a day... If you have not had time to do a full yoga sequence, the lying down twist is a good exercise to do before going into a deep relaxation.

## 193 Floor twist

**Before doing the twist on the floor, ease your lower back by bending your knees and rolling gently on the small of your back.**

▷ **1** Place your hands at the back of your thighs, just below your knees. Practise Reverse Breathing (141), breathing in and pulling the perineum up. Draw your knees closer to your chest, breathing out as you pull your waist back and open the back. Repeat a few times to loosen up your lower and middle back.

◁ **2** Extend your left arm along the floor. Feel the upper back widening and the shoulder relaxing. Gravity is your lever here – the relaxed weight of your upper body and left arm pin you to the floor. Breathe in and, on the out breath, drop your bent legs to the right with your right hand supporting their weight. If you are flexible enough, your legs and feet may come to rest on the floor. If so, leave them there for a few breaths. To make the twist stronger, you can also turn your head towards your extended arm.

▷ **3** Breathe in to bring your legs back to the starting position over your chest, using your right hand to help lift their weight. Repeat the movement to the left and continue several times on each side. Relax with your knees bent to finish.

# Basic kneeling sequence

These movements strengthen and relax the whole body. They will give you a good workout, improving flexibility and lifting your spirits. The movements should be learnt separately, then practised as a routine that flows with the rhythm of your natural breathing. If you have done yoga before, you may recognize a kneeling version of the "sun salute". In this version, you remain close to the floor to avoid straining your abdominal muscles, which are not yet ready for the full sequence. The exercises are also complete in themselves and can be practised separately. Always relax at the end of the kneeling sun salute. You can return to the Swan Pose and rest or lie in Shavasana (197). Try to get into the habit of relaxing, even for a minute, after completing every sequence.

## 194 Swan pose

**In this relaxing pose, the stretched arms help you breathe more deeply in the middle and lower back. This can be very soothing.**

▷ **1** Relax and stretch in this pose, sitting on your heels. Extend your fingers forward for maximum stretch. Press on your hands when you exhale.

◁ **2** Bending your right arm so that your forearm can rest on the floor, stretch your left arm forward as far as you can, extending your fingers. At the same time, allow your spine to extend backwards, breathing into the stretch which reaches from your hand to the base of the spine. Change sides and repeat.

▷ **3** Bend your elbow to open your chest fully. Rotate the shoulder, breathing into the circular movement of your bent arm. Replace your forearm on the floor and work the other side. Change sides and repeat. Rest afterwards with your head and arms down, as before, if you feel tired.

## 195 Cat pose

**This is an easy way to stretch your spine. In a steady "on all fours" position, alternate an upward and downward circling of the back together with an inhalation and an exhalation.**

△ **1** Come on to all fours, with your back flat. Your knees should be hip-width apart: the hip directly over the knee and the shoulder over the wrist. Spread your fingers for good support. Breathing in, arch your spine and tuck your head in.

△ **2** Breathing out, flatten your back at the waist and look up. Repeat. If you wish, you can create a flowing movement, bending your arms to roll back and forth in the stretch.

## 196 Leg stretches

**Lower backache is common in the weeks after giving birth. Leg stretches can both prevent and ease tension, particularly around the sciatic nerve.**

△ **1** Starting in the Cat Pose (195), breathe in and bring one bent knee forward towards your face, keeping the calf muscle and foot relaxed.

△ **2** Breathing out, stretch that leg out behind you (keeping it relaxed). Your body, from crown to heel, stretches in a straight line. Extend your out breath as much as possible.

◁ **3** Turn your extended foot in and drop it on the floor, relaxing your leg and trailing it limply, allowing the hip to drop. From this position, bring your bent knee forward again to repeat the three steps several times. Then change legs.

# Healing relaxation from six weeks





> "As I sit quietly with you my child, I ask that I be made a strong and loving parent. May your life always be filled with light."

This relaxation is not just to recover from your exertions after a yoga session or to rest after a disturbed night. It is for healing, and for integrating the whole experience of pregnancy and childbirth into your life.

The period of six weeks after giving birth is known as "postpartum". The six-week point signals the ending of one phase and the start of another, as you cease to be a "new" mother and become instead a mother. As you pass from one stage to the next it is important to avoid taking any unnecessary physical or emotional baggage with you. You want to move on feeling healed and whole, ready to enjoy your baby.

Six weeks is about the average time it takes to recover from giving birth. For you it may be shorter or longer – you will know when you have reached this dividing line. But even when the birth experience is many months behind you it is still a good idea to do this focused relaxation from time to time. It helps you to assess how well you are moving on into the flow of your life, and free remaining areas of tension.

## conscious surrender

This pose seems very simple, but it involves considerable body awareness, which only comes with practice. Breathe the tension away, then move on to visualizing your happy scene in which you are experiencing total well-being.

From that contented space, look at any unhappy feelings that sometimes afflict you. Be brave and honest with yourself. Acknowledge your own feelings of tiredness and low spirits. Accept them as part of how your life is, and how you are.

We are all just as we are. Judgement and perfectionist standards (your own or anyone else's) have no place here. Simply soothe and care for yourself, just as you would for a dear friend who came to you for loving support. Be your own dearest and most reliable friend – and learn to accept help from this source of inner strength.

You may become aware of other feelings, too. Unacknowledged anger is common: anger at the disruption to your life since your baby was born, anger at feeling disorganized, anger at other people, anger at having to put aside your own interests. These are just a few of the issues that may come up. You may also experience feelings of sadness: grief for the time before you had responsibilities, or

**▽ As you quieten the body and the mind in stillness, allow this conscious relaxation to free you from fluctuating emotions.**

for the loss of your own childhood, or for those golden days when you never seemed to run out of energy.

Mixed emotions are normal at this stage, around six weeks after the birth. They may come as the result of changes in lifestyle, or hormonal changes as your body returns to its pre-pregnant state, or a mixture of both. The first step in dealing with any such feelings is to admit that you feel them. Then tell your "inner friend" all about your sad or angry feelings and ask for understanding, support and healing. These are already there for you – you have only to ask. Emotional burdens can be lifted from you simply by acknowledging them and sharing them with that "inner friend" who loves you and whom you know you can trust. Be humble and true to yourself as you do this.

Having accepted and then released your negative feelings, you can fully experience and share all your feelings of love and joy. Take time to allow them to surface. Tell your baby of your great love, and tell the other members of your family that you love them, too. Draw them all together into the circle of your love. Recognize and be grateful for the deep joy that is welling up within you and radiating outwards to everyone around you. Breathe gently in and out of your heart space for a few moments.

When you are ready, let the vision fade away. Become aware of your breathing and expand it slowly until you are back in focus. Then move your fingers and toes. Finally, s-t-r-e-t-c-h and yawn before starting to sit up. Remember that the deeper your state of relaxation, the more important it is to come out of it slowly.





## 197 Shavasana

**Refer back to the basic relaxation technique, although by now it should be second nature to you. Your position should be a comfortable one that you can maintain without moving. Shavasana, or the Corpse Pose, is a classic yoga relaxation pose. Once you are settled and comfortable, avoid any further movements. Close your eyes and just let go. Scan your body from the inside and, wherever you find any tension, melt it away and nurture that space. Do the same with any images or emotions that arise, connected with your birthing experience.**

**To come out of the pose, expand your breath gently but steadily, until you feel drawn to open your eyes effortlessly. Feel your body come back into focus. Then stretch before you sit up. Relaxation is progressive – each time you practise, it helps you to go deeper next time.**

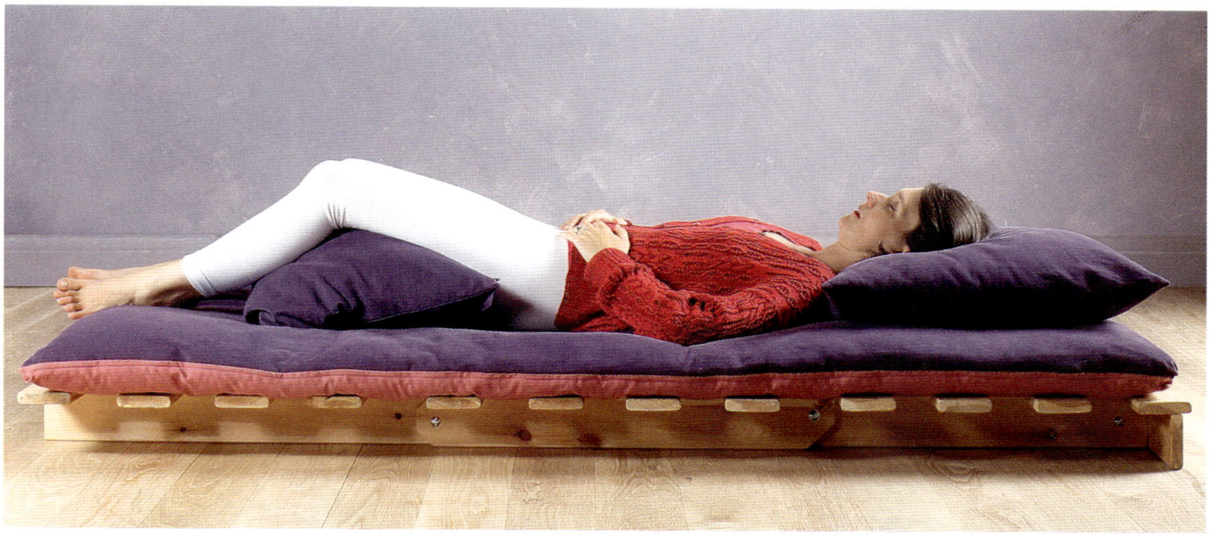

◁ Lie down comfortably, at a time when you can expect to be undisturbed for at least 10 minutes – hopefully longer.

◁ If it is more comfortable, you can have your head and shoulders supported by a beanbag or pillow. Relaxation can be practised in bed when you need it.

# Pulling up





Realigning the spine after giving birth may take time and dedication. But persevere because it is a very important process which lays the foundation for your future well-being as it may determine your long term posture. "Standing tall" refers not only to having a straight back, but also to using your pelvic floor, abdominal muscles and lower back muscles to hold your pelvis in perfect alignment with your spine. Then stretching becomes truly beneficial... You will look and feel amazing.

## 198 Tadasana: standing tall

**This is a classic yoga pose and is used as a starting position for many others. With a vertical support, use your awareness in this pose to realign the spine after pregnancy. You can line yourself up against a wall or the edge of a door, to get into the correct position, and then take a step away without losing your "line". Reverse Breathing (141) will greatly assist you.**

△ **1** With your knees loosely bent and your feet a foot's length away from the door or wall, line up your spine all along its length. Pull up the lower abdominal muscles as you breathe in. Bring the waist back and open the chest as you breathe out. Draw your chin and neck back.

△ **2** Bring your heels close to the door. With your hands, explore the hollow behind your waist. Bend your knees slightly, more if you have done yoga before, to align your spine. Remove your hands. Use Reverse Breathing (141), to strengthen your back muscles, drawing in your pelvic floor muscles – deep as you inhale and further as you exhale.

◁ **3** After breathing in position 2 for a while, straighten your legs again and stand tall against the door. Check your best position today. Breathe deeply, feeling your alignment. Every day will be different.

◁ **4** After doing this you can also practise standing on one leg and circling the other foot inward and outward, exercising your ankles and feet arches.

# Protecting your lower back

Babies soon get heavy and it is easy to strain yourself when lifting and carrying them around, particularly in seats and carriers. Remember that your abdominal muscles are likely to be overstretched from giving birth, so they cannot do their normal job of protecting your lower back. Compensate for any weakness by making the best use of your leg muscles and upper back.



## 199 Standing up, holding your baby

**Your baby may join you on the floor while you practise your yoga, change a nappy, or breastfeed between sequences. Several times a day, practise getting up from the floor, and getting down, holding your baby with your back strong and straight. You will soon develop strength and poise.**

△ **1** Kneel, then rise on to one knee, using your arms and upper back to support the baby's weight.

△ **2** Take your weight on to your front leg, turning the toes of your back foot under, and rise.

△ **3** Straighten your knees only after your spine is erect and you feel balanced.

## 200 Bathing your baby

**It is common for new mothers to strain their backs while bathing their babies. Yoga helps you to develop an awareness of the way in which you reach forward and can lift your baby most easily.**

△ **1** Kneel on one knee, as close to the bath as possible, with a towel at the ready.

△ **2** Take a deep in breath as you lift your baby, completing the lift on an out breath.

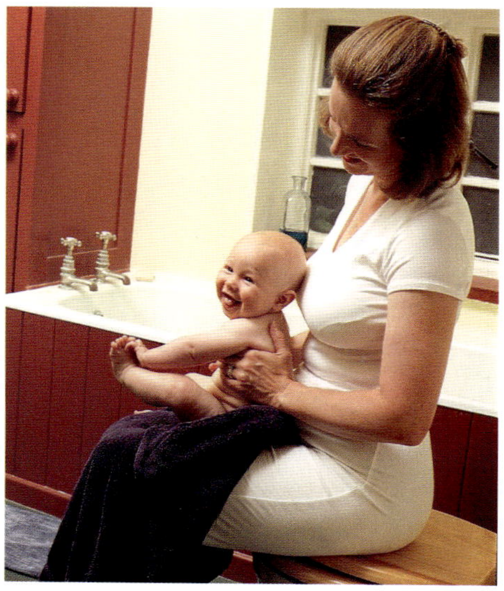

△ **3** Sit upright as you dry the baby.

# Yoga every day

Once the basic techniques in this section have become really familiar to you, any spare time can be used for yoga. Here are some suggestions, and you will soon discover other ideas yourself. Be creative! Remember to use Reverse Breathing (141), and to practise your deep relaxation daily. Always rest for a few moments after yoga breathing and stretching.

## yoga breathing

Get into the habit of using Reverse Breathing (141) at any time of the day or night, whatever position you happen to be in. Every breath in draws the energy of life – of vitality and healing – into the abdominal cavity to strengthen and tone the stretched muscles of the perineum and abdomen. Every long breath out allows the energy of love – of openness and relationship – to lift the chest and the spirits and to open the upper back and the heart space. As these two aspects of universal energy blend, and flow up the spine to the crown of the head, you feel a light energy in and around you. Your mind becomes focused, clear and serene and your posture upright and confident.

The benefits seem purely physical at first but, as you continue to practise, you will find that deep and beneficial changes occur; you you are being healed at many levels. This is the magic of yoga.

## relaxation

This is an essential part of any yoga session. Always include a resting position after every sequence and a relaxation at the end of your session. Rest is healing and deep relaxation will replace lost sleep. Alternate Nostril Breathing (4) is a quick and effective way to centre yourself at any time, and a good way to begin each yoga session.

## good posture

Use Reverse Breathing to help draw yourself upright every time you feel that you are drooping. Use your upper back and leg muscles to take the strain off your abdominal and lower back muscles.

## stretches

Always start your stretches from the lower back. Avoid tensing your legs or arms – stay loose and use your breath to extend further.

## 201 Minding your posture in the kitchen

**While you are waiting for the kettle to boil, or for something to finish cooking, you can realign your posture and practise Reverse Breathing (141) to tone your abdominal muscles in depth from the pelvic floor.**

△ **1** Strengthen your thigh muscles by bending your knees. You can support yourself by bending your elbows behind you and leaning on a table or chair back.

△ **2** Bend and straighten your knees, keeping your spine erect and your chest open. As you stand up, inhale and lift, exhaling as you bend.

◁ You can lean against a wall in any spare moment, drawing up your spine and keeping it in contact with the wall.

▷ Remember your posture when doing housework. Aim to keep your knees bent and your spine erect. Bend your knees before leaning forward or lifting anything.

△ Stand in front of a long mirror from time to time to check your progress.

△ Stop, relax and enjoy life whenever you can – it is time well spent, time that will not return. Babies grow very quickly and the days rush by.

# postnatal yoga six to twelve weeks

Rest, more rest and relaxation come before exercise. Each yoga posture becomes a therapy in itself that stimulates but also calms you, energizes but also nurtures you in a comfortable, effortless way. Take time to watch your body rhythms and your feelings as you stretch more without ever straining, letting your breathing guide you.

# Six to twelve weeks after birth





"Nothing prepared me for the highs and the lows, the challenges, the defeats and the victories. It took weeks to become a mother and still be who I am."

The next set of exercises is more demanding, and should provide just what you need from six weeks to twelve weeks after giving birth. You will have had your postnatal check-up and are now probably ready to move on to some more classical yoga.

Everyone is different, however, and you should consider the progress you feel you have made before moving on. You may have practised less than you would have liked over the last six weeks. You may feel that you still need to stick with the earlier routines for a while longer, for any number of reasons. If this is the case, continue with the exercises you are already practising until you feel truly ready to move on.

The yoga techniques described in this chapter form the foundation for ongoing physical, emotional and mental well-being. One of the ancient yoga texts emphasizes that, "In yoga no effort, however small, is ever wasted." However advanced you may become in your yoga practice, you should still make time to stretch and relax daily, and you should always be conscious of your breathing and your posture. It takes only a minute to practise a few reverse breaths, pulling yourself up from the perineum to the crown and opening your chest and your heart space. Get into the habit of doing this several times every day, wherever you happen to be.

The routines in this section will help you to consolidate the realignment of your spine, and the pelvic strength you have recovered since giving birth. Some more yoga "asanas" (poses) will be introduced, as well as vigorous limbering sequences that really get the energy flowing. You will continue to breathe deeply and to make relaxation your priority – this is an essential ingredient within every movement as well as during your rest afterwards.

Sometimes you may have only a few moments to spare. If your baby needs your attention when you are in the middle of a routine, go back to your starting position and take a deep breath out to relax. Then smile, as you go to greet your baby.

**▽ As you get ready for more active yoga, remember that relaxation is the foundation for renewing your strength and stamina from within. Keep using the relaxations from the first section.**

# More advanced reverse breathing



The following positions – described in order of difficulty – allow you to get a really good "grip" on your pelvic floor muscles as you breathe in and out. You are now using the buttock muscles too. After pregnancy, they may be unfamiliar to you. First become aware of the power of your buttock muscles, tightening them and then releasing them, before practising the exercises on this page.

## 202 Standing against the wall

**Tightening your buttock muscles intensifies the "pulling up" that you practised in Tadasana (198).**

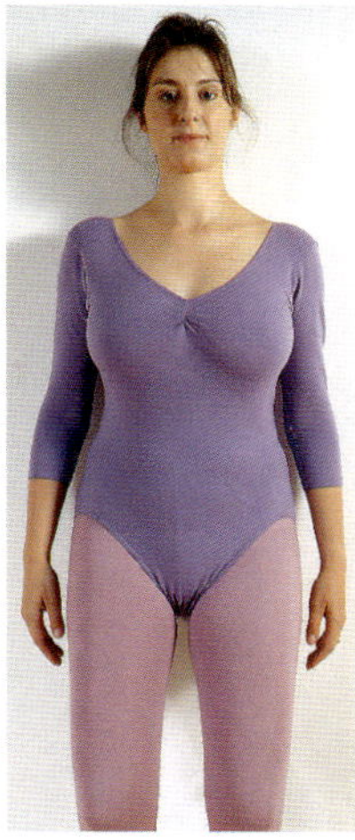

◁ **1** Stand with your heels a short distance away from a wall. Then place your spine against the wall, keeping your knees bent. Tightening your buttocks, breathe in and pull the pelvic floor up. Hold the grip as you breathe out, then relax all the muscles. Repeat several times.

◁ **2** For a more extreme posture, raise your arms against the wall as you breathe in and repeat the exercise several times.

## 203 Raising the hips

**Tightening your buttock muscles as well as practising Reverse Breathing (141) makes this apparently easy raising of the hips from the floor a very powerful toner.**

△ **1** Lie on the floor with your knees bent and feet flat on the floor, hip-width apart. Lengthen the back of your neck and keep your chin tucked in throughout. Place your arms alongside your body, palms down, to support you.

△ **2** As you breathe in, lift your pelvis up from the floor as high as you comfortably can, keeping your inner knees in a straight line. Grip the base of your spine with your buttock muscles and hold as you breathe out. Lift your pelvic floor again as you breathe in again, then relax as you breathe out.

△ **3** On your next in breath, release the buttock muscles and lower your pelvis slowly to the floor, lengthening your spine as far towards your heels as possible. Repeat several times.

## 204 Lying prone

**This position is one that you won't have been able to achieve for some time while pregnant. Now, it offers you a different angle for pelvic floor lifts.**

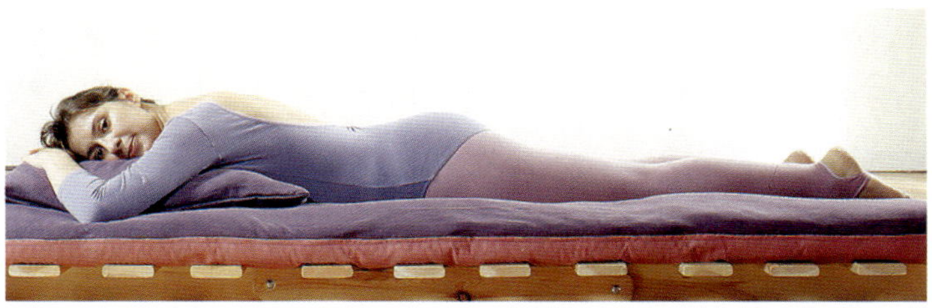

△ Lie on your front with cushions under your breasts and your upper back wide and relaxed, with your elbows bent at eye level and your face turned to one side. Let your feet roll apart. Grip the base of your spine with your buttock muscles. Breathe in and out a few times, then release.

# Standing sequence: stretches and balance

In this chapter, like the last, the yoga poses have been modified to provide you with a gentle progression, and are especially useful for those new to yoga. If you find any of these poses too difficult for now, do not worry, you can simply compose a sequence to suit you from the other poses in this section. Many standing poses can also be practised more easily with your back against a wall. If you stand a half-foot away from the wall, you can then use it as a support for your back by leaning against it while in the pose.

Some standing poses are described here as rhythmical sequences. Movement that flows with the breath is relaxing, effective and more "yogic" than a stretch in which you try and conform to a pre-set notion of how you should look in a posture. Before you feel comfortable holding "asanas", the word for classical yoga poses that implies steadiness of body, breath and mind, you can practise at least some of them using movement and rhythm. When you hold a pose, however, the dynamic is created inside your body with breathing. This is what makes yoga poses enjoyable. Whenever you feel tension, come out of it and relax.

## 205 Dynamic archer pose

**As you become stronger day by day, stand tall in Tadasana (198), which is also known as the Mountain Pose, and feel the strong vertical axis between earth and sky.**

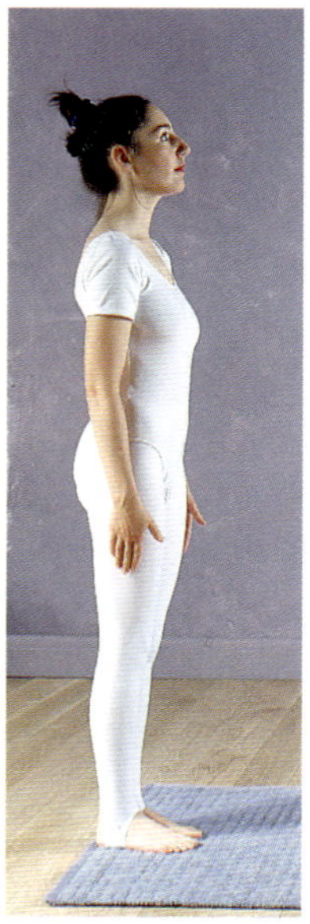

▷ **1** Stand in Tadasana (198). This is the starting pose for standing postures in yoga.

▷ **2** Jump or walk your feet about 1m/3ft apart. Turn your right foot out, your left foot in. Inhale, raising your arms open to shoulder level without tensing them. Exhale bending your right knee and turning your head right, extending both arms as much as you can. Inhale, straighten your legs, centre your head and turn the left foot out, right foot in. Exhale, stretching to the left. Continue alternating sides in an easy rhythm.

## 206 "Easy" triangle pose (Trikonasana)

**Find an easy rhythm, stretching only as far as you can go without disturbing your relaxed breathing. This sequence combines a stretch, the Archer Pose (205), and an open twist in the Triangle Pose.**

◁ **1** Begin in the Archer Pose, above. With your feet still apart and your arms extended, tilt your trunk to the right. Breathe naturally, letting your right hand slide down your right leg to the point where you feel you cannot go any further down without bending forward. Lift the inner arch of your right foot.

▷ **2** Keeping your weight on the left leg, inhale and stretch from your left heel all the way to the fingertips of your left hand. Look at your left hand and stretch more as you exhale. Come back to centre and repeat on the left side.

## 207 "Easy" forward bend

**It is pleasant to let gravity stretch your spine while your shoulders, neck and head can relax completely in this forward bend, which also stretches the back of your legs.**

▷ When you have stretched both sides a couple of times, come back to the centre and lower your arms to flop into a gentle forward bend. Relax your neck. You may like to swing your head and shoulders gently from side to side, to ease your lower back. Bend your knees as you breathe in to come up from this pose.

## 208 "Easy" tree pose (Vrkasana)

**Start with a low chair or stool for this pose and graduate to a higher one as you become more confident and flexible. You may prefer to have your back against a wall to do both this pose, and the Eagle Pose (209), if your balance is unsteady.**

△ **1** Stand in Tadasana (198), facing the chair. Place one foot on the chair and bring your hands into the prayer position, Namaste (180). Use deep breathing to stretch and align your spine and centre your energies. Hold the pose with your body, breath and mind remaining steady.

△ **2** When you feel ready, bring your knee up toward your chest, with both hands clasped below your knee. Keep steady and balanced, with your spine in line. As you breathe out squeeze your bent leg towards your body and release as you breathe in. Breathing deeply, hold the position for a moment. Release, regain your balance and steadiness, then bend the other knee and repeat.

# Standing sequence: stretches and rhythm





Movement and rhythm can make yoga postures dynamic, energetic and fun at a time when you spend a great deal of time at home with your baby. The various walks on this page can be done at any time, with or without your baby, whenever you feel like moving your body. Do not forget to breathe and to relax while you stretch.

## 209 Eagle pose (Garudasana)

**This is another balancing pose, which is very "closing" and excellent for improving concentration. It is easiest to do it quickly, without thinking too much about what goes where. Avoid twisting your spine to achieve the position – it is better to be content with wrapping yourself up more loosely.**

◁ **1** Stand in Tadasana (198) and centre yourself. Rest your hands on the tops of your hips and breathe in. As you breathe out, bend your knees, wrap your right leg around your left leg and – if you can – tuck your right foot behind your left calf. Hold this position, breathing deeply.

◁ **2** Only when you feel comfortable add the arms. Raise your bent left arm in front of your face and bring your bent right arm around it.Bring your palms together. Sit down with your back erect, as if on an invisible chair, and focus on your fingers, directly in front of your face. With practice you will be able to do both movements together on one breath. Change sides and repeat.

## 210 Cross-stride walking

**This is a dynamic movement to do in any odd moments, or to shake yourself out after the static standing poses. It is the opposite to the way most of us walk, and it takes concentration to co-ordinate the right and left sides. Cross-striding is very good for lifting the spirit, and there are dozens of different movements you can create with different rhythms.**

△ **1** Stride briskly with long steps and arms swinging up to shoulder level. Note that your right arm comes forward when your right leg is at the back and your right arm goes back when your right leg comes forward.

△ **2** Now change to cross-stride walking, bringing your right arm and leg forward together, then your left arm and leg.

## 211 Cross-stride prancing

**You can do this using your baby as a "weight", to strengthen your arm muscles and upper back. Grasp your baby firmly with one arm around the chest and the other between the legs so that you can swing him or her vigorously from side to side: your baby might love it. Prance around the room, garden or park with a light step and a light heart.**

△ **1** Walk in a rhythm first, raising one knee at a time while you swing your shoulders to the opposite side of the raised knee.

△ **2** Then rise on to your toes, bring your knee even higher and twist even more, before stepping lightly forward and raising the other knee.



## 212 Walking warrior pose

**To prepare for this movement, stand in Tadasana (198) first. The length of your stride will depend on the flexibility of your hips. Get into a flowing, walking rhythm, extending your stride as your hips loosen. Practise without your baby at first, then invite him or her to join you.**

△**1** Take a long step forward. Bend your front knee. Keep your weight on the outside of your back foot and your spine erect. Breathe in and, as you breathe out, raise your arms straight overhead with your palms facing each other. Look up and stretch more as you exhale. Then lower your arms as you bring your back foot forward for your next stretch.

△ **2** Your baby can join in. Rest him or her on your bent leg with one hand supporting, and stretch the other arm overhead.

△ **3** Change your baby to the other side when you take your other leg forward.

# Kneeling sequence: stretches, bends and twists

Sitting on your knees enables you to lift your lower spine and stretch without straining your lower back and abdominal muscles. Yoga "asanas" in this position straighten your back and make your spine strong and supple. They also tone your thigh muscles in a way that may surprise you at first. They remove fatigue and refresh your whole body with little effort.

## 213 Vajrasana

**This is a classic sitting pose in which you can develop the awareness of your vertical axis – from the pelvic floor to the crown.**

◁ Sit on your heels with your feet stretched out flat behind you and your spine and head erect. You may place a cushion between your buttocks and your heels if this is more comfortable. Use Reverse Breathing (141) to pull up your perineum, bring your waist back, open your chest and "sit tall".

## 214 Kneel tall

**In this dynamic version of Vajrasana, left, the flow of breath assists the lift of the diaphragm in a rhythmical stretch up and down.**

◁ Bring your hands together in front of you. As you breathe in, raise your buttocks, keeping your spine vertical and tailbone tucked under, and lift your arms above your head. Breathe out as you sit back. Breathe in and rise again and, if you can, hold for a few breaths before sitting back.

## 215 Chest expansion

**This exercise is both a stretch and a forward bend. The challenge is to find the position in which your arms can stretch the most while your chest can open the widest. Make sure your neck remains relaxed throughout.**

△ **1** Clasp your hands behind your back, sitting tall. Bring your arms up behind you, keeping them as straight as possible and squeezing your shoulder blades together.

△ **2** Next time you breathe out fold forward from the hips, keeping your arms raised. Breathe in, sitting tall. On the out breath, fold forward from the hips and lift your clasped hands, opening your chest as wide as possible. Keep expanding forward, breathing as deeply as possible.

△ **3** Aim to place your head on the floor (or cushion) in front of you, while still sitting on your heels. Breathe deeply and work to bring your arms higher with each breath out. Release your hands and come up on an in breath, sitting quietly in Vajrasana and observing the effects of the last exercise.

## 216 Kneeling twist

**Twisting in Vajrasana is slightly more difficult than the sitting twists on a chair presented earlier (187–9). Make sure you can kneel comfortably, with a straight spine, before you practise this kneeling twist. It allows further rotation and therefore is stimulating and enjoyable, even more so when you add a circling movement of the shoulder.**

▷ **1** Place the back of one hand against the outside of the opposite knee and the other hand on the floor behind you. These are your levers. Sit up very straight as you breathe in and turn as you breathe out. Improve your twist with successive breaths out. Keep your neck relaxed and turn your head only to the extent that your spine twists. Eventually, you find yourself looking back without strain.

◁ **2** When you are ready, bend your back elbow and put your fingertips on your shoulder. Circle your elbow, loosening your shoulder and upper back. Repeat on the other side.

"Look at today for it is life.

The very life of life."

# Kneeling roll

This sequence offers an expanded version of the Cat Pose (195). It is a stepping stone between the full "kneeling sun salute" (194–6) which keeps you grounded in your practice, and the classic sun salute of all yoga schools. We are giving a great deal of attention to this sequence because if it is not done correctly you may weaken your lumbar area when you move on to the full sun salute. Make sure you use your breath fully in time with the rhythm of this exercise, which is known as the "kneeling wheel".

## 217 Rhythmic kneeling sequence

**Repeat this rhythmic, rolling movement several times to loosen and relax your whole spine. The sequence is based on the Cat Pose (195), kneeling on all fours. Check that your knees are directly under your hips, hip-width apart, and that your hands are under your shoulder joints.**

◁ **1** Begin with your back flat, with your neck and spine in a straight line. If you wish, practise the Cat Pose (195) first, stretching and arching your spine alternately on the in and out breaths.

◁ **2** Lean back as you breathe out, opening up the lower back. Keep your arms fully extended (your hands have not moved at all) and lower your head as you stretch back. Ideally, your head comes to touch the floor while you remain seated on your heels.

◁ **3** Inhale, extending forward on your knees and bent arms until you have to straighten your arms and raise your head to come up, moving your weight on your hands and lifting your shoulders.

◁ **4** As soon as you reach the limit of both your in breath and your stretch, start rolling your shoulders to extend backward with your arms straight on a long out breath.

◁ **5** At the end of your out breath, you are ready to bring your elbows to the floor again and start stretching forward on a new in breath, extending your back fully again, as above. Keep your head relaxed. Enjoy the "wheel" movement with the flow of the breath in and out. Then relax.

# From kneeling to sitting

From kneeling in Vajrasana (213), on your heels (or on a cushion placed on your heels) you can now move on to Virasana, a pose in which you sit between your heels (or on a cushion between your heels). This pose tones your abdominal muscles further and allows you to make Reverse Breathing (141) even more effective. You can use it as a base to stretch backward and up. Virasana makes sitting straight in Dandasana easier as well as preparing you for the forward bends of classical yoga with a fully extended back.

## 218 Virasana

**For this classical yoga kneeling pose you sit between your feet. If you find this pose difficult, place rolled cushions between your thighs and sit on these – it will get easier with practice.**

▷ From a kneeling position, adjust yourself to make a comfortable descent toward a cushion or the floor, supporting yourself with your hands as you lower your buttocks between your feet. Make sure you can sit straight. Practise Reverse Breathing (141) in this position.

## 219 Back arch

**Virasana allows you a full expansion of the chest and a stretch of the spine by moving your hands back in an easy back arch.**

△ Breathe in and, as you breathe out, take your hands back with the fingers pointing forward. Lower your weight on to your palms and breathe in deeply to open the chest and arch the spine. Take several deep breaths in this pose. Come out of it as you went in, crawling your fingers back toward your buttocks.

## 220 Push away

**An upward stretch in Virasana knits your right abdominal muscles back together after pregnancy. If these muscles have split, practise this pose frequently for repair.**

△ Bend your elbows and push your palms away from you, following the seated sequence described in detail in the Sunwheel Stretch (186). This exercise is very effective to tone your right abdominal muscles. Exhale slowly on the way up, breathing in before you start pushing again from below.

## 221 Dandasana

**This is a classical yoga sitting position. The word means "pose of a stick". You can use it to stretch your spine and legs before you relax after completing a sequence of kneeling poses. Put on some more clothes, so that you don't get cold, and place a beanbag, or a big pile of cushions, in position.**

◁ **1** Sit close to the beanbag. Stretch your legs out, with your feet flexed. Place your hands near your buttocks and use them to push your spine upright and at a right angle to your straight legs. Use Reverse Breathing (141) to help you lengthen your lower back. Feel how you are sitting up taller and taller as you breathe. Your leg muscles are also toning as you lift yourself from your buttock bones on the floor.

▷ **2** Raise your arms on an in breath and push away with your palms as you exhale, keeping your head relaxed. Bend your arms again as you inhale and push them further up as you exhale. This is a graceful but very demanding rhythmical stretch in which nearly every muscle in your body gets involved. If you find sitting on the floor too difficult for now, sit on a cushion or on the edge of a beanbag.

▽ **3** When you feel really stretched lie back on the beanbag and totally let go... perhaps alone, perhaps with company.

# Making yoga part of your life

The breathing, movements and relaxation that make up your yoga practice will extend naturally into your everyday life. Take a few moments at frequent intervals to check the pattern of your breathing, the sense of "energy flow" in your movements and the state of relaxed contentment in your heart and mind. Make yoga a part of your life with a few appropriate exercises, wherever you happen to be.

At this stage your life is becoming more outward-looking, as you begin to resume your normal interests outside the home and you may be preparing to go back to work. You need flexible daily routines that suit your baby, your family and yourself.

Caring for yourself is still important. Maintain a special place in your own home where you can turn inward in deep relaxation to address concerns and feelings that are very personal. Your "yoga corner" can become the projection of your inner space, as you and your baby transform week by week.

When you nurture yourself during deep relaxation, you also strengthen the bond with your baby and dissolve stress around you. Yoga practice can become the tool for your transformation into a well-adapted mother. Whether you are at home or at work, you can refresh yourself daily.

## 222 Carrying

**When you are sitting on a chair with your baby on your lap you can practise "pelvic rolls" to ease out your lower back and gain flexibility and awareness in this area. Use them to help you get up from the chair, and practise the same movements in reverse every time you sit down. They can also be used to get in and out of cars.**

◁ **1** Arch your lower back, then tuck your coccyx under. Repeat this in a rolling action.

◁ **2** When you stand up while carrying your baby, tuck your coccyx under and bend your knees while keeping your back straight.

▷ **3** Let your thighs carry your weight, while your arms and upper back carry your baby.

## 223 Easy lifting

**Use this technique for heavy shopping, but remember that babies in seats also constitute heavy loads, and they get heavier as they grow. So you will feel much more comfortable if you apply the principles of yoga from the start.**

△ **1** To loosen up, bend your knees then straighten your legs as you stretch one arm, or both arms. Bend again as you release your arm or arms, and continue swinging in a rhythm; inhale as you stretch, exhale as you release.

△ **2** Pick up your load at the beginning of the upswing movement, as you inhale. Before lifting, your legs are bent and your arm is relaxed.

△ **3** If you are lifting a heavy load, always use both hands. Again, make sure that you are on the upswing, with your legs bent and your arms relaxed, beginning your inhalation. Feel that your abdominal muscles are involved, but do not strain.

▷ **4** Lift as you inhale, keeping your knees bent and your back straight. You may find this makes greater use of your arm muscles, but your back is protected. Put a heavy load down in the same way, but in reverse order, breathing out as you let go of it. Relax your lower back and abdomen as you exhale (all the way down).

# Yoga up and down stairs





If your home has stairs, you will find yourself going up and down them many times a day with your baby. You may also have to carry piles of linen and clothes, and Moses basket, carry cot or baby seat. This sequence will help you to protect your back and also to stretch your spine as you go up and down. Make the stairs a prop to regain or gain fitness each day, with yoga.

## 224 Stairs

**Going up and down the stairs, bending and extending your legs while keeping your back straight can make a striking difference to your energy level at the end of the day.**

▷ **1** Going up, lift your bent knee really high and stretch up before you take your weight on your top foot. With practice, you can learn to inhale as you bend and exhale as you stretch.

△ **2** Practise shifting your weight from your stretched back leg to your front bent leg, extending your leg muscles fully as you go upstairs. Keep your back straight.

△ **3** Going down, bend your knees deeply, keeping your back straight all the time. Inhale as you lift your knee, before lowering your leg down to the next step on the out breath.

## 225 Swing on the banister

**These stretches expand the movements that you make while going upstairs and downstairs. Practise them while leaning on a banister or a table. They will strengthen your lower back and legs to walk upstairs and downstairs without strain.**

◁ **1** Starting in Tadasana (198), bend your knees, keeping your back as straight as possible. Have your hands on your hips or hold on to the banister with one hand. Go down on an out breath, extend back up on an in breath.

▷ **2** From the same starting point, swing your left bent knee as high as you can on an in breath. Keep your standing leg slightly flexed. Let your leg go down to the floor softly as you exhale and push with your foot on an in breath to swing your bent leg up again. Repeat a few times then change legs.

△ **3** Stand on the side of the banister with your legs extended in a wide step, turning your back foot slightly outward. Stretch your arm on the side of your front leg, using the banister, on an in breath.

△ **4** On the out breath, bend your knee and allow your lower back to stretch. This is an easy static version of the Walking Warrior (212). Change sides. Use any convenient support if you do not have a banister.

# Family yoga



When your yoga becomes an integral part of how you move, breathe, think and feel, then every space can be a yoga space for you. You are now ready to include others in your practice from time to time.

It can be great fun to practise together as a family, and keeps siblings and the father involved with you and the new baby. It is best to keep the sessions short and choose simple exercises that children find fun to do. There should be no attempt to achieve a "perfect" pose, even if there is actually such a thing. The breadth and depth of awareness and steadiness that can be achieved in yoga seem to be unlimited. For occasional sessions with mixed ages and mixed abilities, focus on being relaxed, moving from one pose to the next as the energy flows. Lead them by your example, avoid explanation and don't hold any position. Above all, hand out heaps of praise.

"Little one, I embrace your presence in my life, my togetherness with you. When were you not a part of my life and my heart?"

There are times when family practice seems to be the only alternative to abandoning your practice altogether, or carrying on through gritted teeth, trying strenuously to ignore any interruptions. This attitude will spoil your yoga practice, as well as unsettling your nervous system. So make a virtue of necessity, take a deep breath and invite the family to join in. Choose a pose that is suitable for them and also totally familiar to you. Show them how to do it by demonstrating it in a smiling and relaxed manner. Do it with them a few times. Then move on to another pose. When they get bored you can go back to your own yoga practice, still in a serene and happy mood.

△ The example of your breathing helps your children to breathe more deeply.

◁ While you may feel that your partner's life is relatively unchanged while yours is so different now, doing yoga with him or next to him can be quality time.

△ Children like the challenge of simple yoga positions. Help them copy your movements as accurately as possible without strain.

◁ Time to rest with your Legs up the Wall (175). Every moment can also be playtime.

▽ Older children can benefit greatly from joining in and trying some of their mother's stretches.

# Yoga with friends

It makes an interesting change to practise yoga with friends, at your home or theirs. It is always fun for mothers and babies to get together. Most babies are fascinated with other babies, so it will make your own life much easier in the future if you introduce your baby to a number of different (and friendly) people and places as early in life as possible. Your baby will build up trust and confidence through experiencing a variety of different people and faces from the earliest days.

Women who first meet during their pregnancies can become friends for life. They enjoy the fun times together and give each other mutual support through any hard and lonely times. They may also start going to yoga classes together.

There are many exercises you can do with a partner. Be inventive, yet careful. It can be very easy for the "helper" to strain the lower back. As a general rule, let the floor support the weight, rather than either partner. Friends who do yoga together will benefit from the symmetry of postures. Make sure you communicate well so that you both feel equally stretched.

## 226 Leg and arm stretches

**This is a good routine to enjoy with a partner. Sit facing each other on a mat, a little more than a leg's length apart. Through mutual pushing and pulling of arms and then legs in symmetrical dynamic postures, you both energize and have good fun.**

△ **1** Each of you bends the right knee and the right elbow, as you hold hands. Sit up straight, adjusting the distance between you until you are both in a firm sitting position with your arms at shoulder level. Now twist your upper bodies by bending/extending your arms alternately in an easy rhythm. Change legs. Breathe in the rhythm.

◁ **2** Change your hand-hold, so that you are reaching to clasp your partner's opposite hand.

◁ **3** Now work your legs. Lean back on to your forearms and bring the soles of your feet against those of your partner. Keeping contact, "cycle" with your legs – forward a few times, then back.

▽**4** Finish by sitting back to back, using the pressure of your partner's back against your own to achieve a beautiful Dandasana pose (221). Keep your feet flexed and hold the position, breathing deeply and in unison. This breathing together is bonding, and your babies will feel very comfortable sharing the atmosphere that you are radiating.

# postnatal yoga three to six months

The feel-good factor of gentle yoga is expanded by the regular practice of movements and postures that increase new mothers' energy and enjoyment of life day by day. This is the time to replenish or renew your vitality, gaining stamina while remaining centred in mindfulness. Watch your baby copying you.

# Three to six months after birth



This section continues to develop a solid foundation for long-term good posture, pelvic strength and suppleness after your pregnancy and birth. Now is the time for you to influence the state of your hips and your lower back over many years to come. With yoga, you can continue to benefit from the flexibility that the hormones of pregnancy have given you, without over-stretching too soon. The aims are to strengthen and elongate the spinal muscles in your realigned body.

The asanas in this section cater both for those experienced in yoga and for those new to it. You are progressively introduced to classical poses in which the hips are aligned in stretches, twists and bends with the legs open in a wide step forward. While these poses are easy if you have done yoga, you may find breathing deeply in them a new challenge. If you are new to yoga, then getting correctly into the poses as shown here will be your first step.

Once again, this time-scheme is only a general guide. You may feel more comfortable sticking with the earlier routines for a while longer. You may also prefer to take one pose at a time from this section and practise it together with earlier, already familiar poses. It is always best to proceed at your own pace, consolidating your gains and enjoying your progress.

"You are the bows from which your children as living arrows are sent forth."

*The Prophet*

## 227 "Easy" Warrior

**This pose gives you back strong, masculine energy which you may welcome to balance the yielding and softening you needed to welcome your newborn. It helps you to feel "back in your body" and makes you firm, vigorous and strong with breathing in the abdomen, solar plexus and heart combined. The Walking Warrior (212) can still be useful when your baby is awake and wanting your company. Use this standing pose to improve the walking version.**

△ Stand with your legs apart and turn one foot to the side as for the "Easy" Triangle Pose (206), keeping your trunk facing to the front. Breathing in deeply, bring your arms overhead with palms together in a strong, vigorous lift of the upper body. Breathing naturally, improve your position. Open your chest and bring your shoulder blades closer together. Look straight ahead, keeping your chin level and your ears in line with your shoulders. Straighten your arms. When you are ready, breathe out and bend your front knee, keeping your spine erect and weight centred. Breathe in the pose for a moment, then breathe in to straighten your knee and out to lower your arms. If you are experienced in yoga, turn your trunk forward in a classic Warrior Pose.

## 228 Triangle forward bend (Parsvottanasana)

**This pose combines a stretch, a twist and a bend. The more slowly you extend and the more fully you breathe, with your awareness on the base of the spine, the greater appreciation you will get of the calm strength you gain from this pose.**

◁ **1** Start in Tadasana (198). Take a comfortable step forward and turn your back foot out, keeping your weight on the back heel. Clasp both elbows behind your back.

▷ **2** Alternatively, if you can, place your hands in Namaste (180) position, between your shoulder blades, palms together, fingers pointing upward toward your neck.

△ **3** Stretch up and back, all the way from your front foot to the top of your head, breathing in slowly and keeping your weight on your back heel. Take a few deep breaths while stretching.

△ **4** On an out breath, hinge the spine forward from the hips and extend forward slowly, taking a few deep breaths and lifting your breastbone. When you cannot extend any further, drop your head.

◁ **5** If you are experienced in yoga, allow your forehead to rest on your front knee, keeping your weight on the back heel. If this is too difficult, loosen your arms and bring your hands forward, palms on the floor, flexing the knees if needed, to keep your back extended in the forward bend. From either position, come back up slowly, taking a few deep breaths.

# Elongating the spine





As you go through successive stages of feeling aligned and stronger after giving birth, it is a pleasure to recover, or perhaps discover, the joy of stretching your spine. These deceptively simple adapted yoga poses make use of a support – a chair here – to help you enjoy the benefits of a fully stretched back. Feel the downward pull of gravity and the uplift in your lower back.

## 229 Leg-up sequence

**This is harder than it looks! Find a support for your leg at a height that suits your physique and level of fitness – from low to high chair, to table top.**

◁ **1** To begin, stand in Tadasana (198) and circle your straight arms in wide backward sweeps, lifting in the waist, breathing freely.

◁ **2** When you feel loosened up and stretched, place one leg on the chair with the knee straight and the foot flexed. Regain a balanced and upright posture and bring your palms to face each other overhead. Stretch up more on each breath out, squeezing in at the waist. Hold the position for three to five breaths. Relax your leg. Then change legs and repeat.

## 230 Open twist

**A standing version of the sitting twist, this pose uses movement to prepare you for the classic Standing Twist (236).**

△ With your right leg on the chair, place the corresponding hand on the inner side of your thigh as a lever and twist, circling your straight arm. While opening the chest wide, this pose allows a stretch from the standing leg to the extended hand.

## 231 Closed twist (2)

**In this twisting stretch, the pressure of the hand on the outer side of the raised leg allows a rotation of the hips.**

◁ When you twist to the left this time, your leg is on the chair and the back of your right hand is the lever against the outside of your left thigh. Circle your left arm several times in wide upward and backward sweeps, lifting at the waist. Twist both sides equally.

## 232 Forward bend (2)

**The raised leg helps you find more extension in the back as you bend forward, breathing as deeply in your lower abdomen as possible. Open the backs of the knees and enjoy aligning your hips for further stretch.**

△ **1** Rest one straight leg on the chair with the foot flexed. Pull your spine up tall and raise both arms slowly overhead, palms facing each other. Stretch with the breath, then, on an out-breath, hinge forward from the hips with a straight and stretched spine. Hold on to the back of the chair and breathe freely.

△ **2** Alternatively, hold your foot. Keep your legs straight and make sure that your neck and head remain relaxed as you extend in the forward bend. Keep the hip of the raised leg pulled back.

△ **3** To rest after these stretches, kneel down in front of the chair, with a cushion between your heels and your buttocks if you wish, and rest your folded arms on the chair seat. Breathe deeply into your back to relax.

## 233 Upper back strengthener

**This exercise continues toning your central, vertical abdominal muscles as well as strengthening the upper back.**

▷ Sit in an upright chair and raise your baby high above your head as you inhale. Lower the baby slowly into your lap as you exhale, remembering to use your abdominal muscles as you breathe. Repeat whenever you have a spare moment.

# More kitchen yoga



Mothers spend a great deal of time in the kitchen, which often becomes the focus of the home with babies and small children around. However small your kitchen or living area may be, you are likely to have a sink, counter or table which will become an invaluable prop for your yoga practice. These exercises can be done at odd moments when you feel the need for a good stretch.

## 234 Table top spine

**This and the following two stretches involve using a table or counter that is the right height for your legs and current flexibility. For this stretch, it is better for the surface to be too high than too low. It takes considerable awareness to get your spine in a straight line. Start by standing tall in Tadasana (198).**

▷ **1** Put your hands on the table, bend at the hips and walk backward as far as you can, until your spine is stretching horizontally. Avoid sagging in the middle, dropping your head or hunching your shoulders. Ask someone else to tell you where you are not as straight as you could be, and to put a hand on the spot so that you know where to adjust.

▷ **2** To get more stretch, bend your knees and pull the base of the spine further away from your shoulders. Sway your hips right and left, or even circle them with your knees bent to give your lower back a complete stretch.

"Ever serenely balanced, I am neither free nor bound." *Song of the Soul*

## 235 Leg lift

**As you are getting stronger, you can use an extended leg, with a support under the foot, to stretch, bend and twist in a standing posture. This sequence looks deceptively easy (it is an intensive toner of your inner thighs and buttocks).**

◁ **1** If you feel energetic, place one leg on a chair, counter or table. It is better to have it too low than too high for this exercise. Have both legs straight. Your standing leg should be right under your hip. Flex the foot of the raised leg.

◁ **2** On an in breath, raise both arms straight above your head. Exhale and stretch more. Take a few deep breaths in this position before lowering your arms on an out breath. After releasing your arms, bend forward from the hips, sliding your hands down your leg, on an out breath. Slide a little further in the next out breath, extending your lower back. Keep your head relaxed.

△ **3** If you feel ready for more, and can stretch further, hold your raised foot with both hands, keeping your arms and head as relaxed as possible. Inhale and bend forward loosely on the exhale. Come up and rest your legs or move on to the leg twist. Change leg.

## 236 Standing twist

**This is a standing version of the twists shown before, in both Sitting (187) and Kneeling (216) positions. A standing twist adds a further stretch in the leg and buttock muscles to the rotation of the spine from the base.**

◁ With your right leg on the table, place the back of your left hand against the outside of your right thigh and the back of the right hand behind your waist. These are your two levers. Breathe in. Pull the spine up, opening and lifting the chest as you rotate slowly on the out breath. Breathe in again and twist further to the right. Repeat to the left.

# Kneeling balance





As you progress in your yoga practice, make up your own routine, integrating new positions in the first basic sequences. This kneeling balance allows you to experience the full stretch which you will gain later from classical standing balances, while still remaining grounded on one hand and one knee. Balances will help you regain lightness and agility after pregnancy.

## 237 Cat balance

**This is a wonderful stretch, which you can do after completing the Rhythmic Kneeling Sequence (217). Begin in the Cat Pose (195), kneeling on all fours with your knees directly under your hips and your hands under your shoulders.**

▷ **1** With your neck and spine aligned, raise one arm and the opposite leg, making a straight line from hand to foot. Hold the position, breathing deeply, then repeat on the other side.

◁ **2** Now raise the arm and leg on the same side and stretch out straight. Hold, breathing deeply. Feel a stretch down from the hip to the foot and a stretch up from the waist to the hand, creating further space for breathing into. Repeat on the other side.

△ **3** When you have finished, lean back into the Swan Pose (194) for a moment.

△ **4** Or, bringing your arms beside your body, relax in what is known as the Child Pose, breathing deeply. You may like to place a cushion under your forehead.

# Shoulder stretch

The feeding of your baby is well established by now, whether you are still breastfeeding or bottle-feeding at this stage. It is time to stretch anew your arms, shoulders and neck, stimulating the flow of energy in your heart and throat Chakras. The following exercises tone the muscles that support your breasts. They stimulate the production of milk if you are breastfeeding.





## 238 Routine for shoulders and neck

**You have already practised some of these movements separately. Do them as a sequence whenever your shoulders and neck feel tight, tense or sore. Start by loosening your shoulders and neck, sitting in Vajrasana (213): between your heels, with your big toes touching each other. If you need to, put a cushion between your heels and your buttocks.**

◁ **1** Place the fingertips of one hand on your shoulder and circle your elbow several times in each direction.

▷ **2** Repeat with the other arm, then circle both elbows together. Keep your spine stretched tall and your chest open throughout.

△ **3** Now push your palms out in a kneeling version of the Sunwheel Stretch (186), straightening your arms as you push away, breathing out, and bending your elbows as you bring them in, breathing in.

△ **4** Clasp your hands behind you for the Chest Expansion (215), and bring your head to the floor in front of you. Hold the position for several deep breaths, then release your hands and bring your arms beside you in the Child Pose (opposite).

# Sitting poses

After giving birth, some women find that they are less flexible in the hip joints, while others feel they have gained flexibility. Whatever is the case for you, sitting poses allow you to elongate and strengthen your spine in a variety of ways. As you stretch, bend and twist with your legs in different positions, your "sit-bones" are your anchor on the floor and the root of your spinal stretch.

## 239 Seated forward bend (Paschimottanasana)

**Start by sitting tall, with your legs straight in front of you in Dandasana (221), extending from your seat to your crown with your shoulders and head relaxed. Always think of extending with an in breath before you bend on an out breath. If you cannot bend forward without your knees coming up or your abdomen getting squashed, use a belt or a tie round your feet.**

△ **1** Inhale to stretch up your spine. As you exhale, lengthen forward from the hips to reach your toes, or whichever part of your leg you can reach without strain. Keep extending the back of your knees.

△ **2** If this is comfortable, relax by bending your elbows and placing your forearms on the floor alongside your shins. Feel your hips go down on the floor as you extend your spine further with each exhalation.

## 240 Foot to the side forward bend (Trianga Mukhaikapada Paschimottasana) (TMP)

**This is an asymmetric forward bend, so you must take greater care to sit straight. It is best to use a cushion to help you keep your weight down on the side of the straight leg. Spend more time breathing on your stiffer side to give it more stretch.**

◁ Fold one leg and bring your foot beside your buttock, as in Virasana (218). Inhale and stretch your arms forward, keeping your shoulders level. Exhale and clasp your toes. Continue breathing in your lower back, extending more as you exhale. Release. Change legs and repeat.

## 241 "Easy" sage's pose (Marichyasana)

**In this pose you are using one bent leg as a lever to further elongate the spine and release the hips. This is done first as a forward bend and then as a twist, in an easy version of the classical pose in which the bent arm entwines round the front of the knee.**

◁ **1** Bend one knee and bring your heel in against you, with your foot flat on the floor. Hold that knee close to your armpit. As you exhale, stretch forward to grasp the other foot with your free hand. If you are experienced in yoga, do the classic Marichyasana. Extend for a few breaths. Then change sides.



▷ **2** With your legs in the same position, finish this sequence with an open twist, placing your free hand on the floor behind you and stretching your spine up straight before you turn. Extend further with each out breath, keeping your neck relaxed in the twist. Change sides.

# the plough and beyond





This sequence involves positions in which your trunk is inverted, or upside down. For this reason, you should avoid it when you have a period and as long as you feel that your internal energies are involved in clearing your womb and restoring its integrity.

In this sequence, movement and rhythm help you get into the Plough Pose (Halasana) and out of it into a forward bend more easily than by holding these two poses separately. Whether you are new to yoga or have some experience, the rolling plough sequence improves your skills at the stage where you are today. Rolling is also fun as well as stimulating for both you and your growing baby. If you can't get your buttocks off the floor at first, do not worry, just laugh and try the exercise again tomorrow.

## 242 The rolling plough sequence

**The rolling plough sequence is an unconventional, but effective way of taking your feet over your head and extending backwards before stretching forward in a forward bend, which is already familiar to you. Your rolling sequence can be as small, or as acrobatic, as you wish or can have it. Never force it. Repeating a rhythmic backward and forward rolling movement will get you progressively into a full Plough without strain. This is a solid foundation for a shoulder stand, which you can then move to if you are experienced in yoga or may learn as part of a yoga class later.**

△ **1** Lie on the floor with your knees bent, feet flat and arms along your sides.

△ **2** Breathing in, lift your feet toward the ceiling, keeping your knees bent.

△ **3** Breathing out, bend your elbows and bring your hands to support your back, as you roll your hips backwards and up, bringing your knees toward your forehead. If doing this is difficult, move to 6, 7, 8.

△ **4** If 3 is easy, continue rolling your knees to your forehead. If this is as much as you can do now, use your hands to support you as you lift your hips above your head, to get your spine vertical. Take a few breaths before moving to 6, 7, 8.

◁ **5** If 4 is easy, continue your rolling movement to straighten your legs, so that your feet rest on the floor behind you, keeping your arms down beside you. Stretch on an out breath, inhale and start rolling your spine toward the floor, bending your knees.

▷ **6** Holding the back of your knees, keep the momentum of your roll to bring you to a sitting position. If you cannot roll easily, use your hands as a support to sit up.

◁ **7** Sitting up is only a brief intermediate position in your rolling forward, extending your legs straight in front of you...

▷ **8** ...into a sitting forward bend. Stretch as you exhale and start rolling again backward in the rolling sequence that suits you today. Get into a rhythm in which your breathing and movement allow you to roll and stretch in a relaxed way.

# From relaxation to bliss





In the sequences that you have learnt and practised until now, stretching, breathing and relaxing have been equally important. You have probably become more aware of your breathing at all times, of your posture around your home and outside, with your baby and for yourself as a woman. Yoga has reminded you, in practice, how activity alternating with rest is the natural rhythm of life, as natural as breathing in and breathing out, or as day followed by night.

New mothers are often more tired from the constant attention they feel their babies need, day and night, than from lack of sleep. With relaxation, stress can be dissolved every day, as soon as it arrives. You can draw the strength you need to face unexpected challenges from reserves of deep rest. Progressively, as you become aware of your state of relaxation through regular practice of Shavasana (197), the Corpse Pose that renews you, the build-up of tension can be averted instantly, in any position you find yourself in. You learn to "let go", to release, to just be, in a not doing, not wanting state.

At this stage, you are ready to go from relaxation to meditation, which is one of the eight limbs of yoga. In the silence and stillness of relaxation, you can experience wholeness, peace and bliss. For new mothers, surrendering to unconditional love for their babies calls for an adequate source of self-nurture. Learning to "plug in" to the universal life-force at will in relaxation reminds us that this nurturing is infinite. "Plugging in" is simple and the more you practise it, the more rewarding it is for you, your baby and all your loved ones.

"It is vital to ask the spirits for their help or blessing, or you could wait for a long time! They never impose on us, but wait patiently to be consulted."

## 243 Deep rest

**Every day, try to find a moment for relaxing into a deep rest. If your baby is asleep, extend your relaxation as long as you can after yoga. Being a rested mother comes top on your priority list. Bliss comes from this state of deep rest and an open heart.**

△ Find a comfortable position and breathe deeply, concentrating on long breaths out. Let go and relax. Take time to return to activity.

△ Sitting up with an erect spine is the ideal position to meditate, on the floor or on a chair. With practice, three long breaths will take you into this state – known in yoga as Ananda, which means "bliss". This is the meditative state, and the breath is the easiest tool with which to reach this state almost instantly. After a few more breaths, return to your external world, bringing your inner radiance with you. Refreshed and renewed, you can be "out there" again, ready for your baby.

◁ If your baby is crying or unsettled, hold him or her gently and just be – in your heart centre, making contact again with the source of infinite nurturing inside you, letting yourself be held too.

# postnatal yoga beyond six months

Many of the physical dysfunctions that afflict new mothers can be eased or put right with deep breathing in specific yoga postures. A strong, elastic pelvic floor, good posture and better circulation are fundamental for women's well-being. While yoga stimulates the body's internal systems, relaxation can unfold its self-healing capacity.

# Six months and beyond

From now on you can add more classical asanas to your yoga sessions, whether or not you have joined a regular yoga class for further practice. If you have not practised before, it is worth finding the school of yoga that best suits your needs as a new mother.

## different schools of yoga

There are several traditional schools of yoga, each focusing on different aspects of this vast subject. You may need to try out several different classes and teachers before you find the right ones for you. Yoga teachers are usually quite happy to let you join their classes for a week or two before signing on.

Ashtanga Vinyasa and Iyengar yoga are very physical and demanding. Viniyoga focuses on breath with gentle movement. Energy yoga focuses on moving energy through the body using classical breathing, cleansing techniques, visualization and meditation as well as asanas. The Sivananda, Satyananda and Buddhist schools teach this more holistic type of yoga. Many yoga teachers are trained by national associations, which can put you in touch with teachers in your area.

Meanwhile, developing strength and stamina, while moving into more of the classical asanas, will give you an excellent foundation. The focus is still on poses that strengthen and "close" the pelvic and abdominal areas.

## 244 Tree pose (Vrkasana)

**In this pose you should feel rooted, like a tree. Feel how the muscles on either side of your leg and trunk are working together, co-operating in the job of holding you upright and steady. Come out of the pose if you start to wobble. A "smaller" pose, well done, is better than wobbling in a more ambitious one. You can also stand against a wall to start with.**

△ **1** Stand in Tadasana (198) and settle your body and breathing. Then bring one foot to rest on the inner side of your other leg, take your bent knee right out to the side, pull up your spine and join your palms in Namaste (180). Breathe freely. Change legs.

△ **2** Now for the classical pose: hold one foot and bring the sole against the opposite inner thigh, with the bent knee out to the side.

△ **3** Stand up tall and raise your straight arms slowly to the sides and then overhead, palms together, breathing in. Breathe deeply and hold the pose, coming out of it as gracefully as you went in. Repeat on the other side.

## 245 Standing seat (Utkatasana)

**This asana is like sitting on an imaginary chair. Stand in Tadasana (198) and settle your body and breathing.**

◁ **1** Breathing in, raise both your arms straight up overhead. Avoid arching the lower back. Stretch right through from your heels to your fingertips, and take a few deep breaths.

▷ **2** When you are ready, breathe out and bend your knees to "sit down", keeping your spine as nearly vertical as possible, until you are almost squatting, with your heels on the floor. Breathe deeply in the pose.

## 246 Standing forward bend (Padangusthasana)

**This is an inverted pose, with your head lower than your heart. In contrast with the "Easy" Forward Bend (207) your feet are now together and your legs extended. Broaden the upper back and relax your head for a greater spinal stretch.**

△**1** Stand in Tadasana (198) with your feet slightly apart. As you breathe out, bend forward and hold your big toes. Improve your position by looking up as you breathe in and relaxing down even more as you breathe out.

△**2** You can also practise the Chest Expansion exercise (as in 215 and 238, kneeling) in a Standing Forward Bend.

# Yoga for energy

As you are now following more and more the rise and fall of the flow of breath while you extend into the postures, you will be enjoying the special energy yoga brings. Rather than pushing your body to the limit in a workout, breathing in the postures as you can do them today – there is always more to come – stimulates all the systems of your physiology and increases your vital energy. Ups are not followed by downs after yoga. On the contrary, inner strength and enjoyment of life are constantly expanded.

## 247 Triangle pose (Trikonasana)

**In this pose, the straight legs make a triangle. The back foot, firm on the floor, is your base as you stretch your spine vertebra by vertebra from the coccyx to the head, while you reach for the sky with a relaxed but straight arm.**

▷ In the classical pose try to place your feet wider apart than for the "easy" version (206) – about the length of your leg – so there is more stretch. Practise first with your back to a wall, so that your head, shoulders and top hip brush against the wall as you stretch to the side and down. The point is to keep your spine elongating from the side, not to reach down. When you have a good "feel" for the position, practise away from the wall. Hold the position for several deep breaths, then repeat on the other side.

## 248 Downward-facing dog pose (Svanasana)

**This is an inverted position, excellent for stretching and strengthening the whole body. The base of your spine is the apex of the pose, as you extend from the hands up your back and from your feet up your legs.**

△ **1** Start in the Swan Pose (194), sitting on your heels and stretching your fingers forward. Prepare to turn your toes under.

△ **2** Breathing in, raise your buttocks into the air, coming on to your toes, and extending the back. Push your buttocks back and up, bending your knees.

◁ **3** Progressively extend your heels toward the floor, straightening your legs. Make sure you release your neck and shoulders. With each exhalation, let your back grow longer and the top of your thighs stretch. When you are ready, breathe out and place your heels on the floor and your head between your arms, so that you are looking at your navel.

## 249 Upward-facing dog

**This phase is an upward-facing stretch with the spine bending backwards while the weight is on the wrists and feet. The two phases expand the Rhythmic Kneeling Sequence (217).**

▷ From the Downward-facing Dog Pose, bring your hips down without moving your toes but lifting your heels, so that your body is suspended between your hands and your toes. Your head will come up. Gaze steadily forward and breathe deeply. When you feel strong enough, and only then, lift your hips up into the Downward-facing Dog Pose. You can use the breath in these stretches: breathe out to face down and in to face up, in an easy swinging rhythm.

## 250 Equestrian pose

**This pose continues the two phases of the Dog Pose as part of the classic Sun Salute. It is an intense toner of the legs and the hips as well as an energetic spinal stretch.**

◁ **1** From the Downward-facing Dog Pose breathe in, as you swing your right foot forward between your hands. Lean hard to the side opposite your swinging leg, in order to get your chest out of the way.

△ **2** With your left knee on the floor, inhale and raise your arms above your head while dropping your hips.

△ **3** For a stronger pose, keep your back knee a short distance off the floor. Breathe deeply, then return to the Downward-facing Dog Pose on an out breath and swing the other foot forward, breathing in. Change sides, then relax.

# Sunday afternoon yoga



What could be more nourishing to body and spirit than to practise yoga at home with your family – either indoors or outside in the garden on a warm day?

Make your yoga practice an exciting form of exercise, which you can share and enjoy with those around you. Everyone soon rises to the challenge, while yoga ceases to be something esoteric you do in your "yoga corner".

## Walking stretches

**Cross-stride Walking (210) is an energetic and dynamic walking stretch which new mothers can practise in the park while remembering to breathe deeply.**

▷ To get into the swing, begin by walking normally, bringing your right arm and left leg forward together, then your left arm and right leg. Now change it, so that your left leg and arm come forward together, then your right leg and arm, in the Cross-stride Walk.

## 251 Warrior pose

**Both the classical and the "Easy" Warrior Pose (227) can be done with a partner. Stand facing each other with the insteps of your right feet close together and your left legs stretched back. When Dad does yoga too, it can make a good show.**

◁ **1** Keep your shins vertical as you sink your hips as low as possible, each adjusting the position of your back leg – the lower you sink down, the further away your back heel will be. Raise your arms triumphantly, with palms together. Breathe deeply and hold the pose.

△ **2** You can "push hands" in the Warrior Pose, to strengthen your arms and upper back.

◁ **3** Step back and bow deeply to your partner in a Standing Forward Bend 246) with arms folded, before repeating the sequence with your left legs forward. Relax the neck and allow your spine to lengthen.

## Floor exercises

**The whole family can enjoy sitting poses on the grass in the summer. The Rolling Plough Sequence (242) is always good fun, even if it ends in a heap of bodies.**

△ **1** Line up for a Seated Forward Bend (239), stretching forward with straight legs.

▷ **2** Roll back and up into the Plough Pose.

△ **3** Doing your yoga practice outdoors can be invigorating. The Downward-facing Dog Pose (248) is always popular with older children while your baby is asleep.

## Togetherness time

△ Take a quiet walk with your baby. Your body is fit and strong, your mind clear and rested, and your heart full of love. This "walking meditation" can be a celebration of your baby, or you can turn to it for help in calming both you and your baby on difficult days. That's the beauty of yoga. It promotes well-being at every level in your life, just as it is, from day to day.

# First period routine



Up to now you have been working within a particular cycle – that of pregnancy, birth and recovery. Prenatal yoga emphasizes "opening" poses to facilitate the growth and birth of the baby. Postnatal yoga then emphasizes "closing" and strengthening poses to regain pre-pregnancy pelvic health.

The day your first period arrives is the start of a new cycle – that of the monthly "opening" to release waste products from the womb. Here is a suggested routine – a "rite of passage" – to mark this change. It can also be used each month in the first two days of your period. In the yoga tradition, inverted poses are not to be practised during the full flow of menstruation.

## Shavasana (with knees bent) (197)

**This is the end of a cycle that started when your baby was conceived. Now your baby is here. You are bleeding again. Relax to enter this transition.**

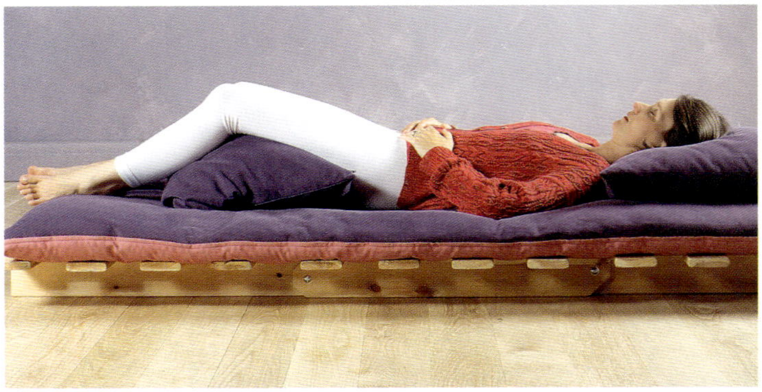

△ Start by lying down on your back on a rug or bed, with your knees bent and your arms loose on each side of your body. Inhale and exhale deeply several times, making a greater contact between your waist and the floor or bed each time you exhale. Make sure your buttock muscles are relaxed after you tighten and release your pelvic floor muscles, inhaling and exhaling in a rhythm that suits you. Then relax.

## Side stretch (179)

**Go back to this early gentle stretch to elongate the lower spine and soothe your pelvic nerves.**

△ Stretch from your heel to your fingertips for a few seconds as you inhale and start exhaling, then release at the end of the exhalation. Repeat a few times, then change sides.

## Forward bend (2) (232)

**This combined stretch and bend can also be practised kneeling on a cushion if you find standing too demanding. It brings oxygenated blood to the pelvis as you breathe deeply and freely, releasing all tension on the out-breath.**

△ **1** Stretch up and forward from your hips, opening the lower back. Breathe deeply, pulling your stomach muscles in toward the spine and drawing up your pelvic floor.

△ **2** Release all muscles on your out breath. This is the opposite of Reverse Breathing (141). Repeat a few times.

## Rhythmic kneeling sequence (217)

**After stretching in the Rhythmic Kneeling Sequence, enjoy resting in the Child Pose (see 237), earthing and drawing up your inner strength.**

◁ **1** Practise the Rhythmic Kneeling Sequence slowly as this will help to loosen your whole back.

△ **2** Relax in a kneeling forward bend, the Child Pose, with a cushion under your forehead, breathing freely.

## 252 Half bound angle pose (Janu Sirsasana)

**This classical yoga pose is most helpful to hold the womb in its optimal position. During your period, breathe freely to relax the perineum in the pose.**

△ **1** Start by sitting in Dandasana (221), with your back and legs straight. Propping yourself up with your hands on the sides of your body if needed, relax your lower back and abdominal muscles on each exhalation for a few breaths. Feel a downward flow of energy toward the floor.

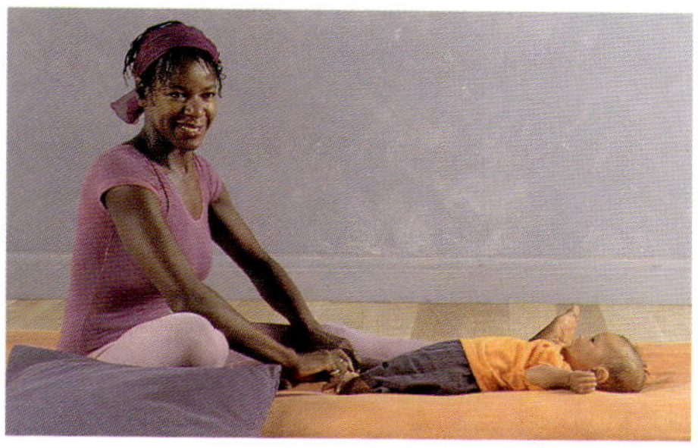

△ **2** Then, keeping one leg straight, bend your other knee and bring the foot against the inside of the straight leg as close to the perineum as possible. Put a cushion under your bent knee if needed. Breathe deeply, drawing in your pelvic floor muscles as you inhale, relaxing totally as you exhale.

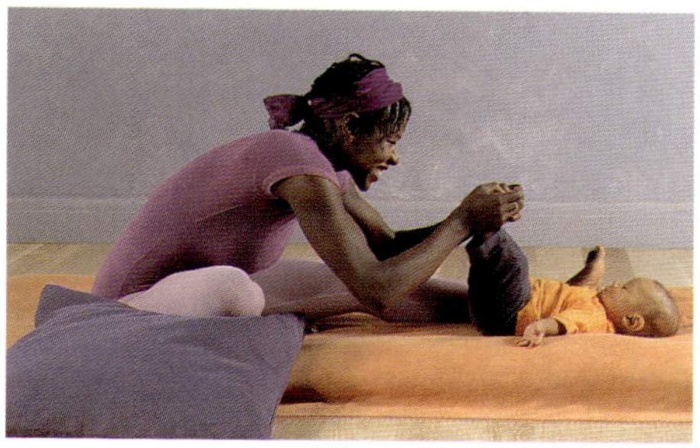

△ **3** Bending from the hips and elongating your spine as much as you can, extend forward, keeping your shoulders and head relaxed. Keep your weight down on the hip of the bent leg on each exhalation. Hold for a few breaths, sit back in Dandasana, then change sides.

## Legs up the wall (175)

**Make the most of your yoga breathing to start your cycle anew and reduce or eliminate pre-menstrual tension and period pains.**

◁ With your hands on your lower abdomen, breathe as deeply as you can, drawing in your pelvic floor muscles as you inhale, relaxing completely as you exhale. Keep your legs relaxed against the wall and feel how their weight helps you breathe deeper into your lower back. If you wish, explore the feeling of "opening" with this breathing.

## Sitting breathing, relaxation and meditation

**As you sit quietly, undoing any tension in your body and mind, explore the infinite potential of the breath to enhance your reproductive health.**

Sit comfortably, against a wall with cushions if this is better for you, or on a chair, so as to keep your back upright. Practise Alternate Nostril Breathing (4) for a couple of minutes, to clear your mind and centre you. Drop your lower jaw and relax along the vertical axis from the crown of your head to your perineum. You will begin to feel aligned, toned and yet open and relaxed at the same time. Feel the palms of your hands soft while your arms are resting on your lap. Feel where you are, right now, in your self as you return to menstruation. Acknowledge any emotions that you have about it and how mixed they can be. Feel them, and let go of them. Find your core self within and acknowledge your feminine energy and its transformation through pregnancy and birth. Feel grateful and blessed for your baby, and the person that you are now becoming.

# Expanding your yoga practice

The "core" of yoga is outlined at the start of this book: that is breath, relaxation, awareness, stretching – especially through the spine – and strengthening. This core remains, however simple or complicated your yoga practice may be. Three sample routines follow, showing how your practice may develop as you grow stronger, while still maintaining the yoga core. You can invent hundreds of permutations of your own, following the same general plan.

You will see that the simpler exercises continue alongside the more advanced ones. When you plan to practise a particular classical posture, you will choose simpler movements of a similar type – backward or forward bending, twists or balances – to use as a preliminary warm-up for the more testing stretches.

Let yoga breathing, relaxation, awareness and posture become part of your life. Your whole attitude will change because you are coming from a space that is more centred, less fragmented; more welcoming, less anxious.

## A sample practice for birth to six weeks

1

◁ **Tadasana (198)**

Start with aligning your spine so that you become aware of your posture after pregnancy.

2

△ **With reverse breathing (141)**

Use this breathing exercise while in Tadasana to tone and strengthen your entire trunk.

3

◁ **Then circle your feet**

The ligaments and muscles of your feet and ankles need strengthening after your change in weight.

4

▽ **Now lie down and rest in Shavasana (197)**

This may complete your session, if it is a very short one. You can continue next time you have a few suitable moments, starting with a short rest, or carry on now.

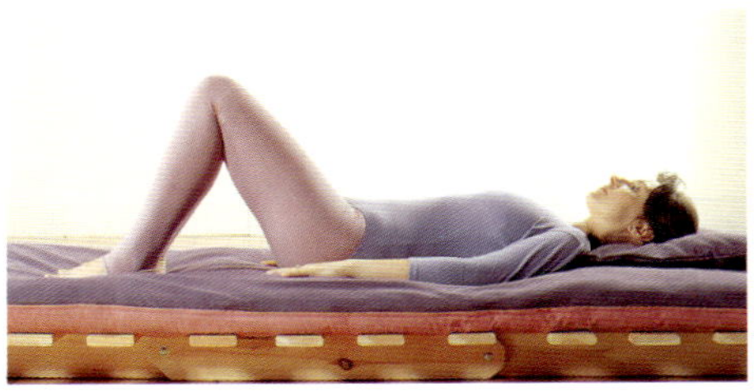

5

△ **Abdominal and pelvic floor muscles, lying down (182)**

Have cushions or a beanbag near you.

6

▽ **Basic kneeling sequence (194–6)**

Spend some time on this sequence, then rest. Stop here, or carry on a little longer…

7

◁ **Legs up the wall (175)**

Rest when you have breathed deeply with each knee bent in turn.

8

△ **Floor twist (193)**

A good way to ease and stretch your lower spine, even if you had a Caesarian section.

9

▽ **Final Rest: Shavasana (197)**

This relaxation should last longer than the rests between exercises, so keep warm.

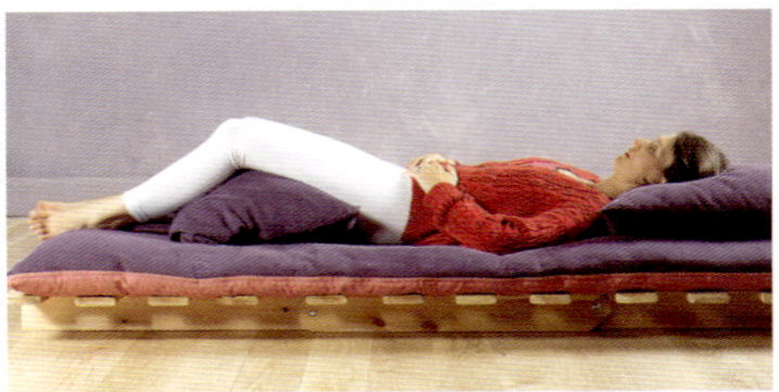

# A sample practice for six to twelve weeks

You can use some of the exercises suggested for birth to six weeks to prepare for stronger stretches. Reverse breathing (141) is essential to tone your abdominal muscles in depth. Whatever your stretch level is, make sure you pay full attention to using the breath in your yoga practice.

1 ▽ **Alternate nostril breathing (4)**

Sit on a firm chair, ready for the next sequence.

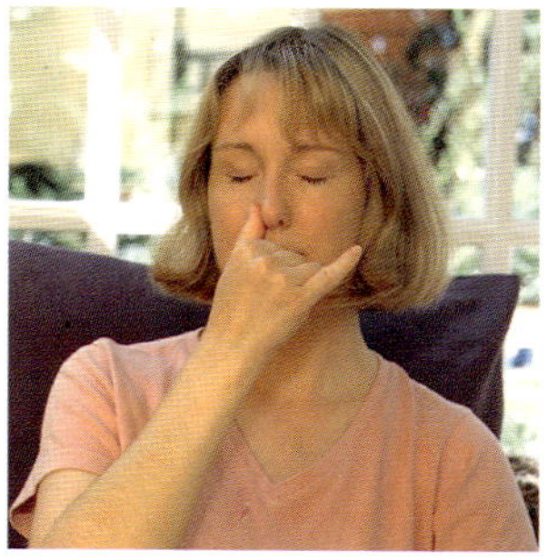

2 △ **Sunwheel stretch (186)**

3 ◁ **Standing against the wall (202)**

Standing tall with your whole spine against the wall, practise Reverse Breathing (141) with your arms lifted.

4 △ **"Easy" tree pose (Vrkasana) (208)**

After practising this pose, your baby may like some attention, so choose something you can have fun with together. Remember to pause and breathe deeply before picking up your baby.

5 ◁ **Cross-stride prancing (211)**

This continues the high-stepping of your previous pose, but is active and energetic. It also has a twisting movement.

6 ◁ **Walking warrior pose (212)**

After this you will both need a rest.

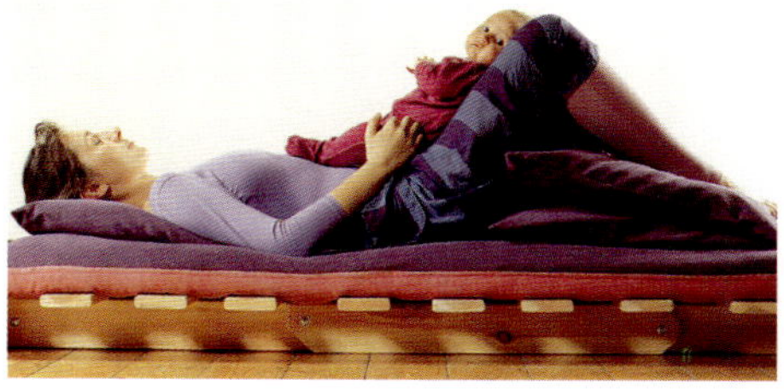

7 △ **Shavasana (197)**

When you decide to continue with your session you will recall that you have done no floor poses so far.

8 ▽ **Basic kneeling sequence (194–6)**

This is always good to do, as it makes the spine flexible and releases tension.

9 ▽ **Rhythmic kneeling sequence (217)**

10 △ **Child pose (see 237)**

Breathe deeply into the back of your lungs and your lower abdomen.

11 ▽ **Final relaxation: Shavasana (197)**

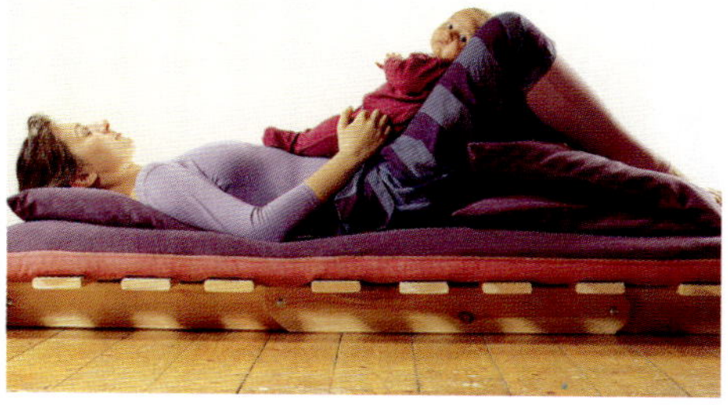

# A sample practice for three to six months

1 ▽ **Reverse breathing, second stage, in Shavasana (142 and 197)**

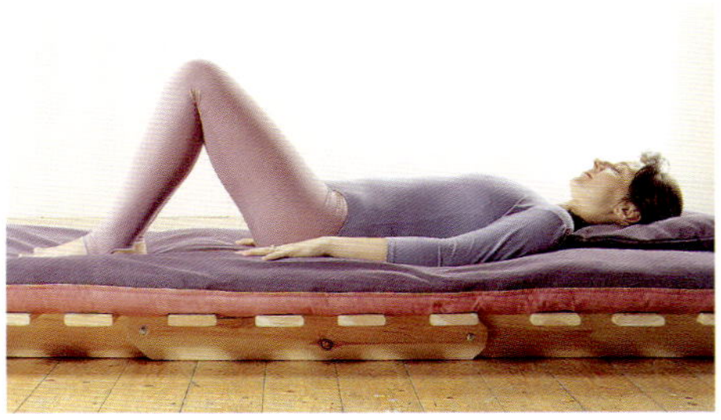

2 △ **Reverse breathing (141) while raising the hips (203)**

This is a backbend.

3 ◁ **Vajrasana (213)**

4 ▽ **Chest expansion (215)**

This is a forward bend, after the backbend.

5 △ **Kneeling twist with elbow rotations (216)**

The basics have been attended to, so now for something new.

6 ▽ **"Easy" sage's pose (Marichyasana) (241)**

7 ▽ **Rest in child pose (see 237)**

8 △ **"Easy" triangle pose (206)**

Repeat a few times on each side, to prepare for the classical version.

9 ▽ **Triangle pose (Trikonasana) (247)**

10 ◁ **Standing seat (Utkatasana) (245)**

Elongate the lower part of your spine as you breathe deeply in this pose.

11 △ **Standing forward bend (Padangusthasana) (246)**

Perhaps you have time for a few more poses while your baby is peaceful. If so, you could add the Downward- and Upward-facing Dog (248 and 249) and "Easy" Warrior Pose (227). If not, don't worry!

12 ▽ **Alternate nostril breathing (4)**

Sit cross-legged for this.

# Useful addresses and resources





**United Kingdom**

*Yoga classes and training courses for conception, pregnancy, birth and beyond:*

**Birthlight**
7 Essex Close
Cambridge CB4 2DW, UK
Tel (01223) 362288
email: enquiries@birthlight.com

**Birthlight/Yoga Biomedical Trust UK**
60 Great Ormond Street
London WC1N 3HR, UK
Tel (020) 7419 7195

*General yoga classes, with trained teachers:*

**The British Wheel of Yoga**
25 Jermyn Street, Sleaford, Lincolnshire
NG34 7RU, UK
Tel (01529) 306 851
www.bwy.org.uk
email: office@bwy.org.uk

*Information and referral to support groups:*

**National Childbirth Trust (NCT)**
Alexandra House, Oldham Terrace, Acton,
London W3 6NH, UK
Tel (0870) 7703236
www.nctpregnancyandbabycare.com

**Foresight**
Association for the Promotion of
Pre-conceptual Care
28 The Paddock, Godalming, Surrey
GU7 1XD, UK
Tel (01483) 427839/419468
www.foresight-preconception.org.uk

**Organization for Prenatal Education**
Tel 01892 784381
Email: contact@ope.org.uk

*Promotion and supply of waterbirth pools:*

**Active Birth Centre**
25 Bickerton Road
London N19 5JT, UK
Tel (020) 7561 9006

**Splashdown Waterbirth Services**
17 Wellington Terrace
Harrow on the Hill
Middlesex HA1 3EP, UK
Tel: (020) 8422 9308

*The Alexander Technique applied to swimming:*

**Aqua Development Programme**
the Laboratory Health Club and Spa
The Avenue
Muswell Hill
London N10 2QJ, UK
Tel: (020) 8482 3000
www.art of swimming.com

**United States**

**Postpartum Support International**
*(for worldwide referral)*
9271 Kellog Avenue
Santa Barbara, CA 93117
USA
Tel 805 967 7636

*Contact network for childbirth information:*

**Midwifery Today, Inc.**
P.O. Box 2672-350, Eugene OR 97402,
USA
Tel 541 344 7438
www.midwiferytoday.com
Email: inquiries@midwiferytoday.com

**Global Maternal/Child Health Association Ltd**
PO Box 1400
Wilsonville OR 97070, USA
Tel 503 682 3600
Fax 503 682 3434
www.waterbirth.org
email: waterbirth@aol.com

**Monadnock OB GYN Associates**
454 Old Street Road
Peterborough
NH 03458, USA
www.waterbirth.com

**Citizens for Midwifery**
PO Box 82227
Athens
GA 30608-2227, USA
www.cfmidwifery.org

*Supply of water woggles*

**Rothama International Corp. (Sprint Athletics)**
St. Louis Obispo
PO Box 3840
CA 93403, USA
Tel 800 235 2156

**Australia**

*Umbrella organization for information and classes:*

**Childbirth Education Association of Australia**
P.O. Box 413, Hurstville BC,
NSW, 1481
Australia
Tel (02) 9580 0399
www.cea-nsw.com.au
email: info@cea-nsw.com.au

# Authors' thanks and acknowledgements

My thanks go first of all to many yoga teachers and to all the *Birthlight* mothers who have helped me develop and refine the approach presented in this book over half a lifetime. Among them is Sally Lomas, radiant in this book with her fourth baby Fyn, who has become a leading *Birthlight* tutor and friend. Thanks to all those people who have supported me in making this yoga more accessible to mothers-to-be, particularly Rhea Quien, Margaret Adey, Elizabeth de Michelis and the Trustees of *Birthlight*. Thanks to Robin Monro for giving Perinatal Yoga importance and recognition at the Yoga Biomedical Trust long before it became common practice. Thanks to Andrea Wilson and Uma Dinsmore, among many special co-teachers, for their unfailing dedication to yoga for mothers.

My most special gratitude goes to my father: he took me swimming as a small child in the Loire near our home in France and his advanced yoga practice was an inspiration. Swimming coaches and yoga teachers from all over the world, too many to be named but all to be thanked, imparted the knowledge that I have drawn on in developing aqua yoga. Thanks to my own four, now grown, "water babies" who patiently shared long practice sessions. Aqua yoga has grown with the help of many friends and advisers of *Birthlight*. Thanks in particular to Sally Lomas, Tricia Beaumont and Louise Pivcevic for their assistance in teaching and to all the pregnant women and new mothers whose feedback has been essential to continue deepening my understanding of yoga in water.

Access to warm pools in Cambridge has been invaluable for *Birthlight* aqua yoga classes since the 1980s. My warmest thanks go to Geoff Barnes for his impeccable upkeep of the Windmill School pool and his great heart, and also to Ruscha, whose beautiful pool at The Wood provided an ideal, conducive atmosphere to convey the power of water in pregnancy. Joanne and Nick also kindly let us use their pool in London.

Thanks to very dear Doriel Hall, with whom friendship has deepened through our collaboration as co-authors, for spurring me to turn my classes into books. Many thanks to Alison and Charlie, and to Bel Gibbs, who kindly opened their homes to be photographed. Thanks to Christine Hanscomb for the outstanding photographs and to Sue Duckworth for not only being an expert stylist but a caring one too. Thanks to Debra Mayhew for her excellent editorial assistance as well as her skills in creating a happy productive team to implement the vision for this book.

My warmest thanks are to my whole family for their love and inspiration. Thanks to Drake for his heartfelt wonder of birth shared with our Amazonian and Hawaiian "families". Thanks to the Amazonian women who showed me the midwifery and mothering of their world. It is my wish that the yoga in this book may be a bridge between them and the magical work of midwives and doulas in the West in order to empower women in pregnancy and birth, helping to alleviate postpartum depression and create what Robin Lim called "wellness after the baby's birth".

## Thank you to the models

Many thanks to the mothers and their families who gave up their time to take part in this book. Katrien Asakura-Vanassche and Kojo Asakura with Koo and Kenji; Miriam Baldor with George and Matthew; Karyn Barnes and Felicity Yeo with Lauryn; Ros Belford with Ismene; Margaret Bishop; Moira Bogue; Simon Bower; Hayley Brewis with Annabel; Karen Brown; Kristin Cauvas; Patricia Cave; Nina Cooke with Louis; Anna Cuirleo; Sally Davis and Andrew Hill with Kate, Zoey and Zan; Claudia Dossena with Isaac; Laura Dymock; Charlotte Forbes with Elsa; Bel Gibbs; Alison Gilderdale with Alice and Luke; Susanna Glimmezveen; Sarah Gostick with Isobel; Rowena Guzy; Pam Ha-Stevenson with Joshua; Stacia Keogh; Victoria Lampert with Harry; Sam Marshall with Molly; Yane Lassen; Sally and Diana Lomas and Aron; Antony Malvasi, Lisa Messenger with Kate; Zoë Moghadas; Rachel Moore; Carol Morgan with Benjamin and Joseph; Angela Nutt with Alabama; Tracy Rodericks with Aidan; Meena Singh with Shanti Lara; Celine Smith; Annie and Bob Taylor; Hester Tingey with Bathsheba; Jane Tudman; Sabine Ulmer-Lake; Mai and Rob Ward with Ruby and Honor; Lucy Witney; Sarah Wood with Harrison; Safuriat Yesufu and Rob with Morton and Emile. Also MOT Models agency and their models Liza Licence and Elizabeth Tarrant. Thanks also to Elizabeth Wright for her photograph of Zoë and Kira.

# index